The History of English Parliamentary Privilege

The History of English Parliamentary Privilege

BY CARL WITTKE

DA CAPO PRESS · NEW YORK · 1970

A Da Capo Press Reprint Edition

This Da Capo Press edition of *The History of English Parliamentary Privilege* is an unabridged republication of the
first edition published in 1921 in Columbus, Ohio, as Volume
26, Number 2 of *The Ohio State University Bulletin*.

Library of Congress Catalog Card Number 74-87623

SBN 306-71810-3

Published by Da Capo Press
A Division of Plenum Publishing Corporation
227 West 17th Street
New York, N. Y. 10011

Manufactured in the United States of America

The History of English Parliamentary Privilege

By

CARL WITTKE, Ph.D.

Assistant Professor of American History in
The Ohio State University

THE OHIO STATE UNIVERSITY

TO
MY FATHER AND MOTHER

PREFACE

My interest in the subject of this thesis was first aroused by a reading of Professor Charles H. McIlwain's *The High Court of Parliament and Its Supremacy.* A short section in the third chapter is devoted to a discussion of privilege of parliament, especially as its history throws light upon the origin, nature, and functions of the High Court of Parliament. The history of privilege seemed to be a subject large enough and important enough to deserve separate and more extensive treatment. The thesis was begun at Harvard, in Professor McIlwain's seminar in the History of English Legal Institutions, and my conclusions are based entirely upon materials found in this country, and particularly in the libraries of Harvard College and the Harvard Law School.

It is impossible to give adequate expression to my very deep obligations to Professor McIlwain. It is no exaggeration to say that had it not been for his careful guidance, his constant encouragement, and the stimulus that came from an intimate relationship with him this study would not have been completed.

Professor Wilbur H. Siebert of Ohio State University was kind enough to interest himself in the publication of my manuscript, and it is largely due to his efforts that it now appears in the university studies.

OHIO STATE UNIVERSITY
June 1, 1921

CONTENTS

CHAPTER I

INTRODUCTION

English Parliamentary Privilege has received some attention in practically every political and constitutional history of England, and at times quite detailed attention in manuals and treatises on parliamentary procedure. Unfortunately, these discussions are generally limited to an enumeration of the ordinary privileges enjoyed by legislative bodies, and to the citation of a number of cases illustrating the procedure in applying these privileges. Sir T. Erskine May's celebrated treatise on *Parliamentary Practice* is still by far the best of all such discussions, and I have found it most useful in the completion of this thesis. As far as May's treatment extends, it cannot be equaled, much less surpassed. But this invaluable discussion is also largely concerned with enumerating and explaining the privileges of the parliament houses for practical purposes rather than with the discussion of the history of these privileges, and the many phases of their development.

My emphasis has been on the theoretical rather than on the practical side. I have made an attempt to discover and explain the theory that underlies the powers claimed and exercised by Parliament in the enforcement of what it considered its privileges. Further, I have stressed the uses and abuses of privilege, its conflict with the law of the land, with other agencies of the government, such as the king and the courts of law, and with the rights of the people. An attempt has been made to make clear the reasons for all such conflicts, the real issues involved, and why and how adjustments and compromises were finally made between the discordant factors. A study of these conflicts has revealed materials that cast abundant light upon the theory that formed the basis of these conflicting claims. In short, what I have written could in no sense be intended for service as a practical manual for the guidance of parliamentarians. I have made no attempt to give an enumeration of cases of parliamentary privilege except as they had real importance in tracing the evolution of fundamental principles.

I have been forced by these investigations to accept conclusions which are at variance with the views of some others who have dealt with this subject. In his admirable work on *The Procedure of the House of Commons* Professor Joseph Redlich holds that the procedure of the Commons bears "no marks of the ideas of feudal law, or the notion of the *parliamentum* as the great court of judicature of the chief vassals," and that in all essentials, "the procedure and order of business have from the first grown out of the political exigencies of a supreme representative assembly with legislative and administrative functions."[1] I hope to present sufficient evidence to warrant the conclusion that this explanation is neither complete nor justified, and that the view of Parliament as a court, "the High Court of Parliament," directly related to the old feudal curia, affords a far more satisfactory explanation for the difficulties an investigation of Parliament's evolution brings to light. I believe one can find much evidence of the relation of Parliament to the old feudal curia in much of its present-day procedure. This is particularly true of the history of parliamentary privilege, as exercised in Parliament and as enforced against the world beyond its walls. I hope to make clear that the idea that Parliament exercised and enforced its privileges as "the High Court of Parliament," the "highest, antientest, and supreamest" court of the realm, was firmly rooted for centuries in the minds of Parliament men, lawyers, and judges, and prevailed to modern times. It was this theory that was applied again and again in settling the vexing problems that were constantly arising from the enforcement of claims of privilege. Professor Redlich believes that expressions of this view, "at times bordering on the fantastic," "were mere cloaks for the political claims to power made by the majority of the House of Commons."[2] Undoubtedly the political motive was present in many cases but certainly there must have been some real basis for a theory so long and so generally accepted. It was not an invention of the time. It was asserted again and again, by judges, members of Parliament, and lawyers, to the close of the nineteenth century.

---

[1] Redlich, *The Procedure of the House of Commons*, translated by A. E. Steinthal. Vol. I, 24, 25. In another place, Professor Redlich offers the following explanation of privilege:— "It may be said that the form in which the notion of a constitutional corporate body has been worked out in the House of Commons has been that of *conferring* upon the highest legislative body certain judicial attributes exercisable solely in the sphere of its autonomous enactments and regulations . . . the extension to the House of Commons of the idea of a 'contempt' (is) the corner-stone of privilege. For thereby, according to English legal conceptions, is the House of Commons *made* into a court of law so far as is necessary to enable it to enforce the appearance of any party before it." Redlich, III, 77, 78.

[2] Redlich, *The Procedure of the House of Commons*. Steinthal's Translation, Vol. I, p. 25, footnote.

Coke's famous Fourth Institute on the *"High and Most Honourable Court of Parliament"* was usually cited as the classical expression of the theory of Parliament's judicial origin. For centuries it was used by the advocates of Parliament's claims of privilege, and it became the basis for many court decisions as well. Because of its importance, and to avoid repetition, it may be well to quote it at length here. In his *Fourth Institute*, fo. 15, Coke has written: "And as every court of justice hath laws and customs for its direction, some by the common law, some by the civil and canon law, some by peculiar laws and customs, etc. So the high court of Parliament *suis propiis legibus et consuetudinibus subsistit.* It is *lex et consuetudo parliamenti* that all weighty matters in any parliament moved concerning the peers of the realm, or commons in Parliament assembled, ought to be determined, adjudged, and discussed by the course of parliament, and not by the civil law, nor yet by the common laws of the realm used in inferior courts; which was so declared to be *secundum legem et consuetudinem parliamenti,* concerning the peers of the realm, by the king and all the lords spiritual and temporal; and the like *pari ratione* is for the commons for anything moved or done in the House of Commons; and the rather, for that by another law and custom of Parliament, the king cannot take notice of anything said or done in the house of commons, but by the report of the house of commons; and every member of the parliament hath a judicial place, and can be no witnesse. And this is the reason that judges ought not to give any opinion of a matter of parliament, because it is not to be decided by the common laws, but *secundum legem et consuetudinem parliamenti,* and so the judges in divers parliaments have confessed. And some hold that every offence committed in any court punishable by that court, must be punished (proceeding criminally) in the same court, or in some higher, and not in any inferiour court, and the court of parliament hath no higher." In discussing the work of the judges summoned to assist the lords in matters of the common law, Coke observed: "Neither doth it belong to them . . . . to judge of any law, custome, or priviledge of Parliament. And to say the truth, the lawes, customes, liberties, and priviledges of parliament are better to be learned out of the rols of parliament, and other records, and by presidents and continual experience, then can be expressed by any one man's pen." [3]

---

[3] Coke, *Fourth Institute,* fo. 50.

England, after the Norman Conquest, was a feudal state. The elements of feudalism probably existed before 1066, but it was the Norman kings who firmly established it as a system. Elements of nationalism may also have existed earlier, but they were undeveloped and negligible. The Norman kings ruled a feudal state. The Conqueror was elected by a National Council, theoretically speaking; in fact, he was head of the state and the nobility, "by the edge of the sword."

The Norman kings were the first in a large body of feudal nobles—nobles who were loyal to their class, rather than to the nation. The wars of the king and nobles were for the most part simply class struggles. From them, to be sure, occasional benefits accrued to the nation as such, but these were largely incidental. The central assembly of the Normans was a feudal assembly, with powers very vaguely defined, irregular in its meetings, and with all the characteristics of feudalism. That means first of all that it was not primarily a law-making body. Its functions were manifold, and not at all clearly defined nor separated from each other. There was no notion at that time of a departmental division of the functions of government into separate "legislative," "executive," and "judicial" departments. Moreover, feudal law existed, and had only to be "found" and "declared," and not "made."

The king was not in any way bound to assemble his council of nobles and seek their advice. It was his privilege to do so, but not his duty. Those who came to the council, came because they had been ordered to appear. The councils were irregular in their composition and in their meetings, there was no conception of such an institution as a "Full Parliament," representing all classes in the state. The King's Council and the Parliament that developed from it was a law court, a body of executive ministers, an advisory council, an exchequer, and various other things, all in one. As Professor Dicey has observed, the Common or Great Council, *Curia Regis,* or *Aula Regia,* "possessed every attribute which has been ascribed to it. It was the executive. It was also a Law Court. It certainly took part in acts of legislation . . . . not the combination, but the severance of judicial and executive powers would have appeared anomalous."[4] The king's answers, given in the Council, were sometimes recorded on the rolls of the court *coram rege,* (the later King's Bench), sometimes on the Chancery Rolls, and sometimes on the

---

[4] Dicey, *The Privy Council,* 7

Rolls of Parliament. "The King in his Council in his Parliament" possibly referred to nothing more than the judicial side of the Commune Concilium.[5]

Parliament was the "highest court in the realm." [6]   As such, it dealt with cases too difficult for the judges of the ordinary courts, and with cases involving new points of law.   In a sense, it resembled a court of equity jurisdiction.[7] With the development of other courts, conflicts arose between them and Parliament.   Parliament not only exercised the general functions of government, which included adjudication, but what was more important, there was no careful differentiation between these functions and powers.   Parliament, as a "Sovereign Law-making Court," "legislated" and "adjudicated," without any clear understanding as to when it was doing the one and when the other.   Serious conflicts with the ordinary courts were therefore inevitable.   They were all the more severe since both parties could claim jurisdiction because of their common descent from the old King's Council.   Both could cite precedents and history to support their claims.   Most of the separate organs that were gradually evolved to carry on the business of government were the offspring of the old feudal curia.   In this common ancestry of Parliament, council, and courts, as Professor McIlwain has put it, we have the key to many an otherwise confused situation, and the explanation of many a later struggle.[8]

---

[5] I am following here the excellent account in Professor C. H. McIlwain's, *The High Court of Parliament and Its Supremacy.*   The same view in regard to the composition and functions of the *Curia Regis* may be found in G. B. Adams, *The Origin of the English Constitution.*

[6] Parliament has been described as "the highest Court in the whole Realm—In which Court all Equity ought to shine forth without the least Cloud or Shadow, like the Sun in its Meridian Glory; where Poor and Rich refreshed with Peace and Ease of their Oppressions, may always find infallible and sure Refuge and Succour   . . ." G. P. (Petyt) *Lex Parliamentaria* (1698), 11 and 12, citing Knyghton, *De Eventibus Angliae.*

[7] "An honourable and worthy Speech, spoken in the High Court of Parliament   . . . concerning the Regulating of the King's Majesty's Prerogative, and the Liberties of the Subjects" (1641), found in *Harleian Misc.*, V, 251, suggests this view.   "My humble Motion therefore is (the speech continues) that an Intimation may go forth, unto the Country, to wish those that are injured to resort to Courts of Law.   And, if there they fail of Justice, in Parliament they may be confident to receive it."   In 1667, a writer on *The Preeminence and Pedigree of Parliament,* speaks repeatedly of the "High Court of Parliament," with its "transcendent and uncontroulable Jurisdiction," and of "this Sovereign Law-making Court."   *Harl. Misc.* I, 34-37.

[8] See Professor McIlwain's *The High Court of Parliament and Its Supremacy,* Preface and Introduction.   The entire essay is a discussion of the court theory of Parliament.   I have found it indispensable in giving me a background for this thesis.   The appendix to G. B. Adams' *Origin of the English Constitution* gives a chart showing all the descendants of the ancient Curia.   A. F. Pollard, in his *The Evolution of Parliament* (1920), writes, "The issue of Simon's and Edward's writs did not evoke a new institution out of the void; they merely grafted new buds on to the old stock of the *curia regis,* and it was the legal sap of the ancient stem that fed and maintained the life of the medieval parliament." p. 45.

When the struggles between Parliament and the Stuarts broke out, Parliament became conscious of its position as a sovereign *legislative* body, as never before. It was then that Parliament began to exercise its legislative functions on a much more extensive scale. It was then that the emphasis was gradually and slowly shifted from the judical and administrative, to the legislative side of Parliament's activities. But this was a mere shifting of emphasis, and many earmarks of the old order remained. "It required the shock of a civil war to teach men that the High Court of Parliament had become the Sovereign Legislature of the Kingdom." [9] The two functions of legislation and adjudication were not then, nor for a long time afterward, clearly defined or distinguished. To show how long the judicial characteristics of Parliament lingered in the minds of Englishmen is one of the purposes of this thesis. It is by no means an exaggeration to say that these judicial characteristics colored and influenced some of the great struggles over privilege in and out of Parliament to the very close of the nineteenth century. It is not altogether certain whether they have been entirely forgotten even now. Nowhere has the theory that Parliament is a court—the highest court of the realm, often acting in a judicial capacity and in a judicial manner—persisted longer than in the history of privilege of Parliament.

Today, of course, the term "parliamentary privilege" arouses very little interest or discussion. We take it to mean freedom of speech within legislative halls, and freedom from arrest and molestation for members while they are performing their governmental functions. A representative may speak his mind openly and fearlessly within the walls of Parliament or Congress, and for what he says there he cannot be called to account by the world outside. He may be censured by the house of which he is a member for disorderly conduct, but that is now considered as purely a matter of internal discipline. Freedom of speech, in the seventeenth century, was made one of the guarantees of the English Bill of Rights, and has ever since been regarded as a bulwark of English liberty. It is also universally conceded that members of Parliament and other legislative bodies must be free from molestations and arrests during Parliament time; if they were not, any number of trivial charges might be invented to prevent a servant of the people from discharging his public duties. In the American Constitution it is provided that Senators and Representatives "shall in all Cases,

---

[9] McIlwain, *The High Court of Parliament and Its Supremacy*, 157.

except Treason, Felony, and Breach of the Peace, be privileged from Arrest during their Attendance at the Session of their respective Houses, and in going to and returning from the same; and for any Speech or Debate in either House, they shall not be questioned in any other Place."[10] Cases of breach of privilege occur rarely today and attract little attention. The vexing problems that arose in years past from the exercise of claims of privilege have been settled with at least the appearance of finality. But it required centuries of wrangling to arrive at that settlement.

The history and evolution of privilege, *per se*, presents many interesting aspects. In addition, it throws much light on the development of English legal conceptions and English institutions. Parliamentary privilege, like its close parallel, prerogative, boasts of a long history, some of it creditable, much of it not.[11] Privilege played an important role in the great political struggles of the past centuries. At times claims of privilege were used to champion the cause of the people; there were also times when privilege became the greatest oppressor of the subject's liberty. Parliamentary privilege has frequently served as a bulwark of liberty and individual freedom, but on the other hand, in the hands of crafty, powerful, and designing politicians eager to perpetuate their control and to gain the utmost personal advantage, privilege has been used as a screen for the basest oppression. There were times when privilege was used to give legal color to a Parliamentary Despotism as oppressive of individual liberty as many kings with their claims of prerogative have been. Particularly was this true when privilege was employed to deprive individuals of the legal remedies afforded by the ordinary courts of the land, by removing to another jurisdiction, that is, before a Parliament house, cases that should never have been taken there. The corrupt Whig Oligarchy that came into power with the Glorious Revolution and remained in so long, were past masters in this art of inventing fictitious claims of privilege.

Very early in the history of Parliament, it became evident that members, to be of any real service, must be free to attend all sessions, unmolested by threats, insults, attacks, or arrests, whether they originated from the Crown, the courts of law controlled by the Crown, or from private citizens. This was especially true in Tudor

---

[10] Article I, Section 6.

[11] Professor Dicey has pointed out the close analogy between privilege and prerogative in his *Introduction to the Study of the Law of the Constitution*, (5th Ed.) p. 357.

and Stuart England, when Parliament, and more particularly the Commons, were struggling for recognition and supremacy against the prerogative and the royally-controlled courts. It was necessary to insist that all legal actions, from whatever source they might come, should be opposed if they hindered members from being actually present in Parliament. A summons or subpoena issued by a law court ordering a Parliament man to appear, arrests in civil causes, and interferences and commitments by order of the Crown were therefore assailed with equal vigor as improper and illegal. Cases of "treason, felony, and breach of the peace," that is, actions in criminal law or offences against the public peace, were always regarded as exceptions to the general rule of privilege, but just what was included under those terms was not always clear and often varied with time and conditions. It was regarded as essential that members should be free to deliberate on public questions without concern for their private estates; their minds must be free from concern for their private fortune while they are engaged in the public service. So it became a "breach of privilege" to institute actions which might involve members' estates while those members were sitting in Parliament. The same reasoning was applied to members' servants who were in attendance upon their masters while Parliament was in session. These two privileges were included in the Speaker's petition at the opening of Parliament until well into the nineteenth century.[12]

Each house guarded its privileges most carefully. Each exercised and enforced them independently of the other, but not by a peculiar separate right, but as part of the High Court of Parliament, and under the Law and Custom of Parliament.[13] Frequently disputes arose between the upper and lower house as to the correct interpretation and application of privilege, during which the houses developed widely divergent and antagonistic points of view. Many bitter and prolonged contests between them were the result. On at least one occasion, not even prorogation of Parliament was sufficient to put an end to the struggle.

What was this peculiar *lex et consuetudo parliamenti* which the two houses claimed to follow in all matters of privilege? According to Coke, it was to be "learned from the rols of parliament," "by presidents and continual experience," and could not be ex-

---

[12] See Anson, *Law and Custom of the Constitution*, Vol. I, p. 151.

[13] I should make perhaps one qualification of this statement—the peculiar claim of "privilege of peerage," made by the members of the upper house.

pressed "by any one man's pen." How might its· principles be discovered then? If Parliament alone knows the extent of this its peculiar law, it cannot be presumed that ordinary courts possess knowledge of it sufficient to enable them to adjudicate properly in matters of privilege coming before them for settlement. All such cases must be settled not by the common or the civil law, but "*secundum legem et consuetudinem parliamenti*," at least that would be the view of Coke and all the other innumerable champions of privilege who agreed with him. What will happen in cases where the *lex parliamenti* and the *lex terrae* seem to conflict? What remedy shall there be and who shall administer it? If we accept the view that Parliament arose as the highest court of the realm, and I believe that was its origin, it cannot be within the power of an inferior court to pass judgment on the acts and decisions of a higher. By this theory, the ordinary common law courts must accept as *lex parliamenti*, inviolable and unchangeable, whatever Parliament or either house of Parliament declares to be its privilege. At first, perhaps, it was essential to make each house the sole judge of its own privileges, but it was not long until this principle was grossly abused. As a matter of fact, both houses, especially in the seventeenth and eighteenth centuries, made such additions to their privileges, and invented so many new ones, that the subject was often the victim of a Parliamentary Tyranny which deprived him of even his ordinary common law remedies and guarantees. During the reign of George I and George II, many cases that were nothing more than trespasses upon a member's estate, and in no way affected his person, were declared breaches of privilege, and were punished by a Parliament house as such.[14] These cases will be discussed at length in later chapters, and attention will be specifically directed to the collision between the law of the subject and the law of Parliament which they involve. By considering such offences as breaches of privilege, they were *ipso facto* removed to a new court and a new jurisdiction for trial—to a court and a jurisdiction where many of the ordinary safeguards of the subject's liberty did not apply.

Many other complications that could and did arise from the exercise of privilege might be suggested. Let us suppose that an offender is committed to prison by order of the House of Commons

---

[14] L. S. Cushing, in his *Law and Practice of Legislative Assemblies*, has given a good general discussion of privilege and its more practical applications. Among other things, he points out this encroachment of the law of privilege upon the ordinary law of trespass.

for an alleged breach of privilege, or imprisoned for a period extending beyond Parliament's adjournment—can he secure his liberty by applying for a writ of habeas corpus? Where shall he apply? To an *"inferior"* court? In such a case, what should have precedence, the law of Parliament or the law of the land? Or should judges regard the former as a part of the latter? If not—and for a long time it was not so regarded—parliamentary privilege would be in the nature of an exception to the ordinary common law of the land, just as prerogative was often declared to be. An extension of privilege would thus constitute an encroachment upon, or a modification of, the *lex terrae*. The result would be legislation by one house, instead of by "the King, Lords, and Commons in Parliament assembled." The basest tyranny might be the result. What could prevent one house from voting such an *extension* of its privileges as to virtually constitute the *creation* of a *new* privilege? An individual's fundamental rights might be violated thereby, and yet, if he applied to an ordinary "inferior" court for relief, he became liable to commitment for defying the authority and privileges of the house that had voted the extension. Attorney-general Sir Fletcher Norton boasted on one occasion that he would pay as little respect to the resolutions of the Commons as "to the resolutions of so many drunken porters at an ale-house."[15] But in the mind of the average subject the prospect of a period of confinement, perhaps in "Little Ease," inspired no little terror. He had no remedy at law, since no court could review the acts of the "High Court of Parliament." There was a peculiar "science" in the *lex et consuetudo parliamenti* which the common law judges did not possess. Even though they might venture a decision, it might be at variance with that of Parliament, and then things would surely "run round," as one judge in consternation once expressed it. On at least one occasion, judges were summoned before the Commons to render account for an unfavorable decision on privilege, and were duly punished for their audacity.

The House of Commons, to comparatively recent times, had a special reason to guard its privileges most jealously and to oppose every attempt on the part of the courts to assume jurisdiction over them. It arose from the fact that by the English constitutional system, the House of Lords is the supreme court of appeal in the kingdom. The final determination of cases coming on appeal from the ordinary courts of England has always been claimed, and for

---

[15] *Hans. Parl. Deb.*, 2d Series, Vol. 16, p. 155.

centuries exercised, by the House of Lords exclusively. Moreover, this determination belonged in earlier centuries to *all* the Lords acting as a body, often ignorant of the law, and always jealous of their special jurisdiction. A case involving privilege, whether directly or indirectly, would thus, if left to the ordinary courts, find its way, like other cases, to the House of Lords, the Supreme Tribunal of England. Because of this peculiar state of affairs, the lower house found itself in an extremely dangerous situation. To allow the courts to pass on questions of privilege, was to submit those privileges to the final arbitrament of the House of Lords. The Commons were fully aware of this situation, and fought several bitter struggles with the upper house over just this issue. They realized that to surrender this right to interpret and enforce their privileges would be—to use their own quaint expression—"to give up all, and like salt that has lost its flavour," "become good for nothing." [16] On the other hand, it became necessary to provide some check upon this power of the Parliament houses, lest "supremacy and impunity go together," and the subject find himself without a remedy. Here is the great dilemma, and it arose from a fundamental defect in the English constitutional system itself. It was solved only after years of painful conflict and confusion between the two houses and the courts. At times, the Commons supported the *lex parliamenti,* and the Lords the *lex terrae,* in these struggles between the two houses. By the very nature of the English constitution, conflicts over privilege were almost always aggravated by the fact that they inevitably assumed the characteristics and proportions of a struggle between the two houses of Parliament, each jealous of the other's power, and fearful of the least encroachment.

Enough has been said to call attention to the numerous problems that a consideration of the history of parliamentary privilege suggests. The discussion of the many struggles over privilege from the point of view that has been indicated, should therefore throw much light upon our conceptions of Parliament, the courts, the common law, the law of Parliament, and their relation to each other. Let me repeat again that it is not at all my intention to give anything like a complete chronological discussion of cases of privilege. I am interested in the theory that lay behind these claims of privilege, and the causes and results of the great struggles that were fought over these issues. It seemed advisable to discuss a

---

[16] *Parl. Hist.,* Vol. 28, p. 1033 and 1034.

number of cases in rough chronological sequence, simply to show the development of such fundamental privileges as freedom of speech, freedom from arrest, etc. But this was done largely in order to make clear what is to follow. In short, this is intended to be not so much a history of privilege as an essay in the interpretation of the great principles underlying parliamentary privilege. It seems to me that the subject is one whose roots extend into the very groundwork of the English constitutional system. Many of the problems raised by claims of privilege were not solved until the nineteenth century, and even then, we could not be absolutely certain of the finality of such solutions.

CHAPTER II

THE PRIVILEGES OF PARLIAMENT

A. The Speaker's Petition

Since at least the early years of the reign of Henry VIII, the Speaker of the House of Commons, at the opening of every Parliament, has claimed by humble petition to the Crown, the ancient rights and privileges of the Commons. This included freedom from arrest; freedom from molestation for members and their servants; freedom of speech in debate; admittance to the royal presence; and favorable construction upon all proceedings.[1] The record of Speakers' petitions to the king may be found in the Rolls of Parliament as early as 1377 and 1406.[2] The general practice has been continued, at least in form, to modern times. This mode of procedure does not imply however that the·privileges enjoyed by the Commons are still dependent upon royal favor. Parliamentarians very early maintained that their claims to privilege rested on the "ancient law and custom of Parliament" and upon such statements and definitions thereof as may have been made from time to time by statute or resolution. Originally, privilege may have been dependent upon royal favor and grant, but the Speaker's petition soon became a mere formality, a part of the customary ceremonial at the opening of each new Parliament. The Commons long ago established the principle that their privileges existed as ancient rights, inherent in them and in no way dependent upon the Crown. As early as 1515,

---

[1] See the discussion in May's *Parliamentary Practice* (11th Ed.) p. 59 *et seq.* May points out that the claim of privilege for the estates of members was not omitted until 1852, and that for members' servants not until 1892.

[2] For the opening of Richard I's Parliament, 1377, we find—"Et puis apres les Coes y vindrent en Parlement devant le Roi, et illoeqs Monsr Peres de la Mare, Chivaler, q'avoit les paroles de par la Coe, faisant sa Protestation q ce q'il y avoit a dire nel' dirroit del soen propre moevement, einz del mocion, assent et voluntee expres de toute la Coe illoeqs esteante: Et s'il avenist q'il y forveiast de rienz, ou par cas y deist chose q ne fust de l'assent de ses compaignons, q'il eut fust par mesmes ses compaignons tantost amendez illoeqs, et devant q'il y partissent de la place." 3 *Rot. Parl.*, 5.

In 1406, the Speaker's Protestation is reported as follows: "Item, Lundy le VII jour de Juyn, les Communes vindrent devaunt le Roy et les Seignrs en Parlement, et illoeques Monsr Johan Tybtot, Parlour pur les Communes, pria a mesme nre Sr le Roy, q'il purra avoir resort a sa primere Protestation fait en Parlement, auxi franchment et entierment come unqes avoit ascun autre Parlour pur les Communes devant ces heures. Quel prier le Roy ottroia."—3 *Rot. Parl.*, 574.

21

the Speaker claimed the "ancient and undoubted rights and privileges" of the Commons in his petition to the king, and the Chancellor "confirmed" them.

The request for access to the king seems to have been included
for the first time in Speaker Riche's petition, 28 Henry VIII. Five
years later, Thomas Moyle followed this precedent, and from then
on the practice became fairly regular.[3] Elsynge says the first
record of a petition for the privilege of freedom of speech is for the
year 1542.[4] In 1566, Onslow, elected Speaker in the middle of a parliamentary session, omitted the prayer for liberty of speech and
freedom from arrest, but in 1572, Speaker Charlton, elected to fill
an unexpected vacancy, returned to the old procedure, and included
all the privileges in his petition. In 1549, however, Onslow's precedent of 1566 was followed by Speaker Foley, who merely protested
his own incapacity to fill such an exalted position and petitioned
for pardon for the errors he himself might commit.[5] It appears
that the omission of the prayer for the usual privileges was due
to the express order of the House of Commons given the day before.[6] Privileges were becoming "undoubted rights." It is not
surprising to find James I questioning the claims of the Commons
and taking exception to their demand for privilege as "their ancient
and undoubted right and inheritance." James, on more than one
occasion, felt it to be his duty to enlighten the Commons in regard
to the real basis for their claims. But the lower house remained
firm, and the only results of such controversies were most emphatic
protests from the Commons and vigorous assertions of their rights.
The relations between James and his Parliaments will be discussed
more fully later.

The Speakers' petitions soon became, and always remained, a
mere formality, based on the custom of preceding years, and pre-

3 Elsynge, *The Manner of Holding Parliaments*, 176.

4 *Ibid.*

5 The speeches of acceptance by most Speakers were curious models of self-abasement. The
following is an extract from Sir Edward Coke's speech before Elizabeth, on the occasion of his
election to the speakership: "As in the heavens a star is but *opacum corpus* until it have received light from the sun, so stand I *corpus opacum*—a mute body—until your Highness's bright
shining wisdom hath looked upon me and allumed me. How unable I am to do this office my
present speech doth tell." Quoted from the *Parl. Hist.* in Jennings' *Anecdotal Hist. of the
British Parliament*, p. 65. Speaker Yelverton (1597) remarked: "Your Speaker ought to be
a man big and comely, stately and well spoken; his voice great, his carriage majestical, his
nature haughty, and his purse plentiful. But contrarily, the stature of my body is small, myself
not well spoken, my voice low, my carriage of the common fashion, my nature soft and bashful,
my purse thin, light, and never plentiful." Quoted in Porritt's *Unreformed House of Commons* (1909 Ed.) Vol. I, p. 438, from D'Ewes, *Journals*, 549.

6 Hatsell, *Precedents of Proceedings of the House of Commons*, Vol. II, 225.

served as another example of the Englishman's fondness for walking in "the deep-trod footprints of ancient usage." The ceremonial at the opening of each Parliament no longer has practical significance, and the Speaker's part therein is nothing more than a sort of public claim and notification to Crown and people that the usual privileges of Parliament will be enforced.[7]

B. FREEDOM OF SPEECH

No privilege of parliament is more essential than freedom of speech. Parliamentary government has been described as "government by talking," and certainly no assembly can become a power in the state unless its members may speak their minds freely and without reserve within the walls of the Parliament building and be immune from punishment and molestation for whatever remarks they may find it necessary to make there in pursuit of their governmental functions. When a legislature is struggling for recognition and control with a Crown and royal courts intent upon maintaining the prerogative, this privilege becomes doubly important.

In 1541, the privilege of freedom of speech, seems, for the first time, to have been included in the Speaker's petition at the opening of Parliament.[8] This does not imply that it was not claimed earlier. As early as the reign of Edward III, it is reported, the House of Commons often discussed and agreed upon laws exactly contrary to the king's prerogative, "yet they were never interrupted in their consultations, nor received check for the same."[9] The first case of importance involving freedom of speech was that of Thomas Haxey. It occurred in the reign of Richard II. Haxey was reported to be the author of a bill before the Commons to reduce the excessive expenditures of the royal household. The measure contained reflections upon the king's extravagance and upon the favorites at court who finally brought Richard's reign to a disastrous close. Richard, probably through the House of Lords or through the Speaker, Sir John Busby, discovered that Haxey was responsible for the measure, and he was promptly condemned to death in Parliament as a traitor.[10] The act was later annulled by Richard, and

---

[7] Hakewell, *Modus tenendi Parliamentum,* pp. 199-220, gives a list of Speakers with comments to the thirteenth year of Charles II's reign. For an historical note on the Speakership, see Redlich II, 156-168. Also E. Porritt, *The Unreformed House of Commons,* Ch. XXI and XXII; and A. I. Dasent, *The Speakers of the House of Commons* (London, 1911).

[8] Elsynge, 176.

[9] Elsynge, 177.

[10] *Ibid.,* 178 *et seq.*

after his reign had come to an unhappy end, was re-annulled in 1399. Haxey petitioned "the king in Parliament" (in Henry IV's reign), for a reversal of the judgment given against him, on the ground that it had been *"encountre droit et la course quel avoit este devant en Parlement."* [11] The petition was granted. But the House of Commons was not content to let the matter rest here. In the same year, 1399, the Commons as a body, petitioned the king for an annulment of the judgment, an admission that it had been erroneous, and a declaration that the whole procedure had been contrary to the usual course in Parliament, and in destruction of the most ancient customs of the Commons. In addition, the Commons demanded that Haxey's estate, which had been forfeited, be restored to him, *"si bien en accomplissement de Droit, come pur salvation des Libertees de ditz Communes."* [12] The king granted the request and the entire proceedings were *"tenuz de nul force n'affect."* The outcome was a distinct victory for the Commons who thus succeeded in having their claim of privilege recognized by the whole Parliament, king, lords, and Commons. In 1401, the king promised not to listen to unauthorized accounts of the proceedings of the Commons in the future. [13]

There was another abuse against which the Commons in particular found it necessary to protest. In many Parliaments there were groups of informers who made it their business to carry reports of the discussions in the House to the ears of the king, long before a decision had been reached in any official way. The attitude of individual members toward certain measures was thus known by the king in advance of official action. In 1400, the Commons petitioned Henry IV that he refuse to give credence to any information or reports that might reach his ear, save those that should come through the regular channels used by the House in communicating with the Crown. Henry announced a desire to comply with the request. [14] The trouble with the informers did not end here, however. In 1455, Thomas Young, a member for Bristol, petitioned "the right wise and discreete Commons," complaining that "notwithstanding that by the old liberte and freedom of the Comyns of this Lande had, enjoyed and prescribed, fro the tyme

---

[11] Elsynge, 180.

[12] 3 *Rot. Parl.*, 434.

[13] Haxey was probably not a member of Parliament, but was present as a priest, representing the clergy. See the discussion in K. H. Vickers, *England in the Later Middle Ages*, 288, 314.

[14] 3 *Rot. Parl.*, 456.

that no mynde is, all such psones as for the tyme been assembled
in any Parliament for the same Comyn, ought to have their fre-
dom to speke and sey in the Hous of their assemble, withoute any
maner chalange, charge, or punycion therefore to be leyde to theyme
in eny wyse"—he, because some of the statements he had made
within the walls of Parliament had been reported to the king, had
been "taken, arrested, and rigorously in open wise led to the Toure
of London, and there grevously in grete duresse long tyme empris-
oned." Young demanded damages for losses to his estate and for
personal injuries received during his close confinement, and begged
the House to plead his cause. The petition was sent to the Lords
and the king ordered them to make reparation to the injured member, according to their discretion.[15]

In 1512, the case of Richard Strode, a burgess of Parliament,
came to the attention of the Commons. The case has a number of
important phases, some of which will be left for later discussion.
Strode was the author of a bill to regulate certain abuses connected
with the Cornwall tin industry. For his interest in the bill, he had
been prosecuted in the Stannary Courts, heavily fined, and imprisoned in Lidford Castle, from whence he was finally released on a
writ of privilege, but only after he had given security "to save
harmless" the warden's deputy who had held him in custody. On
Strode's petition, an "act" was passed by the Parliament, annulling
the judgments and executions against Strode, and providing that
all suits and charges that might be brought against him or his
accomplices in the future—"for any Bill, speaking or reasoning
of any Thing concerning the Parliament to be communed and
treated of"—be considered void.[16]

It was perhaps inevitable that Parliament and the Crown
should clash over the proper interpretation of the privilege of freedom of speech. Naturally, the Crown insisted that it was the Commons or Lords who brought on the conflict by meddling in affairs

---

[15] 5 *Rot. Parl.*, 357. The king ordered that "the Lordes of his Counsell do and provyde in
this partie for the seid Suppliant, as by theire discrecions shall be thought convenyent and
resonable."

[16] 4 Henry VIII, Ch. VIII. See also 1 Hatsell, 86. This case is interesting in another
connection. For a century or more, the dispute raged whether this was a private or a public
act. In 1629, when the privilege of free speech became so important, the judges declared it a
private act, applying only to Strode's case. The Parliamentarians in the struggle with Charles
argued that it was a public bill; the Royalists that it was a private bill. This illustrates the
indefiniteness and confusion that existed in men's minds when it became necessary to distinguish
between private and public acts. For the proof that this affords for the theory that Parliament
was a court and long retained its judicial characteristics, see the discussion in McIlwain, *The
High Court of Parliament and Its Supremacy*, 216-229.

of state which lay outside their proper sphere of action and encroached upon the prerogative. In the reign of Elizabeth, Parliament, and especially the Commons, meddled frequently in matters affecting the succession and in questions of religion. Elizabeth was not a ruler to tolerate these infringements upon what she regarded as her prerogative, "the chiefest flower in her garden, the principal and head pearl in her crown and diadem." In 1558, the Commons began to petition the Queen on the subject of her marriage and the succession[17], but no serious controversy arose until 1566. In that year, a joint committee of the two houses of Parliament presented a petition on the succession, and received the usual non-committal answer. Bold speeches by Dutton, Wentworth, and others, followed in the Commons. What was said, "grated hard on the Queen's Royal Prerogative." Elizabeth was deeply offended, and resolved to silence her critics. A number of Lords and thirty Commoners were summoned before her and received "a Smart Reproof, in which, however, she mixed some Sweetness with Majesty."[18] Further discussion of such matters of state was forbidden. Immediately Paul Wentworth raised the question whether such inhibitions were not "against the liberties and privileges of this House." A long debate followed. Elizabeth summoned the Speaker, and ordered him to stop the discussion, but with no effect. The Queen was forced to yield, and a few days later, the Speaker was able to report that "she did revoke her former commandments; but desired the house to proceed no further in the matter at that time." The House received the news "most joyfully, and with most hearty prayer and thanks for the same."[19] Another Parliament did not meet until 1571. In that session, Wentworth made an address calling attention to the necessity of preserving the liberties of the House against royal interference. At the same time a report reached the House that one of its members, Mr. Strickland, "a grave and ancient man," had been called before the Queen's Council and restrained from attending Parliament, for having moved the reformation of the Common Prayer Book. In defence of the Queen's action, the Treasurer tried to explain that Strickland was not detained for a speech made in the House, but for "exhibiting of a bill into the house against the Prerogative of the Queen." The Commons could not be satisfied by such quibbling, and continued to

---

[17] See Corbett, *Parl. Hist.*, I, 661-664; 695 *et seq.* Also, Redlich, I, 35-39.
[18] Cobb., *Parl. Hist.*, I, 716. See also pp. 708 *et seq.*
[19] *Ibid.*, 716.

clamor for their privileges. Again the Queen yielded and Strickland returned to his seat the following day. Nevertheless, the Speaker soon received another order from Elizabeth to instruct the Commons to waste less time in long speeches, and the Lord Keeper, in his address at the close of the session, could not refrain from criticising "certain of them . . . . who in the proceeding of this session, have shewed themselves audacious, arrogant, and presumptious."[20] In the session of 1575, the House of Commons took up a bill on the rites and ceremonies in the Church, and were ordered not to meddle in religious affairs.[21] It was in this Parliament that Peter Wentworth addressed the House at great length on the infringement of the liberties and privileges of the Commons by the Crown. He called attention to the fact that very often "a rumour runneth about the house . . . . 'Take heed what you do, the Queen liketh not such a matter, whosoever prefereth it, she will be offended with him . . . . ' "[22] The royal messages and commands to inhibit discussion in the lower house he denounced as flagrant violations of the fundamental rights of the Commons. The House stopped him in the midst of his address and ordered him into the Serjeant's custody. Wentworth was then examined by a committee of the Commons, and committed to the Tower.[23] He remained there in prison for over a month—until the Queen offered her pardon and indicated her willingness to have the House release him. In 1587, Wentworth reopened the matter of the privileges of the House by presenting a list of questions concerning the rights of freedom of speech to the Speaker. The latter, instead of presenting them to the House, gave them to a Privy Councillor, and shortly thereafter, Wentworth was again on his way to the Tower. We do not know how long he remained there.[24] In 1592, Wentworth and Bromley presented a petition to the Lord Keeper in regard to the succession. They were called before the Council and committed to the Tower for an indefinite period.[25] In the same session, the Commons debated a bill on the abuses of the ecclesiastical courts. Their proceedings were reported to the Queen in some mysterious way. The Speaker was summoned and the House was ordered not to meddle in matters of state or church. The result was that the

---

[20] Cobbett, *Parl. Hist.*, I, 766, 767.
[21] *Ibid.*, 781.
[22] *Ibid.*, 785, 786.
[23] *Ibid.*, 793-802, *passim.*
[24] *Ibid.*, 851-853.
[25] *Ibid.*, 870.

bill was quashed, and the mover of it was committed,[26] a forceful comment on Tudor control of Parliaments! Yet each Parliament had its brave spirits who kept alive the claims of privilege, in spite of royal persecutions.

James I, continued the struggle between prerogative and privilege. In 1621, the lower house engaged in a long discussion of the Spanish marriage and the affairs of the Palatinate. James was much annoyed and directed a communication to the Speaker "of our high court of Parliament" ordering the Commons to refrain from meddling with the mysteries of state, and advising them that James thought himself "very free and able to punish any man's misdemeanors in Parliament as well as during its sitting as after . . . ."[27] The letter aroused both fear and opposition among the Commons.[28] A select committee was appointed and an apologetic petition was addressed to the king requesting him not to give ear to private reports coming to him concerning the proceedings of the House, and closing with a correct account of the incident that had caused the trouble. It was a week before the king replied. "We wish you to remember that we are an old and experienced king, needing no such lessons, being, in our conscience, freest of any king alive, from hearing or trusting idle reports." Then followed a lecture for the Commons. "We cannot omit to shew you," James continued, "how strange we think it, that ye should make so bad and unjust a commentary upon some words of our former letter, as if we meant to restrain you thereby of your antient privileges and liberties of Parliament. Truly a scholar would be ashamed so to misplace and misjudge any sentences in another man's book. . . . . And though we cannot allow of the stile, calling it, your antient and undoubted right and inheritance; but could rather have wished, that ye had said that your privileges were derived from the grace and permission of our ancestors and us; (for most of them grow from precedents, which shews rather a toleration than inheritance) yet we are pleased to give you our royal assurance, that as long as you can contain yourselves within the limits of your duty, we will be as careful to maintain and preserve your lawful liberties and

---

[26] Cobb., *Parl. Hist.* I, 889.

[27] *Ibid.*, 1326. See also 1301 *et seq.*

[28] Sir Robert Phillips, a member of the House, cried out: "He knoweth not what hath caused this soul-killing letter from the king." (*Ibid.* 1328). Sir George Moore observed, (*Ibid.* 1329) : "Whereas the king is misinformed, that we have meddled with things above our reach and capacity, we have not done otherwise than the Samaratine woman, who, out of her faith, did but touch the hem of Christ's garment; for which Christ did not blame her, but said that her faith had saved her." See also pp. 1338-1338.

privileges, as ever any of our predecessors were, nay, as to preserve
our own royal prerogative."[29]   The Commons were not satisfied
with such equivocation, and insisted that they had their privileges
and liberties "by prescription, time out of mind, and not by toleration."   Sir Edward Coke contended that privileges were an inheritance and not a royal grant.   A committee was appointed to investigate the matter more at length.   In the meantime another letter
arrived from James, this time not officially addressed to the lower
house, in which he asserted his intention to preserve its ancient
privileges.   On December 8, it was followed by another communication from the Crown to the Speaker; apparently it satisfied the
Commons, for they drew up a petition of thanks.   But now came
the report of the select committee, a report which was entered
upon the official Journal.   It re-asserted that privilege was "the
antient and undoubted birthright and inheritance of the subjects
of England."   James flew into a rage, sent for the Journal, and with
his own hands, tore out the report—"*manu sua propria*."   In his
Council, and in the presence of his judges, he declared the protestation "invalid, annulled, void, and of no effect."   James undoubtedly considered the action of the lower house as an invasion of his
prerogative, and shortly thereafter dissolved Parliament, giving
as one of his reasons that the House "either sat silent, or spent
the time in disputing of privileges, descanting upon the words and
syllables of our Letters and Messages."   A few of the "ill-tempered
spirits" he sent to the Tower.[30]

Perhaps the best known case involving the privilege of freedom of speech is that of the arrest of Sir John Eliot, Denzil Holles,
and Benjamin Valentine, by order of Charles I in 1629.   I shall
have more to say of this case a little later; in this connection, it is
almost unnecessary to repeat that these three members of the House
of Commons were prosecuted in the Court of King's Bench, after
Parliament's dissolution, for speeches made in the House which the
king considered dangerous, libellous, and seditious.   The accused
pleaded to the jurisdiction of the court, maintaining that the offence,
if any had been committed, was punishable only in Parliament and
in no other court.   "Words spoken in Parliament, which is a superior court, cannot be questioned in this court, which is inferior."[31]
Judgment was given by the royally-controlled court against the

---

[29] Cobbett, *Parl. Hist.*, I, 1344.
[30] *Ibid.*, 1331-1362.
[31] 3 Howell, *State Trials*, 296.

imprisoned members, and they were incarcerated at the king's pleasure and heavily fined. It was on this occasion that Judge Sir William Jones observed: "We are the judges of their lives and lands, therefore of their liberties."[32] The decision was most unpopular and contributed greatly to the growing opposition to Charles. The Commons never forgot this unwarranted invasion of their privileges, and made freedom of speech one of the fundamental liberties included in the Bill of Rights. But years before, in 1641, the earliest possible opportunity they had, the Commons adopted resolutions declaring the entire proceedings against their members a breach of privilege. The Civil War prevented further action. After the Restoration, the case was reopened. On November 12, 1667, the House of Commons, to remove all possibility of trouble in the future on this point, adopted a resolution declaring Strode's Act of 1521, guaranteeing freedom of speech,[33] a general law declaratory of the "ancient and necessary rights and privileges of Parliament."[34] November 23, the Commons declared the specific judgments against Eliot and the other members illegal and breaches of privilege. Subsequently, Denzil Holles, now Lord Holles, brought suit upon a writ of error returnable in Parliament to annul the lower court's decision, and the Lords ordered the judgment of the King's Bench reversed.[35] After the Revolution of 1688 and the consequent Bill of Rights, the privilege of freedom of speech and debate in Parliament was never again seriously questioned or denied.

Freedom of speech protects members from outside interference only. The privilege does not imply that a member may not be called to account and censured for insulting or discourteous remarks made in a Parliament house. Both houses have repeatedly exercised their right to discipline their members. Many have been brought to the bar for abusive or intemperate language, directed either against a member or against the House as a body. The usual punishment is a severe censure, although other methods of disciplining have been employed. Some have knelt in humble submission at the bar of the House in acknowledgement of their errors; others have been committed into the custody of the Serjeant-at-arms, or to prison; a number have been actually expelled. Some examples will be cited later.

[32] 3 Howell, *St. Tr.*, 306.
[33] See *ante*, 25.
[34] 1 Hatsell, 86.
[35] See 3 Howell, *St. Tr.*, pp. 331 *et seq.*

The privilege of freedom of speech does not permit a member to circulate separate publications of the remarks he has made in Parliament. If such publications should contain matter that constitutes a libel upon the character of an individual, the member is liable to prosecution in the courts. The same reasoning has been applied to reports published by order of a Parliament house, and containing libellous material, but since the great case of *Stockdale v. Hansard,* an act has been passed providing for a stay of proceedings in all cases where it can be shown that the publication is by order of a house of Parliament, and is a bona fide report, printed and circulated without malice.[36]

The case of *King v. Lord Abingdon* settled the law in the case of private publication, by a member, of speeches he has delivered in Parliament. The case was heard in the Court of King's Bench in 1794. Lord Abingdon sent the manuscript of a speech delivered by him in the Lords, to a newspaper for publication at his expense. One paragraph contained a charge of improper conduct against a certain Mr. Sermon of Gray's Inn. Sermon regarded the remarks as libellous and therefore instituted suit. Lord Abingdon admitted the facts but maintained that his speech was not a libel, first because its contents were true, and secondly "as the law and custom of Parliament allows a member to state in the House any facts or matters, however they might reflect on an individual . . . ., and such was dispunishable by the law of Parliament, ... he had a right to print what he had a right to deliver, without punishment or animadversion."[37] The court arrived at a different conclusion. Lord Kenyon admitted that the court could have no jurisdiction if the words had been spoken within Parliament and had been confined to its walls, but declared the present offence to be a private publication of a speech that constituted a libel, because made a "vehicle of slander" against an individual. The jury found for the plaintiff.

In 1813, Mr. Creevey, member of the House of Commons, sent a correct copy of a speech made in the House to a news-editor who had published a defective and inaccurate account of his remarks. The speech dealt with the affairs of the East India Company, and contained among other things a charge of corruption against the Inspector-General of taxes at Liverpool. The latter brought an action for libel in the Court of King's Bench. The

---

[36] See *postea,* 155.
[37] 1 Esp. *N. P. Cases,* 228.

defendant claimed privilege of Parliament, and the right to correct an error in the press by submitting a correct copy of his address for publication. Nevertheless, the jury found him guilty. An application for a new trial was denied by Lord Ellenborough on the ground that no member has a right "to address (his speeches) as an *oratio ad populum* in order to explain his conduct to his constituents," and that the order and procedure of Parliament does not provide that members should print their own speeches.[38]

Privilege does extend to reports and proceedings of Parliament printed by order of either house for the use of members only. This was the ruling in *Rex v. Wright*, 1799. Wright, a bookseller, had printed and published a report of the Committee of Secrecy of the House of Commons, by order of that House, and solely for the use of its members. J. Horne Tooke, whose name was mentioned in one of the paragraphs of the report, took offence at its content and sued Wright for libel. The case was dismissed on the ground that it involved "a proceeding of one branch of the legislature" and therefore could not be inquired into.[39] But where such publications are scattered broadcast, in the world beyond the walls of the Parliament houses, a very different situation arises. If privilege should apply in such cases, the proceedings of Parliament might become "vehicles of slander," and the individual's common law remedy would be seriously impaired. The final solution of this troublesome matter—the conflict between the law of privilege as applied to privileged publications and the ordinary law of libel—did not come until well along in the nineteenth century.

At the present time, the privilege of freedom of speech, as defined and carefully limited by statutes and court decisions, is established beyond question, and is secure from all interference from Crown, courts, or any other source.

C. FREEDOM FROM ARREST AND MOLESTATION

Of equal, if not of greater importance than freedom of speech is the privilege that guarantees to members freedom from arrest and general molestation, whether the interference come from Crown officers, private citizens, or the processes and summonses issued by

---

[38] 1 Maule & Selwyn, *Reports*, 273-283. Justice Le Blanc held that the court had no right to inquire into speeches made in the House, but that such was not the case with a publication, which comes under the common law jurisdiction. Note the distinction between the two bodies of law and the two jurisdictions.

[39] 8 Durnf. & East, 293-299.

the ordinary courts. This privilege, in the early stages of its development, was not limited to members of Parliament; it was extended to their servants and estates as well.[40]

The first case of great importance involves the application of the privilege of freedom from molestation to a member's servant. In the fifth year of Henry IV's reign, the Commons petitioned the king for relief in the case of Richard Cheddre, servant of one of the members. Cheddre had been assaulted during the time of Parliament. That the Commons were conscious of the vital principle involved is shown by the severe punishment they wished to inflict upon the assailant, to prevent the recurrence of such incidents in the future. In the view of the House, the murder of any one coming to Parliament under the king's protection should be treason; maiming or disfiguring a Parliament man should be punished by the loss of a hand, and in their petition to the Crown, the Commons inserted a special prayer requesting the king to refrain henceforth from the exercise of his pardoning power in similar cases unless all parties concerned should first give their assent. Evidently the Commons had learned to distrust royal promises. The assailant was imprisoned, fined, and held liable for damages, and it was resolved that the same punishment should be applied in similar cases in the future. A special act describing this procedure was passed and incorporated in the statute book.[41] Some years later, on the occasion of an assault on one of the knights of Oxford, the Commons referred to the Cheddre incident, and secured another confirmation of their privilege. It was stated that in the event of "any assault or attack made upon any lord Spiritual or Temporal, Knight of the County, Citizen or Burgess, come to Parliament or to the Council of the King at his command" the guilty party should be summoned before the King's Bench, and on conviction, should be held liable in double damages to the injured party, plus a fine and ransom to the king.[42] The wording of the petition in both cases indicates that the Commons regarded this privilege as an ancient part of the law and custom of Parliament, and not created

---

[40] I shall disregard those faint traces of privilege some have claimed to find in the Laws of Ethelbert, Edward the Confessor, and others of the Saxon kings, wherein the king's special peace and protection was guaranteed to those summoned to the witenagemots and synods. The evidence is not conclusive, and it seems better to confine the discussion to records and times where the footing is more secure, and when Parliament as such, took on something more nearly like its present form and composition. But see the discussion in May's *Parliamentary Practice* (11th Ed) p. 103.

[41] 5 Henry IV, Cap. VI.

[42] 4 *Rot. Parl.*, 453. Also 1 Hatsell, 24.

by the statutes mentioned. In Atwyll's case[43],—17 Edward IV—the privilege is said to exist "whereof tyme that mannys mynde is not the contrarie."

Thorpe's famous case in 1453 is not easy to analyze. Thomas Thorpe, Speaker of the House of Commons, had been arrested at the suit of the Duke of York, under an order from the Court of Exchequer, for certain acts of trespass committed since Parliament was in session. The Speaker was found guilty and sentenced to the Fleet prison. Thereupon, the Commons petitioned the king for his release, on the ground that their most ancient liberties and privileges had been violated and that parliamentary business could not be properly dispatched with the Speaker absent.[44] The Duke of York argued that Thorpe should be kept in confinement, since his release on a plea of privilege would result in a failure of justice. The Lords called upon the judges to settle this difficult question. In their reply, they upheld the theory that the High Court of Parliament, the highest court in the realm, and its peculiar *lex parliamenti*, were supreme in cases of this nature, and that privilege could be denied only in cases of treason, felony, or breach of the peace. The decision therefore entitled Thorpe to his release, since he was being held in a civil suit only. Nevertheless, he remained in prison, apparently upon the order of the Lords. The Commons were notified to that effect by the Bishop of Ely, who represented the king, and were instructed to elect another Speaker. They obeyed without further remonstrance.[45] A clear analysis of the case is difficult. It cannot be ascertained with absolute certainty just what steps were actually taken, and in what sequence, but one thing is certain, Thorpe's case was never much stressed by the later champions of privilege. Particularly the Commons were anxious to have some of its features forgotten, for in Thorpe's case, they had applied to the Lords, as well as to the king, for the protection of their privilege, instead of relying on their own powers to enforce their claims. Furthermore, notwithstanding the ruling of the judges to the contrary, the Lords had kept Thorpe in prison, and the Commons had acquiesced in the decision. In after years, the Commons tried to ignore this precedent, and certainly did not follow this course of procedure in subsequent cases. In 1620, Sir Nicholas Rich termed it "a case begotten by the iniquity of the time, when the Duke of York

---

[43] See May's discussion, *Parliamentary Practice* (11th Ed.) p. 104 and 6 *Rot. Parl.*, 191.
[44] 5 *Rot. Parl.*, 239.
[45] 1 Hatsell, 28 *et seq.*

might have an overgrown power in it."[46]   The explanation probably is as true as any.[47]

In 1460, the Commons petitioned for the release of a fellow-member who had been committed to the Fleet prison by the Court of Exchequer during Parliament time.[48]   In a similar case, about a decade later, a burgess was released on the petition of the Commons, but with the reservation specifically made that he was liable to prosecution after adjournment, and that the plaintiff's rights should in no way be impaired by the release.[49]   In 1477, the Commons reaffirmed their ancient privilege "that any of theym shuld not be empleded in any action personell, nor be attached by their persone or goodes in their comyng to any such Parlement, there abydyng, nor fro thens to their propre home resortyng."[50]

The privilege of freedom of arrest was thus recognized by both houses, by statute, by the king, and in the decisions of the judges. Nevertheless, it was not until the middle of the sixteenth century that the Commons began to deliver their members out of custody by the mere display of their own authority, symbolized by their Serjeant's mace.   The Commons, to 1543, appealed to the Lord Chancellor for writs of privilege to secure the release of their members, or had recourse to special legislation.   The year 1543 marks a departure from this form of procedure.   In that year, George Ferrers, a burgess from Plymouth, was arrested in London while on his way to Parliament.   The arrest was the result of a suit brought against him in the Court of King's Bench.   The Commons instructed their Serjeant to demand Ferrers' release.   His authority and power as an officer of the House was regarded as sufficient warrant for his acts, and he was instructed not to wait for a writ of privilege from the Lord Chancellor.   Ferrers' jailors refused to release their prisoner, offered forcible resistance, and in the scuffle that resulted "the Serjeant was driven to defend himself with his mace of arms, and had the crowne thereof broken by bearing off a stroke, and his man was stroken down."[51]   The sheriffs of London arrived at this point and joined the forces of the jailor, and the Serjeant's men, now greatly outnumbered, had to beat a hasty

---

[46] 1 Hatsell, 34.

[47] Pike's discussion of this case is in his *Constitutional History of the House of Lords,* pp. 248-251.   For his discussion of the privileges of the upper house, see Chapter XII.

[48] 5 *Rot. Parl.,* 374.

[49] 6 *Rot. Parl.,* 160.

[50] 6 *Rot. Parl.,* 191.

[51] 1 Hatsell, 53 *et seq.*

retreat. The House of Commons was much disturbed by this contempt of their authority, rose in a body, and proceeded to the Lords, where the Speaker recited their grievances. The Lords decided the "contempt to be very great" and left its punishment to the discretion of the Commons. The latter at once dispatched the Serjeant-at-arms on a second mission to deliver Ferrers. The writ of privilege offered by the Chancellor was rejected and the Serjeant was ordered to proceed without warrant or writ, relying solely on his mace, the insignia of his office. This time the jailor yielded and Ferrers was released. Subsequently the sheriffs, clerks of the Counter, White, who had instituted the suit against Ferrers, and all others involved in the case, were found guilty by the Commons of contempt of their privileges, and were sent to the Tower. The clerk was put in "Little Ease," and the prisoners were not released until the Mayor of London and other influential friends interceded for them. The king became interested in the case—perhaps because Ferrers was also one of his servants—summoned the Chancellor, judges, and Speaker before him, and commended them upon their wisdom and zeal in maintaining unimpaired the privileges of the Commons.[52]

In 1592, Francis Neale, member for Grantham, reported to the House that he had been arrested by Serjeant Lightburn, at the suit of "one Wessellen Weblen, Beer-Brewer;" that he had settled the case by paying the money due, but that he felt it to be his duty to acquaint the House with the facts, to the end that the privilege of freedom from arrest might be preserved without modification. Lightburn and Weblen were at once summoned to the bar, and committed to the Tower. Three days later, they were released, having paid their fees.[53] There are other cases on record in which the lower house granted a discharge only after specified fees had been paid,[54] and such cases suggest a close analogy between "fees"

---

[52] The king's remarks are reported as follows: "Whatsoever offence or injury (during Parliament time) is offered to the meanest member of the House, is to be judg'd as done against the Person and the whole Court of Parliament; which prerogative of the Court is so great . . . as all acts and processes coming out of any other inferior Courts, must for the time cease and give place to the highest." 1 Hatsell, 57. See also Cobb., *Parl. Hist.*, I, 555.

[53] D'Ewes, *Journals*, 518-520.

[54] See a case in 1645. On August 26 of that year the House of Commons resolved: "That this House doth accept of the sum of £600 of Sir John Tirrell, of Essex, to be forthwith paid for the Discharge of his Delinquency and Sequestration. And that, upon payment thereof, an Ordinance be brought in for his Discharge of his Delinquency, and taking the Sequestration off from his Estate, accordingly; he paying the said £600 within ten days." 4 *Com. J.*, 254.

collected by the House of Commons and "fines" assessed by courts of record.

In the procedure of the upper house, the same uncertainty existed for a time as in the Commons, in regard to the proper method to be employed in releasing imprisoned members or their servants. Sometimes writs of privilege were secured from the Lord Chancellor; sometimes the release was secured upon the direct order and authority of the House, symbolized by the demand of the Gentleman Usher of the Black Rod.[55]

In 1621, when parliamentary affairs were in a high state of confusion, the two houses deemed it necessary to adopt a curious and hitherto unheard of rule. The two houses just before adjourning for the summer, a period of over five months, adopted an extraordinary resolution of which Sir Edward Coke was reported to be the author. It provided "that in case of any arrest, or any distress of goods, serving any process, summoning the land of any member, citation or summoning of his person, suing him in any court, or breaking any other Privilege of this House, *a letter shall issue under Mr. Speaker's hand*, for the party's relief therein, as if Parliament was sitting; and the party refusing to obey it, to be censured at the next access."[56] This was an unheard of extension of privilege and might sanction almost any abuse, for release from custody depended entirely upon the Speaker, and what he chose to interpret as privilege of Parliament. This innovation, also, may be attributed to "the iniquity of the times."

In 1625, the Lords were called upon to defend their privileges in the case of the arrest of Lord Arundel. Lord Arundel was committed to the Tower by Charles I for no clearly stated reason, although the general supposition was that it was because of the marriage of the Lord's eldest son with the sister of the Duke of Lenox, a relative of the king. The Lords manifested no desire to provoke a quarrel with the king, but they were eager to learn the cause of the arrest, and to protect their privileges. They prepared to take steps to attain these ends. Charles must have received advance information of this decision, for he immediately sent the Lord Keeper to inform the upper house that Arundel was detained for a personal misdemeanor to the king, and that the offence in no way

---

[55] See May's *Parl. Practice* (11th Ed.) p. 106.
[56] 1 Hatsell, 163.

involved parliamentary matters. The Lords were not satisfied and ordered a search for precedents to be made. A resolution was consequently adopted setting forth the privileges of the Lords, and declaring the king's act to be illegal. Several weeks intervened and the Lords sent another reminder to the king, but still no reply. Then the Lords resolved to suspend all other business "that consideration be had how their privileges may be preserved to posterity." This was sufficient—Lord Arundel was released two weeks later.[57]

One of the great abuses that Parliament had to fight in the maintenance of the privilege of freedom from molestation was the royal practice of "pricking for sheriff" all those whose views were displeasing to the Crown and who must therefore be made ineligible for Parliament. A sheriff, "according to the received rule of our forefathers is tied to his county, as a snail to his shell,"[58] and so became automatically impossible as a member of Parliament. In 1675, the House of Commons appointed a committee "to consider of a proper way of superseding the Commission" making one of their members High Sheriff of the County of York. A resolution was adopted making it a breach of privilege to appoint a member as sheriff during the continuance of Parliament.[59].

It is unnecessary to multiply examples of the application of this privilege of freedom from arrest and molestation. Of the unwarranted extensions of privilege and the consequent conflict between *lex terrae* and *lex parliamenti*, I shall have more to say in a later chapter. Both houses insisted upon their right to commit for contempt and breach of privilege as an inherent right, in no sense dependent upon Crown or courts for its validity.

Tumults, riots, and obstructions in the streets leading to the Parliament houses were reported and dealt with from year to year as breaches of privilege. Sometimes the punishment was left to the Attorney-general; sometimes the houses themselves punished the disturbers.[60] On March 24, 1604, pages took a cloak from one Richard Brooke, "a young youth," servant to a member of Parliament, and carried it to a tavern where they exchanged it for wine.

---

[57] 1 Hatsell, 142 *et seq.* Rushworth *Historical Collections*, pp. 363-371. For other cases, in some respects similar, see Rushworth *Hist. Coll.*, 356, 358, 362, 363; 10 *Com. J.*, 902.

[58] Quoted from *Strafford Despatches*, III, 31, in Porritt's *The Unreformed House of Commons*, Vol. I, p. 383.

[59] 9 *Com. J.*, 378.

[60] See 37 *Com. J.*, 902.

All concerned were called to the bar and punished for breach of privilege.[61]

The practice of granting the privilege of freedom from arrest and molestation to members' servants in time became a serious menace to individual liberty and to public order, and a form of protection by which offenders often tried—and they were often successful—to escape the penalties which their offences deserved and which the ordinary courts would not have hesitated to inflict. Indeed, the sale of "protections" at one time proved a source of income to unscrupulous members, and these parliamentary "indulgences" were on several occasions obtainable at a fixed market price. Neither house, of course, ever gave this abuse its sanction, and both at times made sincere efforts to eradicate the evil.

In 1492, William Larke, servant to a member from London, was arrested and condemned to the Fleet, in a suit of trespass brought in the King's Bench by one Margerie Janyns. Larke claimed privilege of Parliament and petitioned for his release. The king granted the request, but Margerie was to have her judgment and damages at the close of the session.[62] Such a reservation of the legal remedy to the plaintiff after the adjournment of Parliament, was more and more frequently made and was finally stipulated by statute.[63] In the reign of Edward IV, two bankrupt servants, in an attempt to escape their creditors attached themselves to members of Parliament, but their claim of privilege was disallowed.[64] In 1575, the lower house, to check the increasing abuses arising from the practice of allowing privilege to servants, resolved that in the future, to obtain a writ of privilege for a servant, a member must take oath before the Lord Chancellor or the Lord Keeper of the Great Seal that the person concerned was really his servant.[65] In 1584, the Lords refused to grant privilege to a ser-

---

[61] Occasionally privilege was applied in a most amusing way. In 1601 a page was brought to the bar of the House, because he had "offer'd to throng" the venerable Sir Francis Hastings, while the latter was descending the stairs of the House of Commons. The page was committed into the Serjeant's custody, and was released only after humble submission, on his knees. A member moved that the page be carried to a barber and "close cut before his discharge," but the venerable assembly of Commoners decided that it was unfit "for the gravity of the House to take notice of so slight a fault." Townshend, *Proceedings in the Last Four Parliaments of Elizabeth,* pp. 195-196.

[62] 4 *Rot. Parl.,* 357.

[63] See 1 Jac. I Cap. XIII (1604) ; also 12 and 13 Wm. III, C. 3 (1700) ; 11 George II, Cap. 24 ; 10 George III, C. 50 (1770) ; 3 George IV, Cap. 2, s. 4 (1822). By these later statutes action may be brought against members at any time, provided their persons are not touched.

[64] Prynne, *Brief Register,* IV, 765. Other cases in 1 Hatsell, 70.

[65] D'Ewes, *Journals,* 248.

vant of Viscount Brindon because he had not claimed privilege when arrested and because he was "not a menial servant, nor yet ordinary attendant upon the said Viscount."[66]   In 1601, when one of her Majesty's Heralds-at-Arms in Ordinary was arrested, the Lords granted him privilege of Parliament and those responsible for the suit were ordered to appear.[67]   In the same year, privilege was granted to a member's tailor, as "one of his most necessary servants."[68]   Robert Holland, a scrivener at Temple-Bar and his servant were brought to the bar of the House and committed to the Serjeant for having beaten a member's servant.[69]   In James I's reign, a justice of the peace was voted guilty of a breach of privilege for having committed the coachman of Sir Edward Sandys to Newgate;[70] and a "Servant and Bag-bearer to the Clerk of the Commons House" arrested upon an execution, was liberated by order of the House.[71]

June 16, 1610, a committee of privileges of the House of Commons reported that a servant of Dr. Steward, in execution under a warrant from four justices "for getting a woman with child" should have privilege.[72]   A few years later, a member of the lower house announced that a farmer who had been his lessee for many years was now impleaded in one of the courts, and the House ordered that he should have privilege of Parliament.[73]   In 1645, a menial servant of a burgess of Parliament was impressed for military service. The Commons intervened on the ground of privilege and the prospective soldier was freed.[74]   In 1691, a certain Thomas Powley, in execution for £500, tried to escape arrest and payment of his fine by attaching himself to the house of Lord Morley and Mounteagle, in the capacity of gardener.   The matter came to the attention of the upper house and Lord Morley was committed to the Tower, on the charge of having granted a false protection, and an indemnity was granted to the undersheriff who had released several persons

---

[66] D'Ewes, *Journals*, 315.   Other cases in Townshend, *Proceedings*, pp. 85 and 87, and D'Ewes, 677.

[67] 2 *Lords J.*, 240, 238.

[68] Townshend, *Proceedings*, 196.

[69] Townshend, *Proceedings*, 259, 260.   For another case, see Hale, *The Original Institution, Power and Judicature of Parliament*, 178.

[70] Petyt, *Lex Parliamentaria*, 282.

[71] Petyt, 282.   See additional examples in 1 Hatsell, 119, 161; also 2 *Lords J.*, 597.

[72] 1 Hatsell, 133.

[73] Prynne, IV, 845.

[74] 4 *Com. J.*, 316.

on the strength of the illegal protection.[75] In 1745, a peeress by claiming all those employed in her gaming houses as domestic servants, tried to prevent the suppression of her establishment.[76]

It is self-evident what abuses result from such an extension of the principles of privilege of Parliament. By granting privilege to servants and outsiders who had no real connection with Parliament, as these cases clearly show was repeatedly done, these individuals were automatically removed from the jurisdiction of the courts of common law, where their offences should have been tried. For privilege was claimed and enforced under the *lex parliamenti,* and therefore courts which knew only the *lex terrae* could take no cognizance of such cases. Privilege thus became a menace to the rights of the individual, who was deprived in this fashion of his ordinary common law remedy. Occasionally, a judge presumed to interpret privilege according to the rules of the common law or the principles of justice as he saw them—the result was inevitably a conflict between Parliament and the courts. When we consider how often the *lex parliamenti* seemed to encroach upon the *lex terrae,* it is surprising that these struggles did not occur more frequently than they did.

The most disgraceful of all the practices that developed from these extravagant interpretations of privilege was the traffic in "protections." These documents were issued under the hand and seal of members. They usually contained statements to the effect that certain persons were servants of a Parliament man, and demanded—"under the ancient privileges, laws, and customs of the realm heretofore used and approved"— that they be free from arrest, imprisonment, and molestation during the time of Parliament.[77] A protection thus became an ever-ready and convenient means to stop all actions by courts or police officers, and it avoided the necessity of first appealing to Parliament for a writ of privilege. In Parliament, an explanation of the trouble might have been demanded and the justice of the case examined. The original pur-

[75] 15 *Lords J.,* 15, 57. One writer on this period came to the following conclusion: "It has to be admitted that for no purpose was parliamentary privilege more valued than for escaping from the payment of lawful debts." A. S. Turberville, *The House of Lords in the Reign of William III,* 77. (Oxford Historical and Literary Studies, 1913.) Chapter IV, pp. 62-93, deals with Parliamentary Privileges of the Upper House.

[76] 26 *Lords J.,* 492. For an amusing incident involving the arrest of a poverty-stricken Scotch peer in the time of George II, see Fortescue's *Reports,* 165.

[77] One form of protection is given in R. Harford, *The Privileges and Practices of Parliaments in England* (1680) p. 16.

pose of protections may have been excellent, but no procedure lent itself more easily to abuse. There was a time when a regular traffic in protections arose. Both houses did what they could to suppress the evil, and with considerable success. But the danger was real. This privilege of protection was the privilege of "The High Court of Parliament," exercised by the *lex et consuetudo parliamenti*, and no matter how greatly abused or how unjustly extended, no inferior common law court could interfere.

The seventeenth century apparently marks the beginning of the sale and forging of protections. In 1621, Lord Stafford and Lord North complained that forged protections were in circulation. The forgers were apprehended, and sent to the pillory.[78] In 1625, the Lords ordered that George Gardener and George Buttrice be brought to the bar on a charge of counterfeiting protections under the hand and seal of the Earl of Huntingdon. Gardener denied the forgery, but admitted procuring many such protections from a certain Tymothy Chastleton, who made a practice of selling them at a fixed market price. Buttrice also denied the forgery, but admitted having purchased a protection from Gardener. Both were committed to the Fleet. A month later, Gardener confessed to the purchase and sale of ten protections. This time he was sentenced to the pillory.[79] In April, 1640, forged protections, some of them bearing the name of Lord Morley, were selling at £3 each.[80] Protections must have become specially troublesome to the officers of London. In 1641, they complained, in a petition to the Lords, of their "Multitude and Inconveniency."[81]

The practice was not limited to the upper house. On November 2, 1641, the Commons investigated charges preferred against one of their members. It was proved that the burgess had granted protections to as many as twenty individuals who were not his menial servants. These protections he had sold at prices ranging from ten to forty shillings each. One purchaser used his protection against his landlord when the latter came to collect the rent. The member admitted the facts but claimed privilege in defence of his action. He was promptly expelled and the Commons' house adopted a resolution forever disqualifying him from membership in that body.[82] In 1660, a resolution of the Commons declared all

---

[78] 3 *Lords J.*, 170.
[79] 3 *Lords J.*, 509, 525, 550.
[80] 3 *Lords J.*, 64 and 65.
[81] 4 *Lords J.*, 258.
[82] 2 *Com. J.*, 301.

protections null and void,[83] but this did not end the abuse. In the
following year, another forger of protections was brought to the
bar of the House.[84] Two years later, an officer of the excise was
accused of the same offence.[85] In 1689, the House of Commons
declared void all protections and written certificates issued by
members, ordered all those outstanding to be annulled, and forbade
any further issues.[86] This was made a standing order. The Lords
passed a similar order in 1690,[87] and two months later, three of
their number who had violated the order were brought to the bar.[88]
Similar resolutions were passed in 1694, 1712, etc.[89]—but as late
as 1754, the Lords were busy with a case arising from the forging
of two protections.[90] In the act of 1770, no reservation was made
for the privilege of servants; this solved the problem of protections
automatically.[91]

In addition to members' servants, members' goods and estates
were long included under the general claim of privilege of freedom
from molestation. This protection of the property of members was
essential during the early stages of Parliament's development. Without this privilege confiscation of estates or interferences with the
personal property of a member might become the means of har-
rassing members to such an extent that they would be unable to
attend their duties in Parliament. But from extensions of this
privilege—in itself reasonable and necessary, if properly applied—
arose the most flagrant abuses ever practiced under the sanction
of parliamentary privilege. Under the plea of privilege, individuals were summoned to the bar of Parliament for simple cases of
trespass—hunting on a member's land, or fishing in his pond, or
breaking down his fence. By voting offences such as these
"breaches of privilege," they were removed from the jurisdiction of
the ordinary courts and the common law. As in the case of offences
against the old Forest Laws, cases under the *lex et consuetudo parliamenti* were removed from the common law jurisdiction to
a jurisdiction where a separate, peculiar law applied—a law

[83] 8 *Com. J.*, 184.
[84] 8 *Com. J.*, 303.
[85] 8 *Com. J.*, 480. For other cases, see 10 *Com. J.*, 296, 332; 14 *Lords J.*, 457; 461, 462;
5 *Lords J.*, 636.
[86] 10 *Com. J.*, 340.
[87] 14 *Lords J.*, 521.
[88] 14 *Lords J.*, 606.
[89] See 11 *Com. J.*, 219, and 19 *Lords J.*, 431.
[90] 28 *Lords J.*, 201.
[91] 10 George III, c. 50.

that was known only to the body that had brought the indictment. Thus the *lex parliamenti* could infringe upon the *lex terrae*. Furthermore, the scope and content of these two bodies of law, and their relation to each other, was but imperfectly understood for centuries. A later chapter will deal with actual clashes between the law of Parliament and the law of the land in the courts, and the difficulties in working out the proper relation between the two bodies of law. But the instances cited here are of equal importance. They show even more effectively than the contests in the courts what the real difficulty was and what dangers might arise from these unjustifiable extensions of the claims of privilege. The worst abuses were practiced in the seventeenth and eighteenth centuries, by the corrupt, time-serving Whig Oligarchy which had come into power with the Glorious Revolution and which continued "to trade on the credit of the Revolution Parliament."

In 1606, a horse belonging to a member was drafted for use in the postal service. This action was regarded as a molestation of a Parliament man, and the postmaster and his servant were brought to the bar of the lower house for a hearing. The servant was eventually committed into the Serjeant's custody.[92] In 1626, Sir Francis Leake discovered that the claims of privilege might be of service even in family matters. Sir Francis had leased all his possessions to his eldest son, Lord Deyncourt. The latter fell in arrears with his payments, and the father brought suit against him in Chancery. Lord Deyncourt claimed privilege of Parliament and refused to put in an answer to the suit. Fortunately for the father, the House of Lords refused to allow the claim of privilege of Parliament and ordered the suit to proceed.[93] In 1628, when an admiralty officer ventured to attach a ship belonging to the Earl of Warwick, he was ordered before the bar of the Lords and the attachment was discharged as contrary to privilege of Parliament.[94] Twelve years later, a mill in Lincolnshire, owned by the Countess of Exeter was attacked by a mob who "riotously and maliciously threw in a Great Part of the Bank, and broke down a fair Stone-arched bridge." The offence was represented as a breach of privilege and a number of the rioters were apprehended and taken before the Lords. It was only after a promise to build a new bridge had been extracted from the "two principal and ablest Delinquents" that the case was dis-

---

[92] 1 Hatsell, 187, 188.
[93] 3 *Lords J.*, 609.
[94] 3 *Lords J.*, 776.

missed.[95] In 1642, breaking into a Lord's stable and removing several horses was voted a breach of privilege. Several troopers were the guilty parties, and they, with their lieutenant, were ordered to the bar.[96].

The lower house was guilty of the same extensions. In 1643, three offenders "for cutting down and lopping the Timber-trees" on Denzil Holles' estate were sent for by order of the House.[97] May 9, 1662, Richard Shuttleworth was summoned for stopping up "the Lane's End of his Lordship of Barton."[98] In 1664, Gyles Earle, "in breach of privilege" built a wall upon a manor owned by a Lord, and for his offence was fined by the upper house and ordered to tear down the structure again.[99] A half dozen years later, taking a bit of tin belonging to a Commoner was punished as a breach of privilege.[100] In 1670, diverting and stopping a water-course was declared a breach of privilege by the lower house.[101] The Lords, two years later, decided that entering upon and disturbing a fishery and manor of the Lord Fitzwalter was contrary to privilege of Parliament and sent out for the offenders.[102] A little later the same Earl complained that a number of men were fishing on his estate without license. When the Serjeant appeared to arrest the trespassers, he was attacked by the enraged fishermen. The Lords then ordered that Fitzwalter's estates "be quieted to him from time to time by the assistance of the sheriff of Essex, as any occasion or disturbance shall arise thereupon."[103] In 1677, Richard Campion violated the privilege of Peregrine Bartie, member of the Commons, by "pulling down the Scaffolds about the house of the said Mr. Bartie, and . . . . saying that the members of this house were a Company of Rascals, to maintain their privileges against the people."[104] His remark reminds one of Selden's that "the Parliament-men are as great princes as any in the world, when whatsoever they please is privilege of Parliament. No man must know the number of their privileges, and whatsoever they dislike is breach of Privilege."[105] In 1678, an exciseman forcibly entered the

---

[95] 4 *Lords J.*, 188.
[96] 5 *Lords J.*, 636.
[97] 3 *Com. J.*, 65.
[98] 8 *Com. J.*, 424; see also 9 *Com. J.*, 629.
[99] 11 *Lords J.*, 644.
[100] 9 *Com. J.*, 93.
[101] 9 *Com. J.*, 213.
[102] 12 *Lords J.*, 536.
[103] 13 *Lords J.*, 143, 153.
[104] 9 *Com. J.*, 425.
[105] See discussion in G. P. Gooch's *Political Thought from Bacon to Halifax*, p. 74.

house of a burgess whom he suspected of concealing liquor in his cellar. For doing his duty, he was summoned to the bar of the House.[106] A few years later (1690) entering upon the mines of a member of the lower house was punished as a breach of privilege.[107] In 1692, when the Commons learned that the Council of the city of Carlisle had disfranchised one of their number, the act was declared a breach of privilege and the Mayor and several Aldermen were ordered to appear.[108] There are several records of cases in which duellants, who had challenged members of Parliament, were declared guilty of a violation of privilege, and were ordered into the custody of the Serjeant.[109] In 1714, entering and working the lead mines of a member was punished as a breach of privilege.[110] On another occasion, parliamentary privilege served the purpose of a copyright. The House of Lords, in 1721, resolved "that if, after the death of any Lord of this house, any person presume to publish in print his works, life, or last will, without consent of his heirs, executors, administrators, or trustees, the same is a breach of the privileges of this House." Later, this was made a standing order.[111] In 1732, Robert Crabb was openly reprimanded while kneeling in humble submission at the bar of the Lords, for having, within the time of Parliament, "in a forcible manner" broken down a fence rail and driven horses and cattle into the lands belonging to the Earl of Strafford.[112] Several years later, a complaint of a breach of privilege—the killing of rabbits in a member's warren—was referred to a committee of the House of Commons for investigation.[113] In 1745, an attempt was made by several ladies who operated public gaming-houses to escape prosecution by claiming privilege of Parliament for all inmates, "servants" to their ladyships.[114] In 1753, John Joliffe, a member of the lower house, complained that several malefactors had been fishing in his pond and had carried off several stones used as boundary markers, and the case was referred to the Committee on Privileges and Elections.[115] Six years later, fishing in Admiral Griffin's fishery was actually declared a breach of privi-

---

[106] 9 *Com. J.*, 472.
[107] 10 *Com. J.*, 451.
[108] 10 *Com. J.*, 699, 700.
[109] 15 *Com. J.*, 405; 16 *Com. J.*, 562.
[110] 17 *Com. J.*, 591, 639, 640.
[111] See 21 *Lords J.*, 660, 667.
[112] 25 *Lords J.*, 136.
[113] 23 *Com. J.*, 505.
[114] 26 *Lords J.*, 492.
[115] 26 *Com. J.*, 698.

lege and the offenders were committed to the custody of the Serjeant-at-arms.[116] The next year digging up the ground, and carrying off a tree from the estate of a member was considered important
enough to be referred to an investigating committee,[117] and in 1761,
entering the cellar of a member's tenant was punished as a breach
of the privileges of the House of Commons.[118]

The list of citations has been purposely extended to show what
a real danger there was in the rigid application of this theory of
privilege which made Parliament supreme and declared its peculiar
law to be separate from and above the common law. How an extension of its claims to privilege could, and actually did, make Parliament the oppressor of the rights of the individual—at least to the
extent that it deprived him of his common law remedies and the
safeguards and guarantees of individual liberty which common
law courts afforded—the cases cited above clearly demonstrate.
Almost without exception, they involved offences ordinarily triable
in the ordinary courts of the realm; many of them were nothing
more than trespasses. Nevertheless, they were tried in Parliament, by a different and special law and in a court from which there
was no appeal because "there was none higher."

Under the general head of freedom from molestation may be
included the privilege which exempted members from jury duty
or from serving as witnesses during Parliament time. This was
essential to insure the members' constant attendance in Parliament.
Moreover, it was not logical that a summons or subpoena from an
"inferior court" should be permitted to interfere with the personell
or public business of the "High Court of Parliament."

As early as 1290, a case occurred which suggests the privilege
of not being impleaded during Parliament time. The Prior of the
Holy Trinity in London by procurement of Bogo de Clare, had cited
the Earl of Cornwall to appear before the Archbishop of Canterbury. But the Earl had also been summoned by the king to his
Parliament in London. The Prior's order was served *"per medium
majoris Aule Westm'"* during Parliament time. The Prior and
Bogo were summoned before the king and committed to the Tower

---

[116] 28 *Com. J.,* 498.
[117] 28 *Com. J.,* 915.
[118] 28 *Com. J.,* 1107. For other cases, see 26 *Lords J.,* 86; 27 *Lords J.,* 324; 28 *Com. J.,*
598; 3 *Lords J.,* 506; *Ibid.,* 744, 774; 4 *Lords J.,* 155, 168, 169, 276, 295; 16 *Lords J.,* 132, 138;
11 *Lords J.,* 298. Many others might be cited from the Journals of Parliament.

for interference with a Parliament man.[119]   In 1548, the lower house ordered four of its members to excuse the non-appearance of a fellow-member before a justice of the Common Pleas.[120]   Members always insisted upon exemption from jury duty.[121]   In 1584, Anthony Kirke was brought to the bar of the House, charged with having subpoenad a member for the Star Chamber during the time of privilege.[122]   Frequently members who complained to the House that they were being molested by writs and summonses from the courts, were released from these obligations by a Speaker's warrant directed to the Lord Chancellor and asking for a writ of *supersedeas*.[123]   At times, letters from the Speaker were equally effective in securing a stay of proceedings.[124]   In 1607, the House of Commons ordered the Speaker to write a letter to the Barons of the Exchequer for a stay of proceedings.   Hatsell believed this was the first instance of a letter demanding a stay of proceedings directed to a superior court of Westminster-hall, others having been addressed to justices of assize and inferior courts.[125]   In 1680, when the grand juries of Devon and Somerset made presentments against several members, the foreman, two jurymen, the clerk of the assizes, the undersheriffs, etc., were all summoned to the bar of the Commons to answer for their breach of privilege.[126]

At present, the claims of privilege of freedom from arrest and molestation are rigidly limited, and the sphere of their application has been carefully defined.   Members of Parliament may be coerced by practically any legal process that does not involve an actual attachment of their person.   They may serve as witnesses if the courts regard their attendance as essential and if due notice is given to their respective houses.   Permission to attend is almost never refused.   The practice is analogous to the older custom of "waiving privilege," something that could only be done with the consent of the House to which the member belonged.   To assure the unmolested attendance of witnesses summoned before either house of Parliament, or committees of Parliament, the privilege of freedom from arrest and molestation has been extended to them.

---

[119] 1 *Rot. Parl.*, 17.   See also 2 *Rot. Parl.* 196 for an interesting case involving the liberties of a churchman.

[120] 1 *Com. J.*, 11.

[121] See 1 *Com. J.*, 369 ; also D'Ewes, *Journal*, 560.

[122] 1 Hatsell, 97 ; see a similar case in Chancery, D'Ewes, *Journal*, 347.

[123] D'Ewes, 436.

[124] See 1 *Com. J.*, 342 ; 343 ; also 8 *Com. J.*, 601.

[125] 1 Hatsell, 178, 179.

[126] 9 *Com. J.*, 656.

The same is of course true of all officers of the two houses and all those whose personal attendance is necessary to the business of Parliament.[127]

D. PRIVILEGE IN CASES AFFECTING THE HONOR AND DIGNITY OF PARLIAMENT.

In addition to enforcing privileges applying to individual members, their servants, and estates, the two houses were quite as careful to punish breaches of privilege affecting the honor, reputation, and dignity of a Parliament house. Words uttered in debate, or the publication of derogatory or insulting articles in the press, designed to bring Parliament into disrepute, were frequently severely punished under the law of privilege.

In 1588, Thomas Drurie, was brought before the House of Commons charged with "great and deep offences committed . . . . against the whole State of this House." He had publicly declared that he could get no justice from the House and had acted in a manner generally displeasing to that assembly. For his offence, Drurie was committed to the custody of the Serjeant.[128] Libels, whether upon individual members or the houses of Parliament, have been consistently punished as violations of parliamentary privilege. In 1601, a Mr. Doyley lodged a complaint in the House against a publication, "The Assembly of Fools," which he believed to be a libel upon Parliament. The printer was at once brought in, but further examination revealed that the alleged libel was "a meer Toy, and an Old Book, ... a Thing both Stale and Foolish"—for which the member "was well laughed at; and thereby, his Credit much impaired. . . . ."[129] In 1621, the Lords summoned an offender before them for "divers ignominious and base Speeches" against the Prince and Princess Palatine, and the Lords of the High Court.[130] In 1628, the Serjeant-at-arms of the lower house brought in a burgess who, in a rage, had characterized certain Parliament men as "Hellhounds and Puritans."[131] In the same year, a certain Henry Reynde

---

[127] For other examples of the application of privilege, see 8 *Com. J.*, 364, 372, 634; 9 *Com. J.*, 163, 316; 10 *Com. J.*, 537; 48 *Lords J.*, 58, 61-63; 11 *Com. J.*, 784; 15 *Com. J.*, 124; 51 *Com. J.* 614, 661; 14 *Lords J.*, 687; 29 *Lords J.*, 181; 48 *Lords J.*, 58; 8 *Com. J.*, 200; 64 *Com. J.*, 210; 213, 227, 236; 27 *Com. J.*, 540; 3 *Lords J.*, 165, 170; 5 *Lords J.*, 605; 1 *Com. J.*, 353, 378; 10 *Com. J.*, 117, 331; 12 *Com. J.*, 127; 19 *Com. J.*, 667. See also, Townshend, *Proceedings of the Last Four Parliaments of Elizabeth*, p. 254; and G. Petyt, *Lex Parliamentaria*, p. 273.

[128] D'Ewes, *Journals*, 436, 451.

[129] Townshend, *Proceedings in the Last Four Parliaments of Elizabeth*, 217.

[130] 3 *Lords J.*, 155.

[131] 1 Hatsell, 204.

incurred an exceptionally severe penalty at the hands of the Lords
for "ignominious speeches" against Lord Say and Seale, and for
his contempt "of this High Court of Parliament." Reynde was
indefinitely imprisoned, put in the pillory, fined £200, and compelled
to apologize to all the Lords.[132] In 1640, the Serjeant of the Commons' House was instructed to bring in a member of the clergy for
remarks derogatory to Parliament, made in a sermon delivered in
Salisbury Cathedral six year earlier.[133] In 1680, a clerk, Richard
Thompson, was accused in the House of Commons of high misdemeanors against the privilege of Parliament. A committee was
organized to investigate the case, and their report revealed that in
the previous year, Thompson, in one of his sermons, had made an
assault upon Hampden, and had declared that "the Presbyterians
were such persons as the very devil blushed at them." On another
occasion, in the church of St. Thomas at Bristol, Thompson had
pointed his finger at the effigy of Queen Elizabeth, and had called
her "the worst of women," "a most lewd and infamous woman."
The Commons resolved that the clerk had publicly defamed her
Majesty, preached sedition, promoted popery, and vilified the Reformation; and by his endeavor "to subvert the liberty and property of
the subject, and the rights and privileges of Parliament" had become "a scandal and reproach to his function." A committee was
instructed to prepare articles of impeachment, but the dissolution
of Parliament prevented further action.[134] In 1701, Thomas Cole-
pepper, for remarks he had made concerning the previous house,
was committed to Newgate.[135]

In cases of libel of Parliament or its members, and unauthorized and false accounts of proceedings, newspaper publishers were
naturally the chief offenders. The House of Commons adopted
resolution after resolution to prevent news-writers from printing
libellous or unofficial accounts of the proceedings in Parliament.
It must be remembered that the House never officially permitted
the publication of reports of its proceedings, therefore it might
consider any account as unauthorized and a breach of privilege.
Strictly speaking, there is no officially authorized report of debates
today, for the rule was never altered. Any member might announce
to the House that he "espies strangers," and the galleries could be

---

[132] *Lords J.*, 851.
[133] 2 *Com. J.*, 72.
[134] 8 Howell, *St. Tr.*, 2-8.
[135] 13 *Com. J.*, 735. For other cases, see 2 *Com. J.*, 788; 5 *Com. J.*, 469; 10 *Com. J.*, 112;
11 *Com. J.*, 565.

cleared of all present, including reporters, by order of the Speaker. But there is a vast difference between theory and practice.[136] As a matter of fact, reporters now enjoy special privileges in Parliament—members are only too eager to address their constituencies through the medium of the public press—and an authentic report of parliamentary debates is published at public expense. But several centuries ago, this was not the case.

In 1641, an order was passed enjoining all members of the lower house from delivering copies or notes of proceedings to any one outside Parliament.[137] The following year, a printer published a message of the House without license, and was promptly sent for as a delinquent. A resolution was passed at once, by which the printing or selling of accounts of proceedings of the House of Commons under the name of a Journal was made a breach of privilege.[138] A similar resolution was passed in 1694.[139] The next year, two men were brought in for distributing papers contrary to the will of the House.[140] In 1696, John Dyer ventured to give an account of the proceedings of the lower house in a News Letter, and was promptly committed into the custody of the Serjeant.[141] In 1832, the proprietor of the Dublin Evening Mail was taken into custody for printing the report of a committee before it had been liberated for publication.[142]

At present, as I have indicated, the practice is entirely different. Newspaper men are given special privileges in the houses; daily reports of proceedings are the rule, and no objections are raised as long as the debates are accurately reported. Should the publication be made in bad faith however, or for the purpose of libel, the publisher may be summoned. He then becomes liable to censure for *publishing* the debate itself, under the old rule. It is the publication that technically constitutes the breach of privilege.[143]

---

[136] See Redlich, II, 34-38, for historical note on the admission of strangers and the publication of debates.

[137] 2 Com. J., 220.

[138] Ibid., 560.

[139] 11 Com. J., 193.

[140] 11 Com. J., 439.

[141] 11 Com. J., 716.

[142] 87 Com. J., 360. For other cases, see 12 Com. J., 48; 14 Com. J., 270; 20 Com. J., 99; 21 Com. J., 238; 14 Com. J., 270; 30 Lords J., 420; 5 Lords J., 24; 22 Lords J., 129, 149; 68 Com. J., 322; 72 Com. J., 232; 245; 44 Com. J., 463; 48 Com. J., 925; 43 Lords J., 57; 42 Lords J., 177, 181; 60 Com. J., 214; 65 Com. J., 105; 74 Com. J., 533; 75 Com. J., 55. A number of these incidents resulted in extended litigation in the courts, and in some cases, a struggle between courts and Parliament. For this phase of the subject, see a later chapter on the conflict between lex terrae and lex parliamenti.

[143] See May's Parliamentary Practice (11th Ed.) pp. 73 and 74.

Cases of bribery have frequently been included in the class of offences to be punished as breaches of privilege which affect the honor and dignity of Parliament. The giver or receiver of a bribe has, like any other violator of a privilege of Parliament, been punished under the general commiting power each House has ever enjoyed. In 1667, John Ashbournham was expelled from the lower house for accepting a bribe of £500.[144] In 1694, another was committed to the Tower of London for having accepted a bribe of two hundred guineas,[145] and one who had given money to several members to secure the passage of a bill in which he was interested, was committed into the Serjeant's custody for having "been an Occasion of Scandal to this House, and the Members thereof."[146] Authors of letters, offering bribes, were similarly punished, even though no money had actually changed hands.

E. Duration of Privilege

The expression "time of privilege" has, strangely enough, never been clearly defined by parliamentary enactment.

A peer, by the privilege of peerage, is forever "sacred and inviolable." A peeress enjoys the same privilege, but forfeits it upon marrying a Commoner. Representative peers, and all other peers and peeresses of Scotland and Ireland are on the same basis in this respect with those of England.

The House of Commons has never definitely stated just what is meant by "time of privilege." The *lex parliamenti* allows privilege to all members *"eundo, morando, et exinde redeundo."* But what is the proper number of days to be consumed in going to and from the sessions of Parliament has usually been left to be decided when emergencies and specific cases arose. Forty days before the opening and forty days after the close of Parliament has often been regarded as the proper period for privilege, although no legislation has been passed on this point.

In 1586, when a burgess of Parliament had been arrested more than twenty days before Parliament assembled, the lower house decided that twenty days was a convenient and reasonable time of privilege.[147] In 1601, privilege was granted to a member under

---

[144] 9 *Com. J.*, 24.
[145] 11 *Com. J.*, 236.
[146] 11 *Com. J.*, 277. See also 11 *Com. J.*, 274, 331; 14 *Com. J.*, 474; 17 *Com. J.*, 493, 494.
[147] D'Ewes, *Journal*, 410.

arrest in London, after his election, but before a return had been made.[148] In the same year, while discussing the privilege of members' servants in the lower house, a member expressed the opinion that privilege begins fourteen days before Parliament meets.[149] In *Jackson v. Kirton*, the defence pleaded for privilege forty days before and after a Parliament sitting, but the court apparently denied the claim.[150] Prynne believed that privilege began only on the day a member actually had to leave home in order to reach Parliament for the opening session, and extended for a like period after the close of Parliament. He pointed out, furthermore, that members must return to their homes with all possible dispatch and cannot expect protection under a claim of privilege if they linger on private business. In his opinion, eleven or twelve days were sufficient to enable a person to reach the remotest corner of the kingdom.[151] In *Barnes v. Ward,* twenty days were regarded as a proper period.[152] In the case of the *Earl of Athol v. the Earl of Derby* (24 Charles II) it was held that the Lords had privilege twenty days, and that the Commons claimed privilege for a forty-day period.[153] In 1640, the lower house seems to have regarded sixteen days "before the beginning of Parliament, and so many after" as the time for privilege.[154] In 1734, the Court of King's Bench evaded an opportunity to clear up this question, and simply ruled that in the case before them, three days was not a "convenient time."[155] Another reporter, in discussing the case observes in this connection that "this point was not much insisted on, it appearing that the House of Commons had always avoided determining this question and had left it at large to a convenient time, of which themselves were judges. . . . . It doth not appear that they ever entered into the consideration of the nearness or distance of each gentleman's borough; but hold the same general rule, as it is done *in testes* and returns of writs at common law; which are the same near, as in the remotest counties."[156] In the case of *Goudy v. Duncombe* (1847) the court held that for two centuries forty days before and after the meeting of Parliament,

---

[148] Petyt, *Lex Parliamentaria*, 285, 286.
[149] Townshend, *Proceedings*, etc., 225.
[150] 1 Brownlow & Goldesborough *Reports*.
[151] Prynne, *Brief Reg.* IV, 630, 642, 652, 665, 676.
[152] 1 Siderfin's *Repts.* 29.
[153] 2 Levinz, 72.
[154] 2 *Com. J.,* 10.
[155] See *Hollowday v. Pitt,* in Barnardiston's *Repts.,* Vol. II, p. 422.
[156] 2 Strange *Repts.,* 986.

had been considered the convenient or actual time of privilege.[157] The case *In re Anglo-French Co-operative Society* (1880) applied the rule laid down in *Goudy v. Duncombe*, and declared that forty days were allowed by the law of Parliament for the return of members to their residences.[156]

---

[157] 5 Dowling & Lowndes, 209-213. An analogy is pointed out in this case between this practice and the forty days' period allowed for the franking privilege. (See Statute-book, 4 George III, c. 24, s. 1.) An old Irish statute definitely fixed the forty day period for the Irish Parliament (3 Edward IV, C. 1).

[156] 14 Chancery Division, 533-537. Professor Redlich suggests that this practice of allowing freedom of person for forty days after Parliament's adjournment is "a survival from the ancient Teutonic idea of judicial safe conduct." Redlich, *Procedure of the House of Commons*, (Steinthal's Trans.) Vol. II, 153.

CHAPTER III

THE HOUSE OF COMMONS AND ITS JURISDICTION OVER DISPUTED ELECTIONS.

The claim of the House of Commons that it had the sole right to judge and settle disputed elections was never included in the Speaker's petition presented at the opening of each new Parliament. Nevertheless, from the close of the sixteenth century on the Commons have insisted upon this right as one of their undoubted privileges, and therefore a discussion of the action of the lower house in election cases properly belongs in a history of privilege.

Elections to Parliament were notably open to abuse and manipulation. The sheriffs of the counties, royally appointed officials, at times enjoyed practically unlimited power in matters of election. At the dictation of either king or powerful noble, a sheriff frequently made false returns, and in a dozen ways, used his influence to determine the outcome of the elections. Many attempts were made to correct these abuses, by statute or by allowing appeals to the king in Council, but with only limited success.[1] The House of Commons did not claim the right to settle election disputes until 1586. Previous to that time, petitions of electors claiming irregularities or fraudulent returns in elections were referred to Parliament as a whole, to the Court of Exchequer, to the Chancery, or to the king and the lords, but not to the Commons as such.[2] To 1406, the king, in or out of Parliament, took direct cognizance of complaints. After that year, writs were made returnable in Chancery. By an act passed in 1410, the judges of assize were empowered to examine election returns, but the king with his judges or his lords determined their validity.[3] As the lower house continued to develope, it became more and more aware of the importance of this power to

---

[1] A most valuable discussion of election cases is to be found in John Glanville's *Reports of Certain Cases Determined and Adjudged by the Commons in Parliament* (London, 1775). See especially the Introduction. Glanville was chairman of the committee of privileges and elections, and his introduction discusses many of the earliest election cases. The printed Journals of the House of Commons for 1623 and 1624 are imperfect, and Glanville's work is a valuable supplement to the official Journals.

[2] See Glanville, *Election Cases*, Preface.

[3] See discussion in Stubbs, *Constitutional History of England*, III, 421-424. See also, pp. 453-455, 489-500.

judge election cases. A representative assembly, to exercise real power in the state, generally must have the power to decide who is entitled to sit among its membership. To use the words of Selden, an error in election matters, "is like an errour in the first Concoction, that spoils the whole Nutriment." For the Commons it was especially necessary to guard against the influence of king and lords, exercised in the county elections, if they desired to make the lower house something more than the subservient instrument of the upper house or the Crown. Thus far, the principle is simple enough. But when in the case of a conflicting return it became necessary to determine who were the lawful voters in a certain town or county, the case presented real difficulties. Should the House settle this also, or should the final settlement be left to the adjudication of the ordinary legal tribunals? The privilege to vote has generally been regarded as a matter guaranteed by the common law, and under its supervision. If this be true, no voter can be deprived of the franchise by the vote of a single chamber of the legislature, without at least leaving open to him a course of action that would allow him to seek relief and damages in a common law court. At once we are face to face with the great dilemma which arose from the very nature of the English constitutional system. Let the Commons once admit the right of a common law judge to decide a matter arising from a disputed election, and the way lies open for an appeal to the supreme court, the House of Lords, which thus becomes the judge of the composition of the lower house. For the Commons it was absolutely essential to protest against any such procedure which might draw the right to determine their membership "into the insatiable gulf of the Lords' judicature." Here may be found the clue to many conflicts between the upper and lower house. Here also is another example of the friction between the *lex terrae* and the *lex parliamenti*, the Commons frequently applying the latter while the Lords were championing the claims of the common law in these struggles between the two houses of Parliament.

The right to try contested elections was for the first time claimed and asserted by the Commons in 1586.[4] On account of an irregularity in the return for the County of Norfolk, the Lord Chancellor issued a second writ, which resulted in the choice of different candidates. When the Commons took notice of the matter, they were advised by Elizabeth that it was "in truth impertinent" for

---

[4] See Glanville, *Reports of Election Cases*, Preface, XLII-LXI.

them to deal with such a question, "belonging to the charge and office of the Lord Chancellor, from whence the writs for the same elections issued out, and are thither returnable again." The lower house paid little attention to the royal admonition, an investigating committee was selected and a report was adopted in favor of those elected under the first writ. The Committee refused to consult the Chancellor, or the judges, for they "thought them competent judges in their places; yet, in this case, they took them not for Judges in Parliament in this House." The House resolved "That it was a most perillous Precedent that after two Knights of a County were duly elected, any new Writ should issue out for a second election without order of the House of Commons itself; That the discussing and adjudging of this and such like difference belonged only to the said house; That though the Lord Chancellor and Judges were competent Judges in their proper Courts, yet they were not in Parliament; That it should be entered in the very Journal-Book of the house that the said first election was approved to be good not out of any respect the house had or gave the Resolution of the Lord Chancellor and Judges therein passed but merely by reason of the Resolution of the house itself by which the said election had been approved; and That there should no message be sent to the Lord Chancellor, not so much as to know what he had done therein because it was conceived to be a matter derogatory to the Power and Privilege of the said house." [5] Apparently the Queen yielded to this emphatic statement of the rights of the Commons, and the case became a precedent for the future.

In 1592, Thomas Fitzherbert of Staffordshire, outlawed under a *Capias Utlagatum,* was elected to the House of Commons. Two hours after his election, and before the indenture had been returned, he was arrested. Fitzherbert at once petitioned the House of Commons for a writ of privilege. Several questions were thus raised for settlement. Being outlawed, was a man eligible for election to Parliament? If eligible, was he entitled to privilege? After considerable discussion, the House decided that Fitzherbert was a member, but that he was not entitled to privilege, because he had been taken in execution before the return of the indenture of his election, and not *"sedente Parliamento, eundo, or redeundo."* [6] The debates in the Commons reveal two very interesting points of view in regard to the law of Parliament, one considering the *lex parliamenti*

[5] D'Ewes, *Journal,* 393, 397
[6] 1 Hatsell, 107.

as the superior of the *lex terrae*, the other as merely a part of the *lex terrae*. One member, in arguing that privilege should apply in the case, remarked, "And though the Common Law doth disable the party, yet the privilege of the house being urged, that prevaileth over the law."[7] A certain Mr. Brograve disagreed and advised that instructions be obtained from the judges, "whether in this Cause *by the Law* we can grant privilege or no."[8] The supposition probably was that the judges would give their opinion extrajudicially, and not as an actual judgment of the case.[9]

The precedent established in 1586 in the case of the County of Norfolk was definitely confirmed in the great case of Fortescue and Goodwyn, in the reign of James I. In this case the danger to the privileges of the House of Commons came from the interference of the Crown in elections. In the election for the County of Bucks, Sir Francis Goodwyn defeated Sir John Fortescue and was returned as elected. His rival complained to the king and Council that Goodwyn was ineligible, because outlawed, and the Clerk of the Crown therefore refused the writ. James, in his very first summons of Parliament, had especially forbidden the election of outlaws and bankrupts. Fortescue was elected on a second writ. When Parliament met, the sheriff for Bucks returned both writs, the one declaring Fortescue elected, the other containing a statement of the outlawry against Goodwyn and describing him as "not a meet person to be a member of the Parliament house." Goodwyn petitioned the Commons for relief, and the Serjeant was ordered to bring in the Clerk of the Crown, with all necessary papers. March 23, 1604, the Clerk was given a hearing. The House thereupon resolved that Goodwyn was a lawfully elected member, and ought to be received as such. Numerous precedents were cited to support this decision, and the House insisted that by law an outlawry in personal actions (in this case for debt) was no cause to disable a person from being a member of Parliament. James was naturally much displeased by this decision, especially because he seems to

---

[7] D'Ewes, *Journals*, 481.

[8] *Ibid.*, 514. The italics are mine.

[9] See Francis Bacon's speech,—"though we sit here to make Laws, yet until the new Law is made, the old Law is of force, and our Conference with them (the Judges) gives away no resolution from us, but taketh advice from them." D'Ewes, *Journ.*, 515. Another report gives a somewhat different account of Fitzherbert's case. According to this, the House ordered the Speaker to move the Lord Keeper for a writ of habeas corpus to bring Fitzherbert before them. "But the Lord Keeper returned, that in regard of the ancient Liberties and Privileges of this House, the Serjeant at Arms be sent by Order of this House for Mr. Fitzherbert at his own Charge . . ." G. Petyt, *Lex Parliamentaria*, 276.

have had some personal interest in Fortescue's political fortunes. The matter was referred by the king to the "Judges of the Upper House," who decided that no outlawed person could become a member of Parliament. The upper house sided with James, and asked the lower house for a conference on the case. The Commons rejected the request on the ground that there was no necessity for a conference; that judgment had been given; and that "in no sort" should they "give account of their proceedings to the Lords." The upper house retaliated by refusing conferences on other matters, and reported the matter to the king. Thereupon the Attorney-general appeared with another request for a conference, this time from the king himself, who felt himself "engaged and touched in Honor." The Commons sent their Speaker and a committee of members to a conference with the king, but obstinately insisted upon their former resolution in regard to the Lords. James vowed that "he had no purpose to impeach their privilege: *But since they derived all Matters of Privilege from him, and by his Grant,* he expected they should not be turned against him." To the precedents cited by the Commons, he replied "That there were no precedent did suit this Case fully: Precedents in the Times of Minors, of Tyrants, of Women, of simple Kings, not to be credited. . . . ."[10] The precedents from Elizabeth's reign were speedily dismissed with the remark that they were in "the Time of a Woman, which sex is not capable of Mature Deliberation."[11] James insisted that the Chancery was the proper place to decide disputed returns, and that the judges' decision—that outlawry was a ground for ineligibility—ought to be obeyed. With a final injunction to reflect on the matter and confer with the judges if necessary, James left "to ride to Royston a hunting." The lower house refused to yield. They resolved that "what they had done, was well and duly done," and refused to consult with the judges. A formal statement of their position was drawn up, and sent to the king and the Lords.[12] James was forced to adopt a compromise. He urged that both claimants be set aside and that an entirely new election be held, promising at the same time to "confirm and ratify all just privileges:—This

---

[10] 1 *Com. J.*, 158. See also G. Petyt, *Lex Parliamentaria*, 301-304; and 1 *Com. J* 156 *et seq.*

[11] Petyt, *Lex Parl.*, 309.

[12] 1 *Com. J.*, 158, 162, 163. The House resolved that ". . . for any Matter of Privileges of our House, we are, and ever have been, a Court of ourselves, of sufficient Power to discern and determine, without their Lordships, as their Lordships have used always to do for theirs, without us." 1 *Com. J.*, 164.

his Bounty and Amity; as a King royally; as King James, sweetly, and kindly, out of his Good-nature." New writs were issued and with this the incident was closed.[13] In spite of the form of a compromise, the struggle ended in a clear victory for the Commons. A bill was subsequently taken up to disqualify outlaws from sitting in Parliament in the future, but the House seems to have had precedents for its position in the Goodwyn case. In the thirty-fifth year of Elizabeth's reign, John Killigrew, against whom fifty-two outlawries had been returned, and Sir William Harcourt, eighteen times outlawed, had been admitted as members of the House of Commons.[14]

Glanville reports a number of cases arising during the reign of James I, in which the Commons seem to have based their jurisdiction in election cases directly upon their powers as a court. In a disputed election for the County of Middlesex, the House of Commons resolved that it was "a council of state and court of equity, touching things appertaining to their cognizance, as well as a court of law," and "may of themselves question any election, or return, although no party grieved do ever complain."[15] In a case for the County of Cambridge it was declared that "the House of Commons in Parliament, is a distinct court of record of itself. . . . ."[16] Another resolution of the Commons declared that "this court, and council of state and justice, is guided by peculiar, more high, and politic rules of law and state, than the ordinary courts of justice are in matters between party and party. . . . . "[17]

In the case of *Nevill v. Stroud* (1658) the rights of the Commons were recognized without much trouble. The case strikingly illustrates the popular conception that *lex parliàmenti* and *lex terrae* were two entirely separate bodies of law. Nevill had instituted suit against Stroud, late sheriff of Berkshire, for having made a false return in an election to Parliament. The Court of Common Pleas heard the arguments of counsel, and then ordered a transcript of the record to be delivered to the lower house—"this Court doubting whether they have cognizance of this cause; being grounded merely upon the Common Law; of which they have no prece-

---

[13] 1 *Com. J.*, 168-171.
[14] See M. Hale, *Original Institution, Power and Jurisdiction of Parliament*, 169.
[15] Glanville, 118, 119.
[16] *Ibid.*, 85.
[17] *Ibid.*, 59, 60. Borough of Chippenham Case. See also, Case for County of Norfolk, and Borough of Stafford, pp. 4, 27.

dent."[18] The House summoned counsel of both parties to the suit, but a settlement was long delayed. It was almost a year and a half before the case was reopened, and a day set for the appearance of the judges, to explain their record of the case. The judges of the Common Pleas came into the House and reported that "Mr. Nevill hath a Verdict in the Cause; and prayed Judgment: But the Judges . . . . finding that it concerned the Privilege of Parliament . . . . thought (it) not fit to proceed to Judgment, until the Judgment of this House be had therein."[19] A fortnight later, the House ordered the case remanded into the Common Pleas Court, with the advice to transmit it to the Exchequer Chamber for final determination.[20]

In 1674, the right of the Commons to decide disputed elections received the confirmation of the Court of the Exchequer Chamber. In that year, Sir Samuel Barnardiston brought an action against Sir William Soame, sheriff of Suffolk, charging the latter with having made a fraudulent double return in a parliamentary election. Barnardiston obtained a verdict of £800. A motion to arrest judgment was argued in the King's Bench. The Commons recognized the election of Barnardiston and committed the sheriff. Before the King's Bench the defendant argued that the question was one examinable in the Commons, and since they had already punished him, all further proceedings ought to be discharged, for an additional sentence would constitute double punishment for the same offence. The King's Bench dismissed the motion to arrest judgment. Upon writ of error to the Exchequer Chamber, this judgment was reversed. The court definitely recognized the sole jurisdiction of the Commons in election cases,[21] and decided that an action did not lie at common law against an officer for a double return. The House of Lords also upheld the ruling. In the case of *Onslow v. Rapley*, arising a little later, the judges ruled that "it would be a great presumption in this court to meddle in things concerning elections of Parliament."[22]

The Commons continued to apply their privilege in election matters without opposition. In 1694, the Mayor of Liverpool was ordered into the custody of the Serjeant of the House for having

---

[18] 7 *Com. J.*, 599.
[19] 7 *Com. J.*, 671.
[20] 7 *Com. J.*, 824. Also 2 Siderfin's *Reports*, 168.
[21] 2 Levinz, 114-116.
[22] 3 Levinz, 29-30.

made a false return in a parliamentary election.[23] Five years later, a candidate complained to the lower house that "a great many of his (opponent's) Voices were unqualified, by reason they received Alms" and that his rival had spent £300 "on Meat and Drink, presents, money, bribes, promises of leases on houses and lands, etc." The House at once appointed a committee to investigate the case.[24] In 1702, John Packington reported that the Lord Bishop of Worcester had used his influence to dissuade him from becoming a candidate for Parliament, and had threatened to oppose him among the clergy if he persisted in his candidacy. The Lord Bishop carried out his threat among the laity, as well as among the clergy, it seems. The lower house resolved that his acts were "malicious, unchristian, and arbitrary, in high violation of the Liberties and Privileges of the Commons of England," and requested the Queen to remove him from his position as her Lord Almoner. Two days later, the bishop was relieved of his duties.[25] In *Prideaux v. Morris*, the Commons' rights in election cases were once more confirmed, this time by a common law court. In this case, an action arising from a false return, Chief Justice Holt ruled that in the case of a false return where there may be a settlement in the House of Commons, there can be no action by a court because of "the Inconveniency of Contrary Resolutions." ". . . . But where the Right of Election, either is determined, or cannot be determined in Parliament, as in the Case of a Dissolution . . . . an action lies for the false return."[26] In another part of his decision, Lord Holt drew a clear line of demarcation between cases arising wholly in Parliament, and so coming entirely under the *lex parliamenti*, and such injuries as occur and take effect outside Parliament, thus falling within the cognizance of the common law and the common law courts. Determination of who has a legal right to a seat in the House of Commons in a contested election and who shall be returned, is quite different from the determination of who has the elective franchise. The former is examinable and determinable by Parliament alone, and by the *lex parliamenti;* voting is a privilege granted and guaranteed to certain classes of citizens by the common law of the land. Any attempt on the part of Parliament to enter this field of adjudication

[23] 11 *Com. J.*, 201.
[24] 13 *Com. J.*, 89.
[25] 14 *Com. J.*, 37.
[26] Holt's *Reports*, 523.

would be an infringement on the common law that might very well lead to an encroachment upon individual rights and liberties.[27]

In 1702, the House of Commons made an attempt to extend this privilege in elections—now universally recognized by the Crown, Lords, and courts—to include a determination of who composed the legal electorate in a given constituency. It was perhaps a natural step from settling disputed elections to actually determining who were the lawful voters in a given district. The one frequently seemed to involve the other.

On December 26, 1701, a writ was issued for an election to Parliament in the borough of Aylesbury, and the sheriff ordered the constables to proceed with the taking of the vote. Ashby, an indigent who had repeatedly been warned by the overseers of the poor to leave Aylesbury, appeared at the voting place and demanded that his vote be registered for a particular candidate. The Commons, sometime before this incident, had resolved that the franchise in Aylesbury should be limited to all inhabitants not receiving alms. Accordingly, the constables ruled that Ashby was not entitled to vote, because he was not a "settled inhabitant." Ashby then brought suit against the constables, alleging that he was an inhabitant of the district, that he received no alms, and that the constables had falsely and maliciously obstructed and hindered him from giving his vote in the election. Ashby obtained a verdict and £5 damages against White, one of the returning officers, in the County Assizes. The case was taken before the Court of Queen's Bench on a motion to arrest judgment, on the ground that action did not lie. All the judges, with the exception of Holt, ruled that the action was not maintainable. Holt, although standing alone, had a clear conception of the real issue involved. He perceived that grave dangers to the individual were involved in the theory which made each house the sole judge of its privileges, especially if that included the right to extend them as well. He saw clearly that extensions might be made until they would become a menace to those fundamental rights of life and liberty guaranteed to all English-

---

[27] See Holt's opinion in this case. ". . . Whatever falls under the Regulation of Law in such a case, is subject to the Law of the Land; for Laws are to be executed out of Parliament. But for the Rules of the House of Commons, as to their sitting, etc., they are within the House, and the Judges cannot know them, there being no practice of them out of the Parliament; yet if a Law should be made relating to them, or they should become necessary to be determined on account of some other Matter cognisable by the Judges, we must take Notice of and determine them." Holt's *Repts.*, 523.

men by the common law. It required more than a century and a half longer to define the proper relation between the *lex parliamenti* and the *lex terrae;* in the end, the solution adopted was substantially that suggested by Holt in 1700. Holt's colleague, Justice Gould, proclaimed the case of *Ashby v. White* a Parliament matter "with which we have nothing to do," and held that the plaintiff's privilege of voting was not a matter of property or profit, and therefore he had suffered only a *"damnum sine injuria."* The learned judge was evidently afraid to express an opinion that might run contrary to the decision of the Commons.[28] Justice Powys was of substantially the same opinion. He affirmed the absolute right of the Commons to determine their membership. "Besides," he added, "we are not acquainted with the learning of elections, and there is a particular cunning in it not known to us."[29] Justice Powell upheld the supremacy of the *lex parliamenti* in the case and refused to interfere.[30] For Ashby's benefit he suggested that he state his troubles in a petition to the House of Commons, and promised that *after* that body had decided that he had a right to vote, the court would entertain an action for damages. Here we have Justice Powell's suggestion for preventing conflicts between courts and Parliament. The solution was by no means satisfactory. Lord Holt's dissenting opinion—the first clear exposition of what might be termed the modern view of parliamentary privilege—deserves extended quotation. Holt considered the right of election an original right, and a part of the English constitutional system itself. "This right of voting is a right in the plaintiff by the common law, and consequently, he shall maintain an action for the obstruction of it."[31] According to Holt, the law gave a remedy to every one hindered in the enjoyment or exercise of a right, and that remedy was an action at law for damages against the disturber. Furthermore, the case as Holt saw it, involved a matter of property, determinable in the courts, and was not merely a question as to who was entitled to a particular seat in the Commons. He drew a care-

---

[28] See 2 Lord Raymond, 938-942. Justice Gould observed,—"If we should take upon us to determine that he has a right to vote, and the parliament be of opinion that he has none, an inconvenience would follow from contrary judgments." See also the excellent discussion of this case in Broom, *Constitutional Law*, 847-848. For general discussion of privilege, see *Ibid.*, Part III.

[29] 2 Lord Raymond, 945.

[30] "The Parliament have a peculiar right to examine the due election of their members, which is to determine whether they are elected by proper electors, such as have a right to elect; for the right of voting is the great difficulty in the determination of the due election, and belongeth to the Parliament to decide." 2 Lord Raymond, 947.

[31] 2 Lord Raymond, 954.

ful and correct distinction between the question of who has a right to *be* in Parliament, (a matter to be settled by the houses of Parliament) and who has a right to select its membership, an entirely different matter. "We do not deny them (the Commons) their right of examining elections, but we must not be frighted where a matter of property comes before us, by saying it belongs to the Parliament; we must exert the Queen's jurisdiction."[32] The House of Commons, he argued, could neither judge of an individual's complaint nor award him proper damages and satisfaction. In fine, Holt's position was that privilege is no bar to any action. Although an action may be delayed and proceedings in it may be obstructed for a time by reason of a claim of privilege, this does not, to the least degree, take away any legal remedy that may be applicable to the case, when the time of privilege has expired. Further, anything incompatible with the rights of the people, or anything depriving them of their fundamental right to secure reparation for injuries received by applying to the courts of law, can never be a privilege of Parliament.[33] Holt thus announced a new doctrine—the doctrine that there are some fundamental rights of the subject, guaranteed under the common law, which cannot be abridged or altered, not even under the sacred claims of parliamentary privilege. And he called upon the courts of the kingdom to take up the battle for individual liberty, even though it might lead to serious hostilities with an all-powerful Parliament.

January 14, 1703, the House of Lords reversed the decision of the Queen's Bench, and adopted the dissenting opinion of Lord Holt. As might have been predicted, a conflict between the two houses followed. The Commons were in a fury over this violation of what they considered one of their most sacred privileges, and terrified lest the House of Lords, through its appellate jurisdiction, should eventually come to exercise a controlling influence over the composition of the lower house. Before discussing the conflict between the two houses in detail, another case at law, arising directly from the *Ashby v. White* proceedings, may first be disposed of.

Hardly had the Lords given their decision unfavorable to the claims of the Commons, when a certain Paty and four other burgesses of Aylesbury, began an action against the constables of their borough on a charge identical with the one in the preceding case. This incurred the ill will of the Commons who at once ordered Paty

[32] 2 Lord Raymond, 957.
[33] See 2 Lord Raymond, 950-958.

and his associates to be committed by a Speaker's warrant for having brought an action at common law against the constables of
Aylesbury, in contempt of the House. The prisoners thereupon sued
for a writ of habeas corpus in the Court of Queen's Bench. The
judges thus found it their unpleasant duty to decide whether they
had jurisdiction in the case; whether they should order the prisoners before them, or leave the entire matter to the House. The Commons sent no one into court to argue their side of the case. Justice
Gould ruled that the prisoners should be remanded, because committed by a "superior court" whose return of a commitment could
not be reversible for form in an inferior court.[34] The learned judge
then explained that there were several laws in the kingdom, among
which was the *lex parliamenti*, and that the judges "ought not to
give any answer to questions proposed to them about matters of
privilege, because the privileges of Parliament are not to be determined by the common law."[35] Consequently all technical objections to the form of the warrant were overruled.[36] Justice Powell
agreed with the majority of his colleagues in ordering that the
prisoners be remanded "because they were committed by another
law, and consequently we cannot discharge them by that law by
which they were not committed."[37] He concluded with as clear an
exposition of the Parliamentary view of privilege as can be found
anywhere. "There is a *lex parliamenti*," he says, "for the common
law is not the only law in the kingdom; and the House of Commons
do not commit men by the common law, but by the law of Parliament. Consider the judicature of Parliament. The House of Lords
have a power of judicature by the common law upon writs of error,
but they cannot proceed originally in any cause. But they proceed
too in another manner in case of their own privileges, and therein
the judges do not assist, as they do upon writs of error; and their
proceeding in that case is by the *lex parliamenti*. So the Commons
have also a power of judicature (and here the judge quoted Coke's
Fourth Institute)—but that is not by the common law, but by the
law of Parliament, to determine their own privilege, and it is by

---

[34] "If this had been a return of a commitment by an inferior court, it had been naught,
because it did not set out a sufficient cause of commitment; but this return being of a commitment by the house of commons, which is superior to this court, it is not reversible for form." 2
Lord Raymond, 1106. For entire case, see *Ibid.*, 1105 *et seq.*

[35] 2 Lord Raymond, 1106, etc.

[36] See Justice Powys' opinion,—"The house of commons is a court . . . and commitment by a court need not be under hand and seal. And besides, the *consuetudo parliamenti* will
justify this commitment." 2 Lord Raymond, 1107.

[37] 2 Lord Raymond, 1110.

this law that these persons are committed." The House of Commons is the supreme judge of its privileges, and no court, although it might be called upon to judge of privilege, could give judgment contrary to that expressed by the Commons. Powell believed that the High Court of Parliament was a superior court to the one on which he served, and that "though the King's Bench have a power to prevent such excesses of jurisdiction in courts, yet they cannot prevent such excesses in Parliament, because that is a superior court to them . . . ."[38]

Judge Holt again wrote a strong dissenting opinion. His reasoning was as clear and compelling as that set forth by him in *Ashby v. White*. Once more Holt argued for the fundamental rights of the individual. No person's liberty or property, he declared, could be taken away, diminished or encroached upon, except by an act of legislation, which required the concurrence of Queen, Lords, and Commons, and not simply a resolution of one house.[39] "The votes of both houses cannot make law, and so cannot declare it. . . . Both houses are bound by the law of the land, and in their actions, are obliged to pursue it."[40] Holt did not deny the right of Parliament or either house to enforce their just and recognized privileges. What he did combat was the extension of privilege or the creation of new privileges by one house. In this practice, he clearly foresaw the possible infringement of the *lex parliamenti* upon the courts, the common law, and the rights of the subject, guaranteed by that law. And here Holt stood on firmer ground than his colleagues and most of the men of his time. His view was eventually adopted as correct. While courts and judges were still hopelessly wandering through a maze of conflicting principles and unsolved difficulties which the subject of privilege presented, Holt saw where the dividing line between the claims of privilege and the principles of the common law must be run. He seems to have understood the proper relation that must be maintained between them. But while giving all due credit to Lord Holt, one must not fail to appreciate the point of view of the Parliamentarians. The importance of the principle for which they contended so strenuously, cannot be denied. For the House of Commons nothing was more important than to keep questions of privilege out of the ordinary courts of the realm, and thus

---

[38] 2 Lord Raymond, 1110.

[39] "Neither house of parliament, nor both houses jointly, could dispose of the liberty or property of the subject." 2 Lord Raymond, 1012.

[40] 2 Lord Raymond, 1115.

out of the highest court of England, the House of Lords. To do otherwise would be nothing less than signing its own death warrant as a free and independent part of Parliament. The logic of the champions of privilege was unimpeachable. It required centuries, and changes of the most sweeping character in the English framework of government, to reconcile these two points of view.

As already indicated, the decision of the Queen's Bench in *Ashby v. White* was reversed by the Lords on writ of error, and Holt's dissenting opinion was accepted as correct. This was the signal for a prolonged conflict between the two houses. The House of Commons at once adopted resolutions defending its ancient privileges in matters of election, and provoked the struggle by ordering the attorney for Ashby before the bar on a charge of breach of privilege.[41] John Paty and his associates from Aylesbury were also declared guilty of a breach of privilege and contempt of the House for having instituted proceedings at common law against the Aylesbury constables. They were committed to Newgate, and Mead, Ashby's attorney, was put into the custody of the Serjeant-at-arms. A few days later, the prisoners were given a hearing at the bar of the House and were then remanded to Newgate.[42] They attempted to regain their liberty by habeas corpus proceedings in the Queen's Bench, but without success.[43] February 26, four others who had pleaded the cause of the prisoners before the court, were taken into custody by the Serjeant.[44] Simultaneously, the Lords granted them the privilege and protection of their house and warned all keepers of prisons, serjeants, etc., not to arrest them. The following day the Lords explained their position in a number of formal resolutions. They maintained that neither house of Parliament could, by mere vote or declaration, create new privileges unwarranted by the known laws and customs of Parliament; that every injured freeman had a right to seek redress for grievances by an action at law; and that such proceedings against a person not entitled to privilege of Parliament could never be punished as a breach of privilege. The upper house declared the jurisdiction claimed by the Commons contrary to the English constitution, on the ground that every Englishman, when arrested, has a right to apply for a writ of habeas corpus and to demand that his attorneys be free from

---

41 14 *Com. J.*, 431.
42 *Ibid.*, 444, 507, 509.
43 See *ante*, 66.
44 14 *Com. J.*, 552.

punishment for anything they may do in a legal way in his behalf. The Lords considered a writ of error to be the right and privilege of every subject so long as he applied for it in the proper manner.[45] The House of Commons speedily drafted a reply. The Commons disclaimed any intention to deprive a freeman of his right to seek redress for injuries received, but—and here lies the crux of the matter—application must be made "to the proper court," having cognizance of such matters. "For should your Lordships Resolutions be taken as an universal proposition," the Commons' resolutions continued, "all distinction of the several courts, viz., Common Law, Equity, Ecclesiastical, Admiralty, and other courts will be destroyed, and in this Confusion of Jurisdiction the High Court of Parliament is involved."[46] The Commons did not hesitate to draw the analogy between courts of law and a Parliament house, evidently considering both as judicial tribunals, or at least being conscious of the judicial characteristics Parliament still possessed. The lower house contended that certain cases were triable only in Parliament, and cited precedents and judicial decisions to support their view. "To bring such Causes to the Determination of other Courts," the Commons insisted, "strikes at the very Foundation of all Parliamentary Jurisdiction, which is the only Basis and Support even of that personal privilege to which the members of either House are entitled." Therefore, according to the reasoning of the lower house, the prosecution of a case that would draw such matters to the examination of the courts, would constitute a breach of privilege. The House reasserted its claim of being the sole judge of elections, and protested against the release of any one committed by its orders without first obtaining its consent. The action of the Lords was viewed as nothing less than a dangerous encroachment upon the ancient rights of the lower house. The resolutions of the Commons concluded with the sweeping assertion—"The Commons cannot but see, how your Lordships are contriving by all Methods, to bring the Determination of Liberty and Property into the bottomless and insatiable Gulf of your Lordships Judicature; which would swallow up both the Prerogatives of the Crown, and the Rights and Liberties of the People."[47]

These sharp resolutions made little impression upon the upper house, except to prompt another formal statement in reply. The

---

[45] 14 *Com. J.*, 553-559.
[46] *Ibid.*, 560.
[47] 14 *Com. J.*, 563.

Lords admitted the right of the Commons to determine election disputes, but absolutely refused to give up their former contention that a forty-shilling freehold entitled an individual to a vote, and that a deprivation of that fundamental right could only be tried in a court imposing an oath. A deadlock was the result. The Commons produced additional precedents and cited Coke's *Fourth Institute* to explain the law of Parliament. "There are divers Laws within this Realm"—so read one resolution, "of which the Common Law is but One." And "as there are several Laws, so there are several Courts and Jurisdictions, and several Causes proper for those several Laws and the several Jurisdictions . . . . and of these, the High Court of Parliament is the first." Therefore, with "Causes in their Nature parliamentary, the common Law, and the common Law Judges have nothing to do . . . ."[48] The House of Commons proclaimed the *lex parliamenti* "the highest and noblest part of the laws of England, particularly adapted to the Preservation of the Liberties of the Kingdom." In spite of extravagant statements, the House of Commons showed beyond doubt that it understood the situation correctly and knew that permitting writs of habeas corpus upon commitments, and then writs of error to the Lords, "would bring all the Privileges of the Commons to be determined by the Judges, and afterwards by the Lords." It is reported that the Commons had much more to say at the conference, but the Lords broke off the discussion.[49] An order from the Queen, proroguing Parliament, finally ended the deadlock between the two houses. The Commons fired a parting shot by adopting a final resolution declaring all their proceedings to have been "in maintenance of the ancient and undoubted Rights of the Commons of England," and ordering all proceedings, reports, and minutes of conferences to be printed.[50] The prorogation automatically liberated the Alyesbury men, who at once proceeded with their actions at law and obtained favorable verdicts.

The debates in both houses, while this conflict was being waged reveal that most members clung to the traditional view of privilege. But in the lower house there were some who disagreed with the sentiments of the majority and revealed opinions in close agreement with those set forth by Holt. For example, the Marquis of Hardingdon, one of the dissenters, is reported to have said: "When

---

[48] 14 *Com. J.*, 570 *et seq.*
[49] *Ibid.*, 570-575.
[50] *Ibid.*, 575.

a person offers his vote at an election, and is not admitted to give it, and upon such refusal brings his action in the courts of Westminster-hall, . . . if giving judgment upon it be contrary to the privileges of this house, then it is pretty plain, that our privileges do interfere with the rights of the people who elected us. . . . . Gentlemen talk of the law of Parliament; I cannot see how that can give any interruption to the law of the land. . . . ."[51] Another member who later became a judge, expressed similar views, and maintained that as a guarantee of individual rights, the Lords must have the right to determine this matter when regularly brought before them on a writ of error.[52] Sir Joseph Jekyll, afterwards Master of the Rolls, disagreed with the majority because he regarded the right of the elector to vote as a right under the common law, not the law of Parliament, and therefore common law courts were the proper tribunals to pass upon violations of this right.[53] Another member agreed that the lower house had the sole power to pass on election cases and even the voter's rights, "to the end to try who is your member, or to punish the officer as an offender against the court," but believed that any attempt to prevent electors from bringing actions for damages sustained by them as a consequence, would be "not agreeable to the law or constitution of Parliament."[54] Sir Humphrey Mackworth on the other hand, was an out and out supporter of the Commons' Resolutions, and accepted without qualification the view that Parliament was "the highest court of the realm," and that lex parliamenti was supreme. "This is not a case between party and party," he observed, "but between the Lords and Commons; because the determination of the case brings the whole right in question, who have the privilege to judge of the qualification of electors to give their votes in election of members to serve in Parliament, whether the Lords or the Commons . . . ."[55]

The House of Commons, in exercising its right in matters of elections, naturally covered a wide range of cases. In 1750, the House had an offender brought to the bar for having led a mob to the home of the High Bailiff of Westminster while the latter was

---

[51] Quoted in 14 Howell, *St. Tr.*, 732.

[52] *Ibid.*, 743.

[53] "The right of voting is not a parliamentary right, but an ordinary legal one, and the common law Judges have the judgment of it originally; and it is incidentally only that the House has a power of judging of it, and that too according to the rules of the common law . . . This is a right at common law, and this House cannot apply a remedy." 14 Howell, *St. Tr.*, 747.

[54] 14 Howell, *St. Tr.*, 755.

[55] *Ibid.*, 761, also 770-777.

engaged in making the count in a parliamentary election, and for otherwise trying to influence the result. He was committed to Newgate for his contempt.[56] In 1767, a situation very similar to the Aylesbury incident threatened to develop. Complaint was made in the House against three men and their attorneys, charging them with having brought actions of trespass against the sheriff of Pembroke who had refused to accept their votes at a recent parliamentary election. The Commons at once fixed a date for investigating the case. Several postponements occurred, and finally the House learned that the parties concerned had discontinued the suits.[57] In 1770, the Lords resolved "that any resolution of this house, directly or indirectly impeaching a judgment of the House of Commons, in a matter where their jurisdiction is competent, final, and conclusive, would be a violation of the constitutional rights of the Commons, tends to make a breach between the two houses of Parliament, and leads to general confusion."[58]

On February 2, 1780, the House Committee of Privileges reported that the Duke of Chandos, a peer of Parliament, and Lord Lieutenant of the County of Southhampton, had been guilty of a breach of privilege by "concerning himself in the late election."[59] In 1790, the Commons resolved that it was a "High Infringement of the Liberties and Privileges of the Commons . . . . for any Lord of Parliament, or any Lord Lieutenant of any County, to concern themselves in the Elections of Members to serve for the Commons in Parliament."[60] In 1791, the House committed a witness for having made false statements before a committee investigating an election dispute.[61] In 1807, an offender who had tampered with the Speaker's warrant summoning witnesses in an election case was reprimanded at the bar for a breach of privilege.[62] In the same year, the Commons granted privilege and demanded the immediate release of a member who had been in custody of the marshall of the King's Bench and who had now been elected to Parliament.[63] In the year 1811, the freeholders of a constituency petitioned the Commons for privilege to hold another election, one of their representatives having become insane. The Committee of Privileges

---

[56] 26 *Com. J.*, 31, 32.
[57] 31 *Com. J.*, 211, 229, 292.
[58] Quoted in Glanville, *Election Cases*, Preface, LXXXV.
[59] 37 *Com. J.*, 507, 557.
[60] 46 *Com. J.*, 8.
[61] *Ibid.*, 314.
[62] 62 *Com. J.*, 288, 296.
[63] 62 *Com. J.*, 644, 653, 654.

decided that the House had no authority to discharge a member who was afflicted with a curable malady.[64]. In 1818, the author of a letter addressed to a voter to influence his decision was declared guilty of a breach of privilege.[65] In the following year, a soldier, summoned before a committee of the Commons to testify in an election case, was courtmartialled for his neglect of duty, occasioned by his attendance upon the House. The Commons ordered the Serjeant of the Foot-Guards who had made the arrest before them to answer for his act to the House.[66]

From 1586 on then, the House of Commons insisted upon its right to exclusive jurisdiction in matters of election to the House, and was on the whole singularly successful in enforcing its claim.[67] Disputed elections were tried first by select committees, specially chosen for each case. Later a permanent Committee of Privileges and Elections assumed the duties of settling election disputes. Toward the close of the seventeenth century it became the custom for the whole house to vote on these cases. This made possible the many abuses of this privilege under George II and George III, when election disputes were time and again settled by mere party votes, regardless of the merits of the case or the expressed desires of the constituency which the candidate represented. Election cases became mere trials of party strength, and the privilege of the House in such matters became nothing more than a serviceable instrument in the hands of the party in power. The famous case of John Wilkes and the Middlesex election, if the best known, is but one example of this practice.

---

[64] 66 *Com. J.*, 226, 265, 687, 689.

[65] 73 *Com. J.*, 231, 282, 289.

[66] 74 *Com. J.*, 274, 275. For other cases, see 40 *Com. J.*, 846; 39 *Com. J.*, 42, 83; 48 *Com. J.*, 406; 423-426; 60 *Com. J.*, 131; 75 *Com. J.*, 230, 231; 286; 40 *Com. J.*, 889.

[67] There is some difference of opinion as to the date of the origin of the Committee on Privileges and Elections. A committee report in 1820 contains a statement to the effect that the "earliest entry" in the Journals of the appointment of a general committee on privileges and elections is for March 22, 1603, "though there is Reason to believe that the Practice began somewhat earlier." 40 *Com. J.*, 889. In D'Ewes' *Journals* there is an entry for February 7, 1589, which reads as follows: "It is ordered that Mr. Comptroller (and nine others) shall examine such matters of privilege as shall happen at this present session of parliament to come in question, and to make reports thereof unto the House, for the further order and resolution of this House in every of the same cases as shall appertain." D'Ewes' *Journ.*, 429. Redlich says on this point, "In each of the parliaments of 1584, 1585, 1586, 1587, and 1588 a committee touching matters of privilege was appointed for the session. These committees were still comparatively small in numbers. In the parliament of 1589 we find a committee on privilege and one on "writs and returns," i.e., election disputes. From 1592 onwards both of these undertakings were assigned to one and the same large committee, consisting of the privy councillors and thirty or more named members." Redlich, *Procedure of the House of Commons*, II, 207.

Numerous attempts were made to remedy these evils, but with little success, until the whole principle of action was completely changed by the statute of 1868. By the Parliamentary Elections Act of that year, the trial of disputed elections was transferred to the judges of the ordinary law courts, who act theoretically as the servants of the House of Commons in such matters, although their decisions are not in the least affected by that fact.[68] This is nothing less than a return to the procedure of Henry IV's election law of 1410, but such a satisfactory solution of the whole difficulty was impossible until sweeping changes had been made in the composition of the Supreme Appellate Court of England. Under the present arrangement the House takes no notice of proceedings before the court until their termination, when the judges certify the decision in writing to the Speaker. This information is reported to the House, entered on the Journal, and orders are then given to execute the decision.[69]

---

[68] 31 and 32 Vict. c., 125. See also the discussion in Anson, *Law and Custom of the Constitution,* I, 163; and Prothero, *Statutes and Constitutional Documents,* 1559-1625, Introduction, LXXXVII and LXXXVIII.

[69] A good summary can be found in H. E. Paine, *A Treatise on the Law of Elections to Public Offices* (Washington, D. C., 1888). In this chapter very little has been said concerning the innumerable questions of detail which the Election Committees of the House of Commons were constantly called upon to decide. I have been interested primarily in fundamental principles, and in the more general aspects of the jurisdiction of the House of Commons in election matters. Election committees were kept busy deciding such questions as the qualifications and disqualifications of voters and candidates, questions of residence, polling, irregularities in voters' lists, corrupt practices, etc. Abundant information on these points can be found in such election reports as Douglas, *Election Cases,* 15 and 16 George III; Philipps (1780-1781); Fraser, (1790-1792); Peckwell, (1802-1806); Perry and Knapp (1833); Knapp and Ombler (1837); Luders (1785-1787); etc. The introduction of Douglas, Vol. I, contains a good general account of the whole question of controverted elections.

CHAPTER IV

CONFLICTS BETWEEN LORDS AND COMMONS OVER PRIVILEGE.

The actual conflicts arising from the claims of privilege of Parliament might roughly be divided into two classes, the one comprising collisions between the two houses of Parliament, usually the result of varying interpretations of the *lex parliamenti*, the other comprising the far more numerous cases of collisions between Parliament or one house, and the courts. The latter cases naturally involved a conflict between the principles of the *lex terrae* and those of the *lex parliamenti*. It is with a few of the most important incidents in the first class that this chapter deals. The problem of a logical arrangement of these cases has been by no means an easy one, because of the complexity of the issues involved. Practically every notable case in the history of privilege can be discussed from several different points of view, and the present arrangement has been adopted only because it is hoped that it will avoid repetition.

To a large extent, the trouble between the two houses arose from the absolute lack of understanding that existed for so long a time in regard to the judicial functions and powers of Parliament. The Lords, rightly calling attention to their descent from the ancient council of the king, insisted on claiming their full inheritance in the matter of judicial functions. But these had never been carefully defined. The Commons, on the other hand, were part of the "High Court of Parliament" also, and the distinction between their legislative and their judicial functions was likewise extremely vague.[1] The upper house insisted upon its right to sit as the final appellate court of England in all cases coming from the ordinary tribunals of the kingdom. The Commons were jealous of the Lords, fearful of their widening jurisdiction, and not a little concerned lest

---

[1] Selden, in his work *On the Laws of England*, maintained that "the Commons of England have a right in the course and order of Jurisdiction, which (as the known Law) is part of their Liberty; and in the speedy execution of Justice, as well as they have a right to have Justice done." He points out that in former times appeals were regularly made from the inferior courts to Parliament, and that the present arrangement of having the appellate body in the Lords, is the result of an Act of Parliament, and not by a simple order of the Lords alone, "which they might have done, in case the Jurisdiction had been wholly and only shut up in their custody."—Selden, *On the Laws of England* (London, 1760), Part 2, Ch. II, p. 14.

their privileges should in some way become involved in the Lords' judicature. To these difficulties must be added the existing confusion in regard to the exact nature of the *lex parliamenti* and its application.

In 1621, the two houses became involved in a controversy in which the stand taken by both is open to serious criticism. The lower house, stirred to a frenzy by fears of Popery, and moved by an almost fanatical enthusiasm for James' Protestant son-in-law, the Elector Palatine, learned that a certain Edward Floyd, a Catholic and a prisoner at the time, had made slanderous remarks concerning the young Elector and his career in Bohemia. Floyd was not a member of Parliament and in no way connected with the House of Commons or its activities. Nevertheless, the Commons summoned him to the bar, examined witnesses against him, and fined him £1000, condemned him to the pillory and inflicted other punishment of a most cruel and humiliating nature. May 5, 1621, the Lords resolved that the proceedings of the lower house had deeply entrenched upon their privileges, since all such judgments properly belonged to them. The Lords regarded the action of the Commons as an invasion of their judicial rights, for they still claimed the right to exercise original jurisdiction, apparently even over an individual who was in no way connected with their body and who had in no way interfered with their procedure. The Lords requested the judges to search for precedents upon which the Commons might possibly have founded their claims to jurisdiction over Floyd. A conference was arranged between the two houses, and the Commons submitted arguments and precedents to prove that they had ever been a court of record, (and so retained a part of the ancient judicial rights of Parliament), and had always punished delinquents in all cases that involved a member of Parliament, or the privilege of Parliament.[2] The Lords, jealous of what they con-

---

[2] Pollard, in his discussion of this case, argues that " . . . their condemnation of Floyd in 1621 (was) based upon precedent; and represent (s) (an) attempt to retain a share in the common inheritance of parliament, and not a spirit of radical innovation. In the same way, the reference of individual petitions to courts of law did not preclude the passing of private acts of parliament to grant relief or to impose disabilities where other means might fail. . . ." A. F. Pollard, *The Evolution of Parliament*, 249. See also footnotes, *ibid.*, 309, 331. In 1681 the Commons impeached Edward Fitzharris before the Lords for high treason due to his alleged connection with a popish plot. The Lords refused to proceed with the case, arguing that it should be tried at common law. The Commons thereupon resolved, "That for any inferior Court to proceed against Edward Fitzharris, or any other Person, lying under an Impeachment in Parliament for the same crimes for which he or they stand impeached, is a high Breach of Privilege of Parliament." 9 *Com. J.*, 711. See also, 11 *Com. J.*, 577 *et seq.* for Fenwick's case (1696).

sidered to be their judicial rights, held that there was but one question to be discussed in conference, namely, whether the House of Commons could sentence an individual who was not a member of that body, for a matter not concerning the House. The upper house appointed a sub-committee to arrange a second conference, and gave it instructions on no condition to admit the judicature of the Commons. This committee was able to report in a few days that the lower house had acted "out of Zeal," and would now leave Floyd to the Lords, "with the Intimation of their Hope, that this house will censure him also." The record of the evidence gathered by the Commons was sent to the upper house, and there Floyd was once more most cruelly punished.[3] The Commons had contended for a principle that would have enabled them to prosecute any ordinary offender against the law, a principle extremely dangerous to the liberty of the subject, and yet not without some legal justification, derived from the ancient judicial rights of the High Court of Parliament. Moreover, by applying the *lex parliamenti* the case would have been removed from the cognizance of the ordinary courts entirely.

In 1645, the Speaker of the Commons sent a warrant to the upper house requesting the Gentleman Usher of the Black Rod to discharge from his custody a servant of a member of the lower house, who had been committed by order of the Lords. The upper house regarded the Speaker's warrant as a violation of its privileges, apparently because the Commons had neither sent a message nor had requested a conference with the Lords to acquaint them with the circumstances of the case. The Lords expressed a desire to uphold the privileges of the Commons, but insisted that due form must always be observed in the proceedings between the two parts of Parliament. The Commons were anxious to avoid further friction, agreed to a conference, stated their case, and this time respectfully requested the release of the imprisoned servant. This satisfied the members of the upper house and the prisoner was at once discharged.[4]

In the noted case of *Skinner and the East India Company*, the House of Lords and the House of Commons became engaged in a bitter controversy over the jurisdiction of the upper house. The root of the difficulty lay in the claim of the Lords that their house was a court of first instance, even in civil cases. This claim to juris-

---

[3] 3 *Lords J.* 110, 111, 113, 116, 124, 127, 132, 134, 183.
[4] 8 *Lords J.*, 3-10.

diction was based on the powers once possessed by the King in his
Council, and although a number of courts had been evolved since
that time to take care of such litigation, the jurisdiction of the
Lords had never been specifically abolished. In 1668, this state of
affairs led to the memorable conflict between the two houses described below. The immediate cause of the trouble was a petition
of Thomas Skinner to the king, concerning the affairs of the East
India Company. Skinner alleged that while engaged in trade in
the East Indies in 1657, he had been assaulted and robbed of his
goods and estates, contrary to the guarantee of general freedom
of trade in the East Indies. He requested the king to appoint a
court of high constable and earl marshall to hear his grievances,
since he believed the case not remediable by the ordinary courts
of law.[5] Charles, by an order in council, referred the matter to
the Archbishop of Canterbury, the Lord Chancellor, Lord Privy
Seal, and Lord Ashley. Skinner estimated his losses at over £3300;
the East India Company refused to settle at any such figure, and
offered a compromise of £1500. The commission selected by the
king reported that their efforts to arbitrate the differences had
failed, but that the petitioner was undoubtedly entitled to his lands,
and to some compensation for his losses. Thereupon the king sent a
message to the Lords, and requested the upper house to do justice
in the case. Skinner immediately addressed a petition to that body.
The East India Company promptly protested and denied that the
Lords had jurisdiction over the case, since it was "in the nature of
an original complaint, not brought by way of appeal, bill of review,
or writ of error, nor intermixed with Privilege of Parliament. . . . ."
The House of Lords determined to exercise jurisdiction and ordered
counsel to appear before them to argue the case, but for various
reasons the hearing was postponed, and the session ended without
a settlement. Parliament met again the following October. Skinner filed another petition with the Lords; the Company again raised
the question of jurisdiction and maintained that the matter ought
to be tried in the courts of Westminster-hall. Several months later,
the judges, whose advice had apparently been asked by the Lords,
likewise declared the case was remediable in the ordinary courts
of Westminster-hall. No attention was paid to this adverse opinion, and the Lords resolved to relieve their petitioner. A committee was appointed to appraise Skinner's losses and to determine
what damages should be awarded.

---

[5] See Hale, *Judicature of the Lords' House*, Hargrave's Preface, p. 105 *et seq.*

Before this committee could complete its investigation and make a report, the case assumed a far more alarming aspect. The East India Company petitioned the House of Commons for relief from the persecution of the Lords. The petition alleged grave irregularities in the proceedings of the upper house, and denied its jurisdiction. As it happened, several members of the Company were also members of the House of Commons, and these raised the claim of privilege, thus complicating the issue still more. The lower house appointed a committee to investigate the entire matter. Several resolutions were reported, proclaiming the Lords' procedure a breach of privilege which affected the liberties of several Commoners, and denying the jurisdiction of the upper house. On May 1, Skinner was committed by the Commons for a breach of privilege, and the report of the committee was adopted with very little change. The House of Lords retaliated by voting the East India Company's petition to the Commons "a scandalous libel," and ordered the Company to pay Skinner £5000. Each house now set to work framing resolutions to explain its position in the controversy. Conferences, arranged in the hope of bringing about a peaceful settlement, failed because neither side would yield. On May 9, 1668, when both houses were on the eve of an adjournment ordered by the king, the Commons hastily adopted resolutions declaring all who should aid the Lords in executing their orders in the case betrayers of the rights and liberties of the Commons of England, and infringers of their privileges. When a report of these proceedings came to the Lords, they at once requested the king to postpone the adjournment long enough to enable them to vindicate their privileges and to draft a reply to these disrespectful resolutions. Charles gave them the opportunity. The House of Lords then sentenced Sir Samuel Barnardiston, deputy-governor of the East India Company, to a fine of £300, and ordered him into the custody of the Black Rod, for breach of privilege in promoting the petition of his company before the Commons. This accomplished, Parliament was adjourned for three months. No guarantee of peace between the two houses could be obtained in the interval, and two more adjournments and a prorogation followed. It was October 19, 1669, when Parliament reassembled. The lower house at once reopened the controversy, and in quite a novel manner. Since the last Parliament, a book, entitled "The Grand Question concerning the Judicature of the House of Peers stated and argued," had been published by Lord Holles. The author had undertaken the

defence of the upper house in the controversy. The printer and
book-seller was summoned to the bar of the House of Commons, and
was duly punished for his connection with the displeasing publication. Sir Samuel Barnardiston, the deputy-governor of the company who had been punished by the Lords, was also ordered to
appear. His testimony proved most interesting. It revealed that
an entry had been made in the office of the auditor of the receipt
of the exchequer to the effect that Barnardiston had paid the fine
imposed by the Lords, and had thereupon been set at liberty. As
a matter of fact, he had paid no part of his fine, and Barnardiston
reported to the House that he had been "mysteriously liberated on
one of the adjournment days of the last session," and that the
record must have been falsified to make it appear as though the
prisoner had recognized and submitted to the Lords' claim of jurisdiction. The House at once drafted and passed a bill vacating and
cancelling all proceedings against Barnardiston. Naturally, the
Lords rejected it. In their turn, they sent a bill to the lower house
"for limiting of certain Trials in Parliament, and Privilege of Parliament, and for further ascertaining the Trial of Peers and all
others his Majesty's Liege People." The Commons gave this measure a single reading, promptly rejected it, and called for a conference with the upper house. It was granted and resolutions were
presented by the Commons to the effect that every Commoner had
an inherent right to petition their house, and that it was exclusively
for that body to decide whether such petitions were fit or unfit to be
received. The resolutions insisted that no court had power to censure a petition that had been presented to the lower house, unless
that petition had been transmitted to it in the regular manner.
Consequently, the proceedings of the Lords were declared to be a
breach of privilege and in subversion of the liberties of the Commons. The conference closed with a request from the representatives of the lower house that the Lords vacate their illegal judgment
against Barnardiston. Once more the king intervened and pro-
rogued Parliament from December to the following February. During the entire session, not a single act had been passed by the two
houses, so serious had the situation become. When Parliament
met again, Charles earnestly counselled peace between the two
houses. Just four days later, it became known that the Commons
had already fixed a date for reopening the debate on the jurisdiction of the House of Lords. The king then took the matter in his
own hands, and submitted a proposal designed to bring about peace

and to prevent further interruptions of the public business. Charles agreed to order the erasure of all records and entries of this struggle in the council books and in the exchequer, and suggested that both houses do the same with their Journals, so that no trace of the struggle might remain on record anywhere. The houses agreed to the king's suggestion. In the Journal of the House of Commons there is an entry of the king's speech and the resolution to erase. In the records of the House of Lords, neither is recorded, and only a blank space remains to bear witness to the termination of the long struggle.[6]

The Lords, in this extremely interesting contest, had endeavored to establish their claim to original jurisdiction in civil cases, and notwithstanding the king's apparent aid, they failed. The controversy had completely paralyzed all government business for several years. The Lords were forced by the compromise to erase all traces of the quarrel and this included the annulment of the judgments against the East India Company and its deputy-governor. The House of Commons, to be sure, also agreed to the erasure of the records in its Journal, but only after the principles for which it had contended had been practically recognized and granted. The Lords' claim of original jurisdiction in civil cases received a crushing blow, one from which it never recovered. The upper house never again tried to revive the claim.[7]

It was but a few years later when another conflict broke out between the two houses. It far exceeded in intensity and bitterness the one just described, and this time, the issue was the appellate jurisdiction of the House of Lords. The privileges of the two houses became involved, and caused no end of complications. The case arose as the result of a legal controversy between a certain Dr. Shirley and Sir John Fagg. While it was being fought out, in 1675, the Test Bill, proposed by Danby, was also under discussion. Shaftesbury opposed it, and there may be some reason for sup-

---

[6] See 12 *Lords J.*, 240, 242, 243, 247. For an excellent account of this case, see Hargrave's Preface to Hale's *Jurisdiction of the Lords' House*, pp. 105-122.

[7] Pike comments as follows on this case: "The House of Commons took up the ground that if there was no remedy for a wrong in the ordinary Courts of Justice, it could be provided only by the whole body of Parliament. If by this they meant that an Act to create a new remedy could come into existence only in the usual parliamentary course, they were without doubt in the right. If, however, they meant that original jurisdiction had never resided in the Lords, and that the Lords had never had the power of sanctioning a new original writ, they were forgetting the whole history of the Curia Regis, of the King in Council in Parliament, and of the Courts." *Const. Hist. of the House of Lords*, 28. See also Pepys' *Diary* (Wheatley's Ed. 1912) VIII, 1, 3-5, 8-10, 13, for some reference to the case.

posing that the Shirley affair was unnecessarily prolonged by the opposition to block action on the Test Act.[8]

The case arose over a disputed inheritance, the details of which are of no particular importance.[9] Dr. Shirley and Sir John Fagg, a member of the Commons, became involved in litigation which resulted in a verdict for Fagg in the Court of Chancery. In 1675, Dr. Shirley brought the case on appeal before the House of Lords. Besides Fagg, several other members of the lower house were involved. The case had come up, like any ordinary law suit, through the courts to the highest court of England, the House of Lords. The Commons learned of the case, and received information that their member, Fagg, had been served with an order from the upper house to put in an answer to Shirley's petition. At once a message was sent to the Lords, calling attention to the privileges of the lower house, and warning them not to encroach upon them. The Lords promised to observe due respect for the rights of the Commons. Nevertheless, on May 13, Shirley was ordered to the bar of the House to answer for a breach of privilege. He was charged with having prosecuted a suit by petition of appeal before the Lords, against a member during the time of privilege of Parliament. Fagg was instructed to pay no attention to the action brought against him. A messenger of the Commons, armed with a Speaker's warrant, set out to find Shirley. When he appeared in the assembly hall of the Lords, he was met by Lord Mohoun, who snatched the warrant from his hand, and carried it before the upper house.[10] The Commons regarded this as a flagrant abuse of their privileges, issued a second warrant for Shirley's arrest, and addressed a communication to the House of Lords, demanding the censure and punishment of Lord Mohoun. The upper house refused to act, since their member had done "nothing but what was according to his duty," and granted Shirley protection against arrest, on the ground that he had a case pending in the Lords. The next day, the lower house formally declared Shirley's appeal a breach of privilege, and requested a conference to devise a plan to stop the proceedings. At the same time, the Commons learned that another case of a similar character was about to come before the Lords. This was the action of *Stoughton v. Onslow,* the latter also a member of the lower house. Onslow was instructed not to answer to the suit, and

---

[8] See Traill's *Life of Shaftesbury,* Under "Shirley Case."
[9] See *Dict. of Nat. Biography,* under "Shirley."
[10] 6 Howell, *St. Tr.,* 1121-87.

Stoughton was ordered into custody for breach of the privileges of the Commons. On May 17, the two houses held a conference and vainly endeavored to find a prompt and peaceful solution for the distressing situation into which they were unavoidably drifting. The Lords vigorously defended their right to receive and determine, during time of Parliament, appeals from inferior courts, and claimed this right even when members of either house were concerned. Stoughton, the plaintiff in the new case, was given a protection. The Commons were equally determined. They resolved that it was their undoubted right that none of their members should be summoned to attend the upper house during the sitting or privilege of Parliament, and asked for another conference.[11] In the arguments drawn up by the lower house for use in the conference the view was set forth that privilege applied in all cases except treason, felony, or breach of the peace, and that a summons from the Lords, in a matter of appeal, would be a distinct violation of that privilege which gives all members the right to remain undisturbed in the performance of their duties. The Commons proposed a suspension of the case until the end of the session as the only possible way to avoid a deadlock between the two houses.[12] A special conference was demanded to consider Onslow's case. A week elapsed before the Lords replied, and then they agreed only to discuss the general principles of parliamentary privilege, and not their judicial powers or Onslow's particular case. The House of Commons resolved that a conference with such limitations would be of no value, and therefore refused to participate.[13] May 31, the Lords sought another conference. Simultaneously, they fixed a final date for hearing Shirley's appeal. A number of lawyers were appointed by the upper house to represent him at the hearing. The Commons' house agreed to the conference, but on the very next day, on learning from a perusal of the Journals of the House of Lords that another appeal—*Crispe v. Dalmahoy*—was pending, and that Crispe's counsel had received protection from the Lords, the Commons ordered the attorneys to the bar. Dalmahoy was a burgess of Parliament, and so a claim of privilege was made for him also. When the legal advisors of the appellants were brought to the bar, they pleaded ignorance of the House's orders prohibiting the prose-

---

[11] 9 *Com. J.*, 340.

[12] The Commons maintained that even though the contention should result in a failure of justice, "it is not to be remedied by the House of Lords alone; but it may be by Act of Parliament." 9 *Com. J.*, 342.

[13] 9 *Com. J.*, 346, 347.

cution of such actions, and alleged that they had been compelled to take the case by the upper house. In spite of their plea, they were taken into custody. Fagg, who in spite of the order of the House to the contrary, had appeared in the Lords and had filed an answer to Shirley's appeal, was committed to the Tower. June 1, the upper house voted the whole House of Commons guilty of a "great indignity to the king's majesty in his highest court of judicature . . . . and an unexampled . . . . breach of privilege against the House of Peers." The Gentleman Usher of the Black Rod was given instructions to summon all necessary assistance, and liberate Crispe's lawyers who were then in the custody of the Serjeant of the lower house. This brought the two houses to the verge of using physical force in the struggle over their privilege. Black Rod found but one of the attorneys, and he was taken "into his care." The following day, the Lords, by message, asked for another conference "concerning the dignity of the king, and the safety of the government." At the same time, they granted protections to all of Crispe's counsellors. It appears that they had not yet been placed under arrest by the Serjeant. The House of Commons repeated that the limitations placed by the Lords on the scope of the conference were unreasonable, and in turn, demanded a conference to deal with the privileges of the upper house, and Onslow's specific case. Serjeant Norfolke, who had failed to arrest all of Crispe's counsel, was committed to the Tower and the king was asked to appoint another Serjeant-at-arms. Norfolke managed to slip into hiding, and so his punishment had to be deferred. However, he was deprived of privilege, and an under-serjeant was made responsible for his arrest. Armed with a new warrant, the new Serjeant was sent out to arrest Crispe's attorneys. The House of Lords retaliated by ordering the Lieutenant of the Tower and all jailors not to receive them, because they were under the special protection of the upper house. Another conference was finally arranged, but since each house upheld its old contention, very little could be accomplished. The Lords declared the acts of the lower house nothing less than infringements upon all the sacred rights of the subject, and the guarantees of due process of law. On June 4, the Serjeant of the House of Commons was given the order to proceed to Westminster-hall with his mace, and arrest all lawyers concerned in these cases, no matter where he might find them. The Serjeant obeyed instructions to the letter; he brought his prisoners to the bar, and all were committed to the Tower as violators of the privileges of the Commons. It appears that the seizure was made at the very bar of the court, thus constituting an invasion of the sanctity of Westminster-hall. Naturally, it caused a veritable storm of protest in the Lords. The upper house at once took up "the great Breach of Privilege committed in Westminster-hall." Witnesses were summoned who testified that the Serjeant of the Commons had entered the Court of Chancery, had seized his victims at the bar, and had actually refused to allow one of them to "go on in the cause that he was pleading." The fact that all had displayed their protections from the Lords had not embarrassed the Serjeant in executing his orders. The House of Lords now instructed the Gentleman Usher of the Black Rod to arrest the Serjeant of the Commons and to liberate his prisoners. A petition was simultaneously dispatched to the king, requesting him to appoint a new Serjeant to fill the vacancy that would occur when Black Rod had executed his orders, and the Lords resolved to do no further business "till they had received full satisfaction and vindicated themselves in this breach of their privileges." [14] Black Rod set out to execute his orders, but found the men he wanted safely lodged in the Tower. The Lieutenant of the Tower refused to release them, since they were committed by warrant of the House of Commons, and so could not be delivered without an order from that body. Black Rod found it impossible to arrest the Serjeant, because the latter kept himself within the safe confines of the Speaker's chamber. At this point in the controversy the king intervened and tried to bring about a peaceful settlement. Anticipating the Lords' request, he appointed a new Serjeant for the Commons. The House of Lords then demanded the dismissal of the Lieutenant of the Tower, but this the king refused to do. The Commons requested another conference, granted privilege to their Serjeant, and ordered the arrest of any one who attempted to molest him. They reasserted their right to arrest a Commoner guilty of a violation of their privileges, and claimed that they were only engaged in an honest defence of their privileges and were in no way trying to infringe upon the rights of the Lords. One of these resolutions was to the effect that the House of Lords had no jurisdiction in cases of appeal from any court of equity. The statement was of course contrary to fact and the law. The Commons concluded with a sweeping assertion of the supremacy of the *lex parliamenti* over the *lex terrae*. "As to what your Lordships call

---

[14] 6 Howell, *St. Tr.*, 1159.

a transcendent invasion of the rights and liberty of the subject, and against Magna Charta, the Petition of Right, and many other laws; the House of Commons presume that your Lordships know, that neither the Great Charter, the Petition of Right, nor many other laws, do take away the law and custom of Parliament, or of either House of Parliament."[15]   Where could one find a statement more dangerous to the liberty of the subject?   If accepted as true, it removes all check upon what Parliament, or either house, may do under the sanction of *lex parliamenti;* and it makes a single Parliament house when acting by that law, the supreme and sovereign power in the realm.   Parliament could justify any discretionary power under this interpretation of the *lex parliamenti.*

To return to the case itself.   There appeared to be no hope for a peaceful solution and the transaction of all state business was hopelessly blocked.   Consequentlly, the two houses were summoned to Whitehall, where the king, in a carefully prepared and moderate address asked them to grant full conferences, so that steps might be taken to bring an end to the disorder in Parliament.[16]   The king's efforts ended in failure.   Two days later, the Lords sent four writs to the Lieutenant of the Tower, demanding the persons of all those confined in the Tower by order of the House of Commons. The prisoners were not released, and four additional writs were sent, with a penalty of £40 attached to each, should the Lieutenant refuse to bring his prisoners before the Lords on the following day. Before the day set for the hearing of the Shirley case arrived, the Commons granted Fagg their protection and again ordered him not to appear in court.   They voted all who should try to execute any sentence against their member guilty of a breach of privilege, and "betrayers of the Rights and Liberties of the Commons of England."[17]   The Lieutenant of the Tower was given a protection, and was instructed not to liberate any one committed for breach of privilege, during the session, except upon order or warrant from the Commons.   The Lieutenant found his position becoming more and more untenable as the day for the hearing drew near.   In this dilemma, he called upon the House of Commons for advice.   He was told to pay no attention to writs of habeas corpus that had come to him from the Lords, and new resolutions were drawn up to the effect that a writ of habeas corpus was not a sufficient or proper

---

[15] 9 *Com. J.*, 354; also 6 Howell, *St. Tr.*, 1162.
[16] 9 *Com. J.*, 355.
[17] *Ibid.*, 355, 356.

way, during the session of Parliament, to liberate a person committed by the House of Commons for breach of privilege, even
though the prisoner be wanted in the House of Peers. The Lord
Keeper was informed of these resolutions, "to the end that the
said Writ of Habeas Corpus may be superseded as contrary to Law
and the Privileges of this House."[18] According to the view of the
lower house, even such a fundamental guarantee of the common law
as the right to a habeas corpus writ, must yield to the claims of the
law and custom of Parliament. Charles determined to prorogue
Parliament to the following October. But almost immediately upon
its reopening, Shirley presented a new petition, praying that his
case against Fagg might receive a speedy hearing. A long debate
followed in the House of Lords. Some counselled against renewing
the controversy; others insisted that the Lords must vindicate their
claim to appellate jurisdiction from the lower courts. The address
of the Earl of Shaftesbury on this occasion—whether his remarks
were the expression of his convictions, or merely designed to pro-
long the conflict,—was strikingly prophetic, in the light of the later
history of the House of Lords, and its influence in English political
affairs. "This matter," he warned the peers, in advising them to
insist upon their jurisdiction, "is no less than your whole judicature; and your judicature is the life and soul of the dignity of the
peerage of England; you will quickly grow burdensome if you grow
useless; you have now the greatest and most useful end of parliaments principally in you, which is not to make new laws, but to
redress grievances and to maintain the old landmarks. The House
of Commons' business is to complain, your lordships to redress, not
only the complaints from them that are the eyes of the nation, but
all particular persons that address you."[19] After much debate, the
upper house fixed November 20 as the day for hearing Shirley's
appeal. On November 15, the Commons again adopted resolutions
declaring the prosecution of this case a breach of privilege, and
ordered Fagg to offer no defence. November 18, they requested a
conference, to avoid reopening the quarrel between the two houses.
The Lords consented to a conference, but at the same time, assigned
counsel for Shirley's case. On November 19, the Commons discovered that several appeals from courts of equity were pending
in the House of Lords, and at once resolved "That whosoever shall
solicit, plead, or prosecute an Appeal against any Commoner of

[18] 9 *Com. J.*, 357.
[19] Quoted in 6 Howell, *St. Tr.*, 1173, 1174.

England, from any Court of Equity, before the House of Lords, shall be deemed and taken a Betrayer of the Rights and Liberties of the Commons of England."[20] This resolution was posted in conspicuous places at Westminster-hall, Serjeants' Inn, the Chancery, and elsewhere. On November 20, Shirley was once more ordered into the custody of the Serjeant-at-arms. The Stoughton-Onslow case also being up for consideration, Stoughton was ordered into custody, and Onslow was instructed not to plead. Before these orders could be executed, Shirley appeared before the Lords, with Richard Fallop as one of his counsel. The latter, none too anxious to become entangled in the quarrel between the upper and lower house, begged to be excused, on the ground that he was unacquainted with Chancery proceedings. The Lords ordered him to plead, and promised him their protection. Another of the lawyers assigned to the case pleaded illness and absolutely refused to appear. Fagg, in obedience to the mandate of the House, made no defence. The Lords then granted Shirley, Stoughton, and Wallop their protection, and adjourned to November 22, evidently happy to have been able to proceed this far without the interference of the Serjeant of the Commons. One of the Lords moved to ask the king to dissolve Parliament, but after long debate, his suggestion was negatived by the close vote of 50 to 48. The king made further trouble impossible by proroguing Parliament to the following February. No further record of the case is given in the Journals of either house.[21]

The Lords apparently emerged as victors from this prolonged struggle between the two houses. The matter was not reopened by the Commons. Shirley's particular appeal, it seems, was never revived, but the House of Lords continued to exercise their appellate jurisdiction and their claim was never again seriously disputed. The claim of the Commons that any one bringing an appeal to the Lords from a court of equity in a case involving a Commoner was guilty of a breach of privilege, was most extravagant, and had no legal basis. The whole history of the case shows most strikingly how confused men's notions in regard to the judicial powers of

---

[20] 9 *Com. J.*, 380.

[21] See 6 Howell, *St. Tr.*, 1121-1187. Also Lord Holles—*The Case Stated concerning the Judicature of the House of Peers in the Point of Appeals.* (1675). In 1697, when the upper house ordered the discharge of a person committed by order of the House of Commons, the lower house protested, had him rearrested, and resolved that no person committed by that house "can, during the same Session be discharged by any other Authority whatsoever." 12 *Com. J.*, 174. The incident passed without further trouble, although it might well have precipitated another contest between the two houses.

Parliament were, even as late as the close of the seventeenth century, and it proves how easy it was to provoke a contest between the two houses when both believed their privileges were involved. All legislative business was practically at a standstill while the two houses were engaged in this struggle over their judicial power, and prorogations had to be resorted to to prevent really serious consequences from the deadlock.

The Lords regarded it as absolutely essential to their existence as a potent factor in the state to defend their judicial powers, even against the law of privilege. The Commons were equally concerned lest their privileges should be affected by the Lords' judicial rights. The Lords were ready to admit that no member of the lower house could be arrested or his duties interfered with, but that, in their eyes, could not obstruct the usual method of judicial procedure nor the remedy of the appellant. Today the House of Lords has exclusive jurisdiction in error, but it is no longer the whole membership of that house which gives the judgment. Neither house of Parliament claims any original jurisdiction except over its members and their privileges, and the latter have by this time been closely defined and regulated by statute, resolution, and numerous court decisions.[22].

---

[22] In *King v. Flower* (1799) counsel for the defendant argued that the House of Lords had no power to punish, either by fine or imprisonment, a commoner who was guilty of a contempt committed outside the House. Flower had been committed to Newgate by the Lords for breach of privilege, arising from a libellous article in The Cambridge Intelligencer reflecting upon the character of the Lord Bishop of Landaff. The Court of King's Bench refused to accept the opinion that such cases were triable in the common law courts. The judges held that in the case before them the Lords had sat in a judicial capacity, as a court of record, and as such, had the power to fine and imprison. The case simply involved the Lords' privilege of protecting themselves against libellous publications, and therefore, the argument of Flower's counsel could have little effect upon the court. 8 Durnf. & East, 314-325.

CHAPTER V

THE CONFLICT BETWEEN LEX PARLIAMENTI AND LEX TERRAE.

By far the most important phase of the history of privilege remains for discussion, namely, cases involving a conflict between Parliament or either house of Parliament, and the ordinary courts of the realm; between the claims of *lex terrae* and *lex parliamenti*. They were of significance because of the fundamental nature of the issues involved. A full statement of the main facts in each important litigation is unavoidable. These cases reveal the real problems the conflict between the law of the land and the law of Parliament raised, and show how long it was before a satisfactory solution for the difficulty could be worked out. An issue that remained confused and without anything remotely resembling a final solution to the opening of the nineteenth century and beyond, was certainly of more than ordinary significance.

It may prove profitable to recall briefly what has been said earlier in regard to the nature of Parliament and its claims to privilege. Coke, it will be remembered, described Parliament as a court, determining and adjudging matters "not by the Civil Law, nor yet by the Common Law of this Realm used in inferior courts," but *"secundum legem et consuetudinem Parliamenti."* His interpretation of the character and powers of Parliament was, almost without exception, applied and accepted in the great cases over privilege that occurred from his time to the middle of the nineteenth century. Traces of this separate body of law for Parliament men and parliamentary affairs may be discovered even before Coke. In 1341, King Edward III tried to compel his chief minister to answer to certain charges in the court of exchequer. The Lords insisted upon a trial in Parliament and by his peers.[1] In the case of Robert De Veer, Duke of Ireland (1387-8) the justices and serjeants maintained that the case should be tried only in Parliament, since it involved a peer. Further, it was to be tried by no other

---

[1] "Hon'rable Seigneur, a la reverence de Vous semble d'un assent as Prelatz, Countes & Barouns, q-les Piers de la terre ne devent estre aresnez, ne menez en Juggement sinoun en Parlement & p lour Piers." 2 *Rot. Parl.*, 127b-131.

law than the "Ley & Cours du Parlement," and *not* "par cours,
processe, et ordre use en auscune Court or Place bas deins mesme le
Roialme; quex Courtes et Places ne sont qv Executours d'anciens
Leys et Customes du Roialme, et Ordenances et Establisements de
Parlement," etc.[2] A citation in the Rolls of Parliament for the
reign of Richard II specifically distinguished the civil and common
law from the law of Parliament. We find—"En ycest Parlement,
toutz les Seignrs si bien Espiritels come Temporels alors presentz
clamerent come lour Libertee & Franchise, q les grosses matires
moeves en ces Parlement, & a movers en autres Parlementz en
temps a venir, tochantz Pieres de la Terre, serroient demesnez,
ajuggez, & discus par le cours de Parlement & neyme par la Loy
Civile, ne par la Commune Ley de la Terre, usez en autres plus bas
Courtes du Roialme: quell claym, liberte & franchise le Roy lour
benignement alloua & ottroia en plein Parlement."[3] This statement
of Parliament's supremacy over other courts, and of its special law,
anticipates Coke's by about three centuries, and one could hardly
say, in this instance, that it was a "mere cloak for political claims
to power," however much that interpretation might be used to explain the constitutional arguments employed in the political struggles of the sixteenth and seventeenth centuries.[4]

Thorpe's case of 1453 has been discussed in an earlier chapter.[5]
It will be recalled that the opinion of the judges was sought in that
case to determine whether privilege was involved, and how it should
be applied. "To the which question, the chefe Justice, in the name
of all the Justicez, after sadde communication and mature deliberation amonge them, aunswered and said; that they ought not to
answere to that question, for it hath not been used afore tyme, that
the Justicez shuld in eny wyse determine the Privileges of this high
Court of Parliament; for it is so high and so mighty in his nature,
that it may make lawe, and that that is lawe it may make noo lawe;
and the determination and knowledge of that Privilege bellongeth
to the Lordes of the Parliament, and not to the Justicez."[6] The
judges thus recognized the supremacy of the "High Court of Parliament," but not without some qualifications. They admitted
that privilege applied in all cases except treason, felony, or breach

---

[2] 3 *Rot. Parl.*, 286a-b.
[3] 11 Richard II, 1387. 3 *Rot. Parl.*, 244a-No. 7.
[4] See Redlich, *Procedure of the House of Commons* (Steinthal's Trans.) Vol. I, p. 25, foot-note.
[5] See *ante*, 34.
[6] 5 *Rot. Parl.*, 239.

of the peace, but denied the right of Parliament, by a general *supersedeas*, to stop all proceedings and deprive the plaintiff of his remedy, at law. Parliament, in their own words, "must not lette the processe of the commune lawe" nor "put the partie compleyant withoute remedie."

In the case of the *Executors of Skewys v. Chamond* (37 Henry VIII) suit had been instituted in the Court of King's Bench against Chamond, the sheriff of Cornwall, to recover the amount involved in a suit of indebtedness brought by the late Skewys against another party. The latter had been in the sheriff's custody but had been liberated on receipt of a writ of privilege from the House of Commons which claimed the prisoner as a burgess of Parliament, and therefore entitled to privilege. Here was a case, like so many others that followed it, in which the individual might be deprived of his legal remedy, if the writ of privilege from the Parliament house were considered valid. A writ of this sort was practically a command to the sheriff to free his prisoner even though the result might be a failure of justice. The judges of the King's Bench, on the theory that Parliament was the highest court of the realm, allowed the claim of privilege and freed the sheriff from all blame.[7] But, in this particular case, the court saved to the plaintiffs their remedy at law, by ruling that the prisoner had not been discharged forever from the execution of the judgment, but only during the time of privilege.

In the first year of the reign of James I, the entire Parliament became absorbed with the settlement of Thomas Shirley's case, who had been elected a member of the Commons in James' first Parliament. Four days before Parliament met, he was arrested at the suit of a London goldsmith, and imprisoned in the Fleet. On learning of the arrest, the House of Commons ordered its Speaker to send a warrant to the Clerk of the Crown, for a writ of habeas corpus, to bring Shirley into the House. The warrant for the writ was issued, and three days later, the warden of the Fleet brought his prisoner to the bar. At that time, the House was busy with the Fortescue-Goodwyn case, and so Shirley was left in prison for a while longer. Several weeks elapsed. Finally another warrant was issued to bring Shirley before the Commons, but on the day

---

[7] See the opinion, "This court of parliament is the most high court, and hath more privileges than any other court in the kingdom . . . and although Parliament should err in granting this writ, yet it is not reversible in another court, nor any default in the sheriff." 1 Dyer *Repts.*, 60.

set, he did not appear. Then Sympson, the creditor, and Watkins, the serjeant who had arrested Shirley, were committed to the Tower. The case naturally raised the question whether the warden would be held responsible by the courts for Shirley's debt, if he gave the prisoner his release. April 17, a bill was introduced, and twice read, to meet this difficulty, and four days later, this special bill to relieve Shirley and to free the warden from liability, was sent up to the House of Lords. Meantime, to protect creditors as a class against losses when debtors were released by claims of privilege, a general act had been introduced. The Commons became impatient because the Lords delayed action so long, and made a special plea that action might be taken immediately upon the proposed measures. April 30, the Lords passed the special bill. By its wording, it invoked the aid of the king and the Lord Chancellor in enforcing the privilege. Suddenly the Commons awoke to the realization that the measure, as it then stood, would be fatal to their claim of sole jurisdiction in matters of privilege. Consequently, on May 4, the House of Commons rejected a motion to ask the king's assent to the bill, and proceeded to issue a writ to release their imprisoned member by virtue of the authority vested in a Parliament house. The warden refused to liberate Shirley until the king's assent to the bill should have been obtained. On May 7, the warden was committed for contempt. The next day, he was brought to the bar, and this time he offered to release Shirley provided a writ was secured from the Chancellor. The Commons were incensed by his obstinacy, sent the warden to the Tower, and instructed their Serjeant to release their fellow-member by show of his mace. But when the Serjeant tried to execute the order, he encountered the warden's wife. The latter put up such stout resistance that he had to return to the House empty-handed. By a small majority, the Commons now resolved to send a squad of members to batter in the doors of the prison. Fortunately, before the resolution could be carried out, wiser counsel prevailed. May 10, a new bill was passed and sent to the upper house, where it was approved two days later. This act was like the first, save that it omitted all reference to the king and chancellor. It protected the rights of the creditor, and saved the warden from legal proceedings. The warden still refused to surrender his prisoner, and was committed to "Little Ease." After four days he yielded and permitted Shirley to re-enter the Commons. After humble apology at the bar, the warden was also released. The lower house won a great victory in principle. The first act passed requested the Chancellor to "wthout delaie direct yor writt to the Warden of yor matie said Prison of the Fleete" for Shirley's release; the warden to incur no legal liability, and the creditors to have their rights when Parliament adjourned. The second act merely asserted the privilege, and protected the warden, and omitted all reference to the Chancellor.[8]

In 1604, a committee of the lower house, appointed to report on the liberties and privileges of the Commons, proclaimed the House of Commons "a Court of Record," and "so ever esteemed," and asserted that "There is not the highest Court in this land that ought to enter into competency either for dignity or authority with this High Court of Parliament, which with your Majesty's Royal Assent gives Laws to other Courts, but from other Courts receives neither Laws nor Orders."[9]   The language of the report obviously confuses the double function of Parliament as a legislature and as a court.   Frequently, the judicial characteristics of Parliament served as a basis for its legislative activity.   This was especially true during the period of transition from a court, with primarily judicial functions, to a sovereign legislature.   For a long time there was no clear-cut division between these two functions of Parliament, and in this confusion lay the basis for much of the trouble between Parliaments and the courts.[10]   The committee concluded its report with an unqualified endorsement of the theory of the supremacy of the High Court of Parliament when acting by the *lex parliamenti*.   They could not believe "that the Judges' opinion, which yet in due place we greatly reverence, being delivered what

---

[8] Shirley's arrest was declared to be "contrarie to the liberties, priviledges, and freedome accustomed, and due to the Comons of yor highness Parlyment, who have euer used to enioye the fredome in coming to, and returning from the Parliament, and sitting there without restraint or molestacon.   And yt concerneth yorr Comons greatelie to haue this fredome and privileig inviolablie observed, yet to the end, that no pson be preudiced, or damnified herebie." These two bills were private bills, and have never been printed. They do not appear in the *Statutes of the Realm*.   **Mr. G. W.** Prothero has printed them in the *English Historical Review* for October, 1893, together with an excellent account of the entire case, to which I am much indebted. See *Engl. Hist. Rev.* vol. 8, pp. 733-738. Also 1 *Com. J.*, 149, 154.

[9] In 1593, the Speaker of the Commons began the closing speech of the session with these words, "The high court of parliament most high and mighty prince, is the greatest and most ancient court within this your realm . . ." Cobb. *Parl. Hist.*, I, 889-890.

[10] "*A Brief Discourse concerning the Power of the Peers and Commons of Parliament, in Point of Judicature*," written in 1640, contains the following, . . . "Now began the frequent Sending of Writs to the Commons; their Assent was not only used in Money, Charge, and Making Laws, for, before, all Ordinances passed by the King and Peers, but their Consent in Judgments of all Natures, whether Civil or Criminal." *Harl. Misc.* VIII, 605.

the Common Law was, *which extends only to inferior and standing Courts,* ought to bring any prejudice to this High Court of Parliament, whose power being above the law, is not founded on the Common Law, but have their Rights and Privileges peculiar to themselves."[11] In 1675, the Commons were even more specific, and boldly claimed for the law and custom of Parliament a power transcending the sacred guarantees of Magna Charta and the Petition of Right.[12]

Rolle's case (1629) shows the claim of privilege in conflict with an alleged right to collect taxes. It is not necessary to discuss the political phases of the noted controversy between Charles and his Parliaments over tonnage and poundage. Taking the arguments in the case at their face value, they are of interest because they show the conflict between the privilege of Parliament exempting members' goods from molestation, and the law—or alleged legal right—to levy taxes. Rolle, a member of the House of Commons and a merchant, complained to the House that his goods had been seized by customs officials for non-payment of taxes and duties. While the Commons were discussing the question, they were interrupted by a communication from the king. Charles made what he hoped would prove a conciliatory address, pleading for harmony and better understanding between Crown and Parliament, and offering to drop the whole affair if the House would only grant him the old taxes of tonnage and poundage. The Commons rejected the offer. Two weeks later Rolle reported that his warehouse had been locked, and that he had been served with a subpoena to appear in the Star Chamber. The House at once ordered the messenger who had served the subpoena to the bar, and subsequently, the customs officers were also brought in. Their plea was that they had acted under a commission under the great seal, and that privilege applied only to the person and not to the goods of a member. After extended debate, it was resolved to grant Rolle privilege of Parlia-

---

[11] 1 Hatsell, 239. James I, in his speech to Parliament in 1609, remarked, " . . . there are two special Causes of the People's presenting Grievances to their King in the Time of Parliament. First, For that the King cannot at other Times be so well informed, . . . Secondly, The Parliament, which is the highest Court of Justice, and therefore the fittest Place where . . . Grievances may have their proper Remedy. . . ." *Harleian Misc.* I, 12. (London Ed. Printed for T. Osborne, 1744-6).

[12] See *ante*, 86. The Shirley-Fagg Case.

ment for his goods.[13]   March 10, Charles dissolved Parliament. Among his other reasons for the dissolution, Charles included the trouble over the Rolle case.   He declared he would never permit the extension of privilege of Parliament to members' goods, since that would mean a practical exemption from taxation during Parliament time.[14]

It has generally been admitted, especially in more recent years, that one of the greatest bulwarks of English liberty, guaranteed by the law to every Englishman, is the right to procure a writ of habeas corpus when committed to prison for some alleged offence.   But what should be the procedure in the case of an offender committed for breach of privilege by a house of Parliament?   That commitment is presumably made by *lex parliamenti*, while a writ of habeas corpus is a matter of the common law.   Should the prisoner receive his writ and a hearing in one of the ordinary courts of the kingdom? Since Parliament repeatedly insisted that no court could have cognizance of matters relating to commitments by either house, it was inevitable that conflicts should arise between claims of privilege and the alleged right to a writ of habeas corpus.

Parliament asserted its position by frequent resolutions and orders.   When in 1642 the Commons learned that certain offenders committed by them had procured writs of habeas corpus returnable in the King's Bench, they resolved "That neither the Court of King's Bench, nor any other Court, hath any Cognizance or Jurisdiction touching the Commitment of any Person who stands committed by order of both or either of the said Houses of Parliament," and maintained that courts, on learning of such commitments, "ought to surcease any further proceedings thereupon and leave the cause to both or either of the said houses, by whom and by whose authority such person was so committed."[15]   In 1647, the lower house adopted

---

[13] Debates in the Commons.   Sir John Eliot—"The heart-blood of the commonwealth receiveth life from the privilege of this House."   Littleton—"The Parliament only can decide privilege of parliament, not any other judge or court . . .   For the judges to determine privilege of parliament, were to supersede and make void the law. . .   The king is never so high in point of state, as in the parliament."   Banks—"The courts at Westminster do grant twelve days privilege to any man, to inform his counsel; much more the courts of parliament are to have their privilege.   The king's command cannot authorize any man to break the privilege."   Cobb. *Parl. Hist.* II, 478, 479, 480.

[14] Extracts from Charles' address— . . .   "Some have not doubted to maintain, That the resolutions of that house must bind the Judges, a thing never heard of in ages past." (The house) "have of late swollen beyond the rules of moderation, and the modesty of former times; and this under the pretence of privilege and freedom of speech whereby they take the liberty to declare against all authority of council and courts at their pleasure."   Cobb. *Parl. Hist. II,* 500, 501.   For entire case, see *Ibid.,* 437-501 *passim.*

[15] 2 *Com. J.,* 960.

a somewhat more conciliatory attitude. The Serjeant-at-arms was instructed to make returns of the bodies of all prisoners, and the causes of their detention whenever he should receive writs of habeas corpus from any of the law courts, but the judges were warned to give notice before discharging or bailing prisoners, committed by the House and brought before them.[16]

In 1653, Parliament and the courts came in conflict in the case of Captain Streater. The case occurred during that period of English history when the House of Lords had been temporarily abolished, and when Parliament therefore consisted only of the Commons' house. That state of affairs had no noticeable effect upon Parliament's claims of privilege, nor upon the theory upon which these claims were founded. The Commons defended their claim with their usual zeal and with all the old stock arguments. Captain John Streater had been committed to the Gate-house by order of Parliament, that is, the Commons' house, for certain seditious pamphlets for which he seemed to be responsible. The warrant for the commitment was correctly signed by the Speaker, and demanded Streater's confinement until he should be liberated by a subsequent order of Parliament. The prisoner applied for a writ of habeas corpus, and on November 23, 1653, he was granted a hearing before the Upper Bench in Westminster-hall. Streater contended that the return was too general and showed no lawful cause for his imprisonment; that the writ of commitment failed to specify the time and place where the alleged offence had been committed; and that an order of Parliament must show legal cause for commitment. Extracts from Streater's argument before the court deserve quotation. He upheld the rights of the ordinary courts to enforce the *lex terrae*, at all times, and against all classes of offenders. "Parliament ever made laws, but the judges of the law judge by those laws," he insisted. "Who will question but that the warrant of a justice of the Peace, showing lawful cause of commitment, is of greater force in law, than an Order of Parliament, shewing no cause for commitment. . . . . It is not to be imagined, neither do I think, that the Parliament expected that their order, the inferior part of their power, shall take place of the superior part of that

---

[16] 5 *Com. J.*, 221.

power, the law and acts of Parliament that command law."[17] Streater's views clearly illustrate the double nature of Parliament, as a legislature and as a judicial tribunal, for Streater evidently tried to distinguish between what Parliament enacts as a legislature, and what orders it may issue as a court. The two often conflicted.

The Attorney-general appeared for the Commons. His argument—if it may be styled an argument—was very brief. He simply informed the court that Streater was committed by an order of Parliament, "which is not to give an account to the court," and that it was the pleasure of Parliament to keep the prisoner in confinement until released by an order from the same source. The judges decided against Streater, and their opinion adhered to the traditional conception of privilege. "Mr. Streater," they began, "one must be above the other, and the inferior must submit to the superior; and in all justice, an inferior court cannot control what the Parliament does. If the Parliament should do one thing, and we do the contrary, here, things would run round."[18] The objection to the warrant because it failed to show lawful cause for the arrest was overruled on the ground that no inferior court could call to account a superior tribunal.[19] Judge Nichols confused the judicial power of Parliament to punish for contempt, with its legislative powers, and apparently was not clear as to where the dividing line could be drawn between these two functions. He declared that "what the Parliament does, we cannot dispute or judge of: their laws are to bind all people; and we are to believe they had cause for what they did. . . . . Why, their power is a law, and we cannot dispute any such thing. . . . ."[20] The power of a house of Parliament to commit offenders has invariably been supported by the same reasoning that underlies the power of any ordinary court to commit for contempt. Should the High Court of Parliament be without a power enjoyed by the meanest of the courts in the land? And yet, it was at times extremely difficult to differentiate between this judicial characteristic of the High Court of

---

[17] 5 Howell, *St. Tr.*, 381. For entire case, see pp. 365 *et seq.*

[18] 5 Howell, *St. Tr.*, 386.

[19] "We are judges of the law, and we may call inferior courts to account why they do imprison this or that man against the known laws of the land; and they must show cause to any man. In this case, if the cause should come before us, we cannot examine it, whether it be true or unjust; they have the legislative power." . . . *Ibid.*, 386.

[20] *Ibid.*, 387.

Parliament and its law-making power, when it became, in later centuries, a sovereign legislature.[21]

Streater was remanded to the Gate-house. The proceedings of which an account has been given, occurred in Michaelmas Term. Between this and Hilary Term, Parliament was dissolved. Streater naturally assumed that the order of commitment was now void, because of the dissolution of the body that had ordered the imprisonment. On January 23, 1654, the first day in the new term, Streater moved for a second writ of habeas corpus. It was granted but several postponements occurred, and it was February 7 before the prisoner obtained a hearing. The Attorney-general again represented the Commons, and argued that the recent dissolution of Parliament had not altered the case in the least. "When kings die," he asserted, "it is true that Commissions do cease; but when Parliaments dissolve, their acts do not cease. Besides, a Parliament is a Supreme Court, and they do constitute other courts; and therefore it is not for other courts to question the proceedings of a Parliament."[22] The judges decided that the Attorney-general need not prove that Parliament had had sufficient cause for committing the prisoner. Twisden argued the case for Streater, and undoubtedly presented much the better argument. He placed special emphasis

---

[21] Professor Redlich insists that the House of Commons was never recognized as a court, and asserts that "though it made repeated claims to be a court of justice, it was never able to sustain them." Certainly the House based its right to commit offenders upon the power it retained as part of the High Court of Parliament. This reasoning was accepted as valid for centuries and to modern times, not only by members of both houses, but by courts, king and people. Indeed, some of the most emphatic assertions of this theory will be found in the cases that occurred in the last century. Redlich makes much of the fact that the House of Commons never had the power, possessed by every judge, to administer an oath. But the members of the House were under oath, they had the power to examine witnesses at the bar or in committee, and to punish them for perjury. No court could do more. On many occasions, witnesses were brought to the bar to answer to charges of prevarication. Redlich admits that the House "has some judicial powers, inasmuch as it can decide questions of privilege and can protect its privileges . . . by corresponding executive power." "In this way the House of Commons is invested with a certain measure of public authority such as is only otherwise given to the royal councils summoned for the purpose of giving legal decisions. It may be said that the form in which the notion of a constitutional corporate body has been worked out in the House of Commons has been that of conferring upon the highest legislative body certain judicial attributes exercisable solely in the sphere of its autonomous enactments and regulations. The extension to the House of Commons of the idea of a 'contempt' (is) the corner-stone of privilege. . . . " Redlich, *Procedure of the House of Commons*, III, 77, 78. I have tried to show that the Commons were not "*made* into a court of law" by a legal fiction, but that the houses exercised their privileges as part of the High Court of Parliament, whose judicial functions were established long before Parliament became a sovereign legislative body; that the judicial characteristics of Parliament were even used to effect the transition from a court to a legislature; and that traces of Parliament's functions as a court still remain, especially in the field of privilege.

[22] 5 Howell, *St. Tr.*, 391.

upon the difference between an order of Parliament, and an act of Parliament. His clear distinction is especially noteworthy at this time when the confusion between adjudication and legislation by Parliament was still so great. Twisden was certainly correct in maintaining that a dissolution ought to vitiate the orders of the preceding Parliament. If it were otherwise, a prisoner might be held in confinement indefinitely, even though he sued for his liberty in the courts. Depriving a prisoner of his remedy at law for an indefinite period would be nothing less than an absolute failure of justice. Streater's counsel concluded with the excellent summary— "My Lord, a Parliament may determine (i. e., end) and all Parliaments do determine; and when they do, their orders should determine with them. It is true that acts of Parliament do continue; but this is but an Order of Parliament, and not an Act of Parliament. My Lord, we must come hither to be relieved; this is the place, this is the court appointed for relief in this case." [23] The court ruled that "Another Parliament must be another session, and therefore an order cannot be in force until another session." [24] In other words, a dissolution vitiates the orders of the dissolved Parliament. Any other ruling would have been a serious menace to the liberty of the subject.

On June 9, 1675, a Commons' resolution definitely forbade the summoning of offenders committed for breach of privilege before the Lords, by writ of habeas corpus. The Lord Keeper was informed of the resolution to the end that the writs issued might "be superseded, as contrary to law, and the privileges of this house." [25] This is but one of the many times when a resolution of the lower house upheld the doctrine that the *lex parliamenti*—the law of privilege—was superior to, and must receive precedence over, the *lex terrae,* even though such a fundamental guarantee of individual liberty as the right to the writ of habeas corpus was involved. [26]

In 1676, the Court of King's Bench had before it the case of the Earl of Shaftesbury, committed by the House of Lords "for high Contempt" of their body. In this case, again, our interest is not in its political phase, but only in that which concerns the law of privilege. Shaftesbury had been committed to the Tower, during the

---

[23] 5 Howell, *St. Tr.,* 402.
[24] In the opinion of the court we find the statement—"If they (the Parliament) had made an Act of Parliament, or passed a Judgment of parliament, it had been another case."
[25] 9 *Com. J.,* 357.
[26] See 14 *Com. J.,* 565.

king's and Lords' pleasure.[27] The prisoner then applied to the judges of the King's Bench for a writ of habeas corpus, and succeeded in getting a hearing. The Earl offered a number of technical objections to the form of the commitment, among others that the form left considerable uncertainty whether it was a conviction or merely an accusation. His counsel laid great stress upon the dangers to the liberty of the subject that would arise from such methods of procedure, and contended that even such "a supreme court" as the House of Lords must act under the limitations of the common and statute laws.[28] "The House of Peers is an high court," he argued, "but the King's Bench hath ever been entrusted with the liberty of the subject, and if it were otherwise (in case of imprisonment by peers) the power of the king were less absolute than that of the Lords."[29] Serjeant Maynard and the Attorney-general argued the case for the Lords. Their main contention was that the upper house constituted the supreme court of England, and therefore could not be controlled in its procedure by the inferior court of King's Bench. They based the procedure in this case against Shaftesbury upon the *lex parliamenti*, and pointed out that "The Judges in no age have taken upon them the judgment of what is *lex et consuetudo parliamenti*."[30] It was admitted that if an action before the court raised a question of privilege, the judges might judge of it as *incident* to the suit to be settled by them, but where, as in this case, "an *original* matter arising in Parliament" was involved, the court had no right to assume jurisdiction, since offences of this nature were punishable by Parliament only. The distinction was frequently made between pleas of privilege incident to a suit of which the court is possessed, and such original matters that arise directly by order of a house of Parliament, and within Parliament.

Shaftesbury personally addressed the court. His argument was a plea for the subordination of the *lex parliamenti* to the *lex terrae*, and a plea for the rights of ordinary courts to check encroachments by privilege of Parliament upon the guaranteed liberties of the subject. The Earl admitted that the Lords were the supreme court of the realm; but he refused to concede that they

---

[27] See 1 *Modern Repts.*, 144 *et seq.* Also 3 Keble, 792-796.

[28] "Though the house of lords is the supreme court, yet the jurisdiction is limited by the common and statute law; and their excesses are examinable in court; for there is great difference between the errors and excess of a court, between an erroneous proceeding, and a proceeding without jurisdiction, which is void, and a mere nullity." 1 *Modern Repts.*, 148.

[29] 1 *Modern Repts.*, 150.

[30] 1 *Modern Repts.*, 153.

were above the law. He seemed to hold to the idea that there should be a fundamental law with which all legislation and all orders of Parliament houses should be in accord, for he contended that the Court of King's Bench "will and ought to judge of an act of Parliament void, if it be against Magna Charta" and therefore "much more may judge an order of the house, that is put in execution to deprive any subject of his liberty."[31]

The court upheld the claims of the upper house. While admitting grave irregularities in the return—enough to make the return "ill and uncertain," if it had emanated from an ordinary court of justice—the judges ruled that these objections could not apply to the Lords, "this High Court," where ordinary rules of procedure did not apply.[32] The judges accepted as correct the distinction urged by the Attorney-general between cases involving privilege only incidentally and those involving it directly. Of the former the courts of Westminster could take cognizance; over the latter—and in this class Shaftesbury's action was included—they had no jurisdiction.[33] Following the decision in Streater's case, Judge Wild maintained that had the session of the Lords been at an end, Shaftesbury would have obtained his discharge. Since such was not the case, the court refused "to intermeddle with the transactions of the High Court of Peers in Parliament during the session, which is not determined."[34] Chief Justice Rainsford, in complete accord with his colleagues, observed that "The consequences would be very mischievous if this court should deliver a member of the House of Peers and Commons who are committed, for thereby the business of Parliament may be retarded; for it may be the commitment was for evil behaviour, or indecent reflections on other members, to the disturbance of the affairs of Parliament."[35] Shaftesbury was remanded to the Tower. Here he remained in confinement until another session of Parliament, when the Lords voted his application to an inferior court for a writ of habeas corpus a breach of privilege. Shaftesbury was finally brought to the bar, where he humbly, and upon his knees, sought the pardon of the upper house for his offence, and received his discharge.[36]

---

[31] 6 Howell, *St. Tr.*, 1294-1296.
[32] 1 *Modern Repts.*, 157.
[33] 6 Howell, *St. Tr.*, 1296. Justice Jones held that the case was "a direct Judgment on the Proceedings of the Lords; and each Court allow the Customs of the other, which is the Law of the Court, and must be intended as judged by themselves." 3 Keble, 792-6.
[34] 6 Howell, *St. Tr.*, 1296.
[35] 6 Howell, *St. Tr.*, 1296; also 1 *Modern Repts.*, 157.
[36] 6 Howell, *St. Tr.*, 1297.

In Murray's case (1751) the King's Bench again refused to release a prisoner who had been committed by the House of Commons for a contempt of privilege, on a writ of habeas corpus. The judges made a most interesting interpretation of the Habeas Corpus Act. "It could never be the intent of the Statute"—the judges insisted—"to give a Judge at his chamber, or this Court, power to judge of the privileges of the House of Commons. The House of Commons is undoubtedly an high Court; and it is agreed on all hands that they have power to judge of their own Privileges; it need not appear to us what the contempt was for; if it did appear, we could not judge of it."[37]   Justice Foster held that the lower house had the power to commit, like "all courts of record."[38]   Even though Murray lost his case, the argument of his counsel is important. It uncompromisingly opposed the idea of a parliamentary omnipotence in matters of privilege. Murray's counsel insisted that his client was entitled to bail under the Habeas Corpus Act, "the bulwark of English liberty." Deprived of the benefit of that act, the prisoner would have to remain in prison indefinitely. "It is well known," he continued, "that the House of Commons cannot take bail, and if this court will not admit the prisoner to bail, it will be in the power of the House of Commons to perpetually imprison. The habeas corpus act is of higher authority than an order of the Commons, who are but one branch of the legislature; and however their orders may bind themselves, yet nothing less than an act of Parliament shall bind the whole body of the people and the nation. Liberty is the birthright of every subject, and he has a right to apply *here* for it."[39]   The argument correctly pointed out the dangers of one-house legislation under the guise of privilege, and also the possible encroachment of the *lex parliamenti* upon the common law rights of the subject.

The conflict between the operation of the habeas corpus act and the orders of Parliament arising from claims of privilege lasted much longer than 1751. The question was a matter of dispute and friction until well into the nineteenth century, and it will be necessary to deal with additional cases in a later chapter.

In 1629, Sir John Eliot, Denzil Holles, and Benjamin Valentine stood before the court of King's Bench, charged with having

---

[37] 1 Wilson, 299. See also 1 Hatsell, 308.

[38] "The law of parliament is part of the law of the land, and there would be an end of all law if the House of Commons could not commit for a contempt; all courts of record (even the lowest) may commit for contempt." 1 Wilson, 300.

[39] 1 Wilson, 299.

made seditious speeches in Parliament. The case has of course been amply discussed from all angles because of its importance in the constitutional revolution of the seventeenth century, but only that phase which deals directly with privilege of Parliament is of importance here.[40] Sir Robert Heath, representing the king, charged Eliot with having said, in a speech before the members of the lower house, "That the Council and Judges had all conspired to trample under foot the Liberties of the Subjects." Holles and Valentine it will be remembered, had held the Speaker in his chair while the speech was being made and therefore they were held to be equally guilty. The defendants of course pleaded to the jurisdiction of the court, and claimed that the offence, if any had been committed, was punishable in Parliament, because committed wholly within its walls. The court seems to have been determined to give judgment favorable to the king long before the arguments had been concluded.[41] Counsel for the defendants were several times interrupted in their arguments. They insisted, in the first place, that privilege guaranteed that debates in the lower house should remain unrevealed to the world outside, until the House saw fit to make them known through its usual channels of communication.[42] Secondly, that the liberty of accusation was a privilege of Parliament and "determinable in Parliament, and not elsewhere." Further, this accusation in Parliament "is in a legal course of justice, and therefore the accuser shall not be impeached."[43] Parliament was declared to be a superior court and the right to detain the Speaker in his chair one of its particular privileges. It was further argued that there could be no failure of justice if the court should dismiss the case, because the next Parliament might punish the offenders if it saw fit to do so. Again, the case being "great, rare, and without precedent," could only be decided by Parliament, apparently because that was the highest court in such matters. Valentine's defence was grounded on the court theory of Parliament, and on the contention that Parliament acted by a special law, above the con-

---

[40] See *ante*, 29.

[41] See Chief Justice Hyde's interruption, "That is no new question, but all the judges in England, and Barons of the Exchequer, before now, have often been assembled on this occasion, and have with great patience, heard the arguments of both sides and it was resolved by them all with one voice, That an offence committed in parliament, criminally or contemptuously, the parliament being ended, rests punishable in another court." 3 Howell, *St. Tr.*, 294.

[42] Parliament "is a Council, and the Grand Council of the king; and councils are secret and close; and none other have access to those councils of parliament, and they themselves ought not to impart them without the consent of the whole house. . . ." 8 Howell, *St. Tr.*, 295.

[43] *Ibid.*, 295.

trol of the ordinary and inferior courts, whose judges, at best, were mere assistants to Parliament. "If this court shall have jurisdiction," it was asserted in conclusion, "the court may give judgment according to law, and yet contrary to parliamentary law, for the Parliament in divers cases hath a peculiar law. This court of Banco Regis is *coram ipso rege;* the king himself, by intendment, is here in person. And . . . . it is 'Supremum Regni Tribunal,' of ordinary jurisdiction. But . . . ., the Parliament is a transcendent court, and of transcendent jurisdiction. . . . ."[44]

Sir Robert Heath answered for the king. He contended that while the House of Commons had a right to make complaints in a parliamentary manner, its members should not move things that tend to the distraction of the Crown and the government. He denied that the House of itself was a court of justice, and upheld the right of the court to punish the offenders on the ground that subsequent Parliaments could not punish an offence committed in a preceding session because ignorant of all the details."[45]

The judges of the King's Bench assumed jurisdiction over the case. Judge Jones ruled that an offence "committed criminally in Parliament, may be questioned elsewhere, as in this court." It could hardly have been expected that the suggestion to leave settlement of the case to Parliament would meet with the approval of a royally-controlled court, and it was dismissed with the statement that a Parliament was not a constant court, did not examine under oath, and had a constantly changing membership.[46] Chief Justice Hyde dealt extensively with the alleged conflicts between inferior and superior courts. In part, his opinion reads as follows: "As to what was said, That an inferior court cannot meddle with matters done in a superior; true it is, that an inferior court cannot meddle with judgments of a superior court; but if particular members of the superior court offend, they are oft-times punishable in an inferior court, as, if a judge shall commit a capital offence in this court he may be arraigned therefore at Newgate."[47] Justice Whitelocke found an easy solution for the trouble by declaring the case to be one concerning a burgess "become mutinous," and therefore

---

[44] 3 Howell, *St. Tr.*, 299 *et seq.*

[45] "The House of Commons is not a court of justice of itself. The two houses are but one body, and they cannot proceed criminally to punish crimes, but only their members by way of imprisonment; also they are not a Court of Record. . . Even sitting the parliament, this court of Banco Regis, and other courts, may judge of their privileges, as of a parliament-man in execution, &c., and other cases." 3 Howell, *St. Tr.*, 305.

[46] *Ibid.*, 306, etc.

[47] *Ibid.*, 307.

no longer entitled to privilege. Another of the judges claimed that all offences against the Crown were examinable in the King's Bench.[48] Eliot and the others involved with him, were fined and imprisoned at the king's pleasure. A dozen years elapsed before the case came into prominence again. In 1641, the Commons declared the whole procedure a breach of privilege, and awarded damages and compensation to the members who had suffered in defence of their privileges, and in 1688, the Lords reversed the judgment against Holles.[49]

---

[48] Justice Croke remarked, "It hath been objected, 'That the Parliament is a higher court than this.' And it is true: But every member is not a Court, and if he commit offences, he is punishable here." 3 Howell, St. Tr., 309.

[49] See ante, 30. The arrest of the five members in 1641, because of alleged treasonable activities with the Scots, brought forth heated debates in the Commons. Each side went to extremes in its zeal to defend its position. Very few understood the principles on which the solution of the conflict between the claims of privilege and the law had eventually to be made. Clarendon apparently did forecast the modern solution. In the debate in the Commons, Grinston argued, "Parliament had always claimed and exercised power and jurisdiction above all other courts of judicature in the land. . . What circumstances . . . had given such awful predominancy to the very name of Parliament in this nation. It was because the ordinances and statutes of that high court struck with terror and despair all such evil-doers as were malefactors in the State. It was because, not alone the meanest of his Majesty's subjects, but the greatest personages of the kingdom were in danger, if infringers of the law, to be called in question by this highest court and to be punished by it. . . ." Quoted in Forster, Arrest of the Five Members, 272-273. See also, Sir John Forster's Sir John Eliot. Clarendon's view of privilege, if enforced at the time it was stated, might have made many of the beneficent results of the revolution impossible, nevertheless, it was, in substance, the view ultimately accepted. His observations on the arrest of the five members deserve extended quotation. "It is not to be believed how many sober, well-minded men, who were real lovers of the peace of the kingdom, and had a full submission and reverence to the known laws, were imposed upon, and had their understandings confounded, and so their will perverted, by the mere mention of privilege of Parliament, which, instead of the plain and intelligible notion of it, was, by the dexterity of these boutefeus, and their under-agents of the law, and the supine sottishness of the people, rendered such a mystery, as could only be explained by themselves, and extended so far as they found necessary for their occasions, and was to be acknowledged a good reason for everything that no other reason could be given for. "We are," they say, "and have always been confessed, the only judges of our own privileges ; and therefore whatsoever we declare to be our privilege, is such: otherwise whosoever determines that it is not so makes himself judge of that, whereof the cognizance only belongs to us." And this sophistical riddle perplexed many, who, notwithstanding the desperate consequence they saw must result from such logic, taking the first proposition for true, which, being rightly understood, is so, have not been able to wind themselves out of the labyrinth of the conclusion: I say the proposition rightly understood: they are the only judges of their own privileges, that is, upon the breach of these privileges, which the law hath declared to be their own, and what punishment is to be inflicted upon such breach. But there can be no privilege, of which the law doth not take notice, and which is not pleadable by, and at, law. The clearness of this will best appear by instance: If I am arrested by process out of any court, I am to plead in the Court, that I am a member of Parliament, and that, by the privilege of Parliament, my person ought to be free from arrests. Upon this plea, the Judge is bound to discharge me ; and if he does not, he is a criminal, as for any other trespass against the law ; but the punishing the person, who hath made this infringement, is not within his power, but proper to that jurisdiction, against which the contempt is, and therefore that House, of which I am a member, upon complaint made of such an arrest, usually sends for the persons culpable, and the party at whose suit the arrest is made, and the officers which executed it, and commits them to prison, till they make acknowledgment of their offence. But that House never sends, at least never did till this Parliament, any order to the court, out of which

In *Hodges v. Moor*, a case that arose during the reign of Charles I, the King's Bench refused to accept a letter from the Speaker of the Commons, asking the judges to stay proceedings in the case of a burgess of Parliament. The judges held that it should have been a writ of privilege, and that "Parliament only privileges the person of Members of it, and not stayes the proceedings" of the King's Bench.[50]

In Charles II's reign, the case of *Lake v. King*, an action for libel, came before the King's Bench for adjudication. Lake complained of a libellous article which had been printed and published by King. It appears that the defendant had sent an article to the committee of Parliament for grievances, charging Lake with extortion, oppression, etc., in the performance of his duties as vicar-general to the Bishop of London. The plaintiff maintained that these charges constituted a false and malicious libel, while the defendant insisted that they were part of a privileged publication, since they had been presented to the committee in the form of a petition. This petition had been printed by King and copies had been delivered to the members of the Commons—"for the better manifestation of the grievances contained." The court gave judg-

---

the process is issued, to stay the proceedings at law, because the privilege ought to be legally pleaded. So, after the dissolution of Parliament if I am arrested within the days of privilege, upon any plea of privilege the court discharges me; but then the party that arrests me escapes punishment till the next parliament. . . Again, if a man brings an information, or an action of the case, for words spoken by me, and I plead, that the words were spoken by me in Parliament, while I was a member there; and that it is against the privilege of Parliament, that I should be impleaded in any other place, for the words I spoke there; I ought to be discharged from this action or information, because this privilege is known, and pleadable at law; but that Judge can neither punish, nor examine the breach of privilege, nor censure the contempt. And this is the true and proper meaning of the old received axiom, that they are judges only of their own privileges. And indeed these two, of freedom from arrests of their persons (which originally hath not been of that latitude to make Parliament a sanctuary for bankrupts, where any person outlawed hath been declared incapable of being returned thither a member) and of liberty of speech, were accounted the chiefest privileges of Parliament. . . But that their being Judges of their privileges should qualify them to make new privileges, or that their judgment should create them such, as it was a doctrine never before now heard of, so it could not but produce all those monstrous effects we have seen; when they have assumed to swallow all the rights and prerogatives of the Crown, the liberties and land of the Church, the power and jurisdiction of the Peers, in a word, the religion, laws and liberties of England, in the bottomless and insatiable gulf of their own privileges." Clarendon, *History of the Rebellion* (Oxford Press Ed., 1839), II, 183-186.

[50] Noy, 83. In Latch's *Cases*, p. 48, the case is reported as follows: "Moor, ayant un Parliament Protection, procure le Speaker Finch, al inditer son Letter en nosme del Parliament al B. R. de stayer Judgment. Et le Court fuit grandement offend a c, et voyl aver return un sharp respons al Parliament, si ne ad estre dissolve; quia est envers le Sacrament des Judges a stayer Judgment; nec p Grand Seal, nec Petit Seal, p le Statute. Mes le voy en teil Case est a Procurer un Supersedeas, que est un Special Breve appoint en ceux Cases, & est d'estre allow esteant le legal course; Mes l'Epistre n'est d'estre regard." See also, *Hodges v. Devant*, Latch's *Cases*, 150.

ment for King, because it was the order and course of proceedings
in Parliament to print and deliver copies, etc., whereof they ought
to take judicial notice."[51]

In 1689, the House of Commons actually summoned two judges
of the King's Bench to the bar, to answer for a judgment they had
given adverse to the claims of the privileges of the lower house,
and strangely enough, the judges appeared and submitted themselves to examination. They made every effort to defend their
decisions, took refuge behind nice, technical distinctions, and tried
hard to escape punishment. It was truly a great day for privilege
when two judges of the King's Bench were forced to give an account
at the bar of the Commons for a judgment given by them in regular
session of court! The case shows most strikingly to what extremes
the Houses of Parliament might and did go to enforce their claims
of privilege. The incident arose from the action of *Jay v. Topham*.
Topham was the faithful Serjeant of the lower house, and most
zealous in enforcing its mandates and privileges. "Take him Topham" became almost a synonym for commitment by the House of
Commons. But now, Serjeant Topham reported to the House that
he had of late suffered greatly from several prosecutions at law,
arising from his execution of the orders of that body against a certain Jay, who had brought suit against him in the court of King's
Bench. The Serjeant had pleaded to the jurisdiction of the court,
and had explained to the judges that he had simply acted as the
official agent of the Commons. But the plea had been disallowed,
and judgment had been given for Jay. To get relief, Topham now
appealed to the House of Commons. The matter was at once referred to the Committee of Privileges for examination. On July 6,
that committee reported, and the House resolved, that the judgments against their Serjeant were illegal and a violation of Parliament's privileges. The judges who had made the unfavorable ruling, Sir Francis Pemberton and Sir Thomas Jones, were ordered
to attend the House. On July 10, they presented themselves, apparently willing to be interrogated. Judge Pemberton addressed the
Commons in a long and carefully prepared speech. He disclaimed
all intention to question the jurisdiction of the House, or to deny
its privileges. But in the present case, he maintained, the plea
should have been in bar, and not to the jurisdiction of the court.
"The order of this house was sufficient to take any one into custody,"
he admitted, "but, if this be pleaded to the jurisdiction here, the

---

[51] Saunders *Repts.*, 131b.

hands of the court are closed; so that whether he had such an order or not, is not to be enquired of by the court. But if it be pleaded in bar, so it is a good bar, and he will have as much advantage as any, and all people must allow it is a good bar. Therefore, I would pray you that you would consider that in this case here is nothing of your privileges, nothing of the jurisdiction of this court is called in question, but only the manner of making use of it. . . ."[52] The judge's contention was correct in principle, but the Commons were not convinced by his explanation, and ordered him to appear again on a later date. On July 19, Pemberton made a second plea. He informed the House that he had searched the records carefully, but had found no precedents to warrant a decision other than the one he had given; that the matter had come before him in a judicial way, and therefore he had examined the case. "Then I considered," he continued, "that where justifications are made, by virtue of acts of Parliament, and everybody must acknowledge that court is of a higher nature than the King's bench, yet that was not enough to exclude the king's court from their jurisdiction. . . . . Therefore, I thought that the high authority and high nature of this court, could not exempt the King's Bench, being a court of law to examine, whether what was alleged to be done was done in pursuance of your authority or not? . . . . We did not question the legality of your orders, nor the power of them; but the great business was, whether he (Topham) has pursued this order of the House of Commons, and that was the thing properly examinable. . . . ."[53] Pemberton insisted that his sole object had been the protection of the plaintiff, since the House of Commons never gave damages or examined witnesses on oath, and he expressed a willingness to apologize if he had erred or been over-zealous in the case.[54] Judge Jones appears to have been much more alarmed by these proceedings than his colleague, and his defence was more apologetic. He also denied all intention to interfere with the privileges of the Commons, pleading his own service in two Parliaments as a guarantee of his sincerity.[55] Jones lamented the fact that

---

[52] 12 Howell, *St. Tr.*, 825.

[53] 12 Howell, *St. Tr.*, 828.

[54] "If I was mistaken in this case, it was an error of judgment, I had no mind or design to meddle with the affairs of the house, nor to pry into what was done here; my desire was to do justice." 12 Howell, *St. Tr.*, 830.

[55] "Mr. Speaker, in the first place, I seriously profess before God and this honorable house, that I never have designed to interfere with the authority and privileges of this house . . . truly, I did always conceive that for anything transacted (by the authority of the Commons) no other court had any jurisdiction to hear and determine it." *Ibid.*, 830.

Topham had not produced a copy of the Journal of the Commons, to prove his authority; if he had done that, no judge would have doubted his power. Topham had absolutely refused to make any answer to the charges brought against him.

The Commons remained unconvinced, and resolved that Pemberton and Jones, by "giving judgment to overrule the plea to the jurisdiction of the court of King's Bench . . . . had broken the privileges of the house." For that breach of privilege they were ordered into custody, and "lay till there came a prorogation,"[56] another example of the triumph of the *lex parliamenti* over the ordinary courts and the ordinary laws of the realm.

A case of the greatest importance, which has not always received the attention it merits, was that of Sir William Williams, arising from the publication of Dangerfield's Narrative.[57] Sir William Williams was prosecuted and fined £10,000 in the King's Bench for having signed, in his official capacity as Speaker of the House of Commons an order for the publication of Dangerfield's Narrative, alleged to be libellous upon the character of the Duke of York. The argument of Sir Robert Atkyns in defence of the Speaker was without question one of the most remarkable expositions of the court theory of Parliament, and of the wide application of the *lex parliamenti*, ever made. Atkyns applied *lex parliamenti* to cases coming before Parliament on appeal, and made *lex parliamenti*, and not *lex terrae*, the basis for the judicial decisions. The conflict between the two bodies of law, while men argued and thought as Atkyns did, was unavoidable.

Williams had acted for the House, in his official capacity as Speaker. He was not the author of the libellous book of information, and had merely ordered it to be printed. All this had been done during the time of Parliament.[58] Williams therefore pleaded privilege of Parliament.

Atkyns' plea in his behalf brought out most clearly the judicial characteristics of Parliament, and the fusion of its legislative and judicial functions. He maintained that what had been done in the

---

[56] 12 Howell, *St. Tr.*, 830 *et seq.*, for entire case.

[57] Professor McIlwain has said: "The great case of Sir William Williams has hardly received the notice it deserves in our histories of the English Constitution. Along with the cases of the *Seven Bishops*, and *Godden* v. *Hales*, it must be considered one of the immediate causes of the Revolution. It was the occasion of one of the most important clauses in the Bill of Rights, and probably therefore of the like provision in the Constitution of the United States." McIlwain, *The High Court of Parliament and Its Supremacy*, 242.

[58] See 13 Howell, *St. Tr.*, 1370 *et seq.* Also Robert Atkyns, *Parliamentary and Political Tracts*, pp. 1-120.

case before the court, had been done "in a course of justice" and "in the highest court of the nation, (i. e., Parliament) according to the law and custom of Parliament."[59] It was apparently his belief that the High Court of Parliament must be bound by, and must act according to, some law; but that law was not necessarily the law of the land. It was just in that respect that Parliament differed from the ordinary courts of law. Parliament had a special body of rules—the *lex et consuetudo parliamenti*—by which it could practically do what it wished without being challenged for the exercise of its powers elsewhere. Sir William Williams had, according to Atkyns, acted merely as "the servant or minister of Parliament." And since the case arose from matters transacted in Parliament, and by Parliament, "this court of King's Bench ought not to take connusance of them; nor hath it any jurisdiction to judge or determine of them."[60] In his *Parliamentary and Political Tracts*, Atkyns has elaborated his views. He begins with the statement that Parliament is one entire body—all three estates constituting "one body corporate." As such, Parliament has three powers—the legislative, and in that capacity Parliament is the "Three Estates of the Realm;" the judicial power, exercised as the "Magna Curia" or "High Court of Parliament;" and the counselling power, as the "Commune Concilium Regni."[61] In Williams' case, Atkyns based the argument on Parliament's character as a court. "It is the proper work of this supreme court to deal with such Delinquents, as are too high for this Court of King's Bench, or other ordinary courts, against whom, through their Potency and mighty Interest, common Right cannot be had; it must be understood in ordinary courts."[62] Atkyns then points out that matters done in Parliament can only be judged in and by Parliament. Because Parliament gives law to all the other courts of the kingdom, he regards it as absolutely absurd to assume that it should be subject to, or receive law from, any of these ordinary courts. "The greater is not judged by the less."[63] Furthermore, Parliament is, and must always remain, "the immediate court for examining the judgments of the Court

---

[59] 13 Howell, *St. Tr.*, 1370, etc.

[60] 13 Howell, *St. Tr.*, 1370.

[61] Atkyns, *Parliamentary and Political Tracts*, 69.

[62] See also the statement in another place: "This great Court encounters only with Great Offenders. It is like the Imperial Eagle—Aquila non capit Muscas; it leaves them to this and other inferior Courts, but that takes to task the Animalia Majora." Atkyns, *Parl. & Political Tracts*, 72.

[63] *Ibid.*, 95.

of King's Bench, and if they be erroneous, they reverse them."[64]
Atkyns apparently also applied the law of Parliament to cases
coming before Parliament on appeal. He contended that Parliament, acting by the *lex parliamenti*, acts by an entirely separate
code from that of the ordinary common law, and a code that can be
found nowhere else than in Parliament. The Court of King's
Bench, like "all the Courts of Common Law," judges "only by the
ordinary rules of the Common Law." "But the proceedings of Parliament are by quite another Rule. The matters in Parliament are
to be discussed and determined by the Custom and usage of Parliament, and the course of Parliament; and neither by the Civil, nor
the Common Law, used in other Courts. . . . . The Judges of this,
and of the other Courts of Common Law in Westminster, are but
Assistants and Attendants to the High Court of Parliament, and
shall the Assistant judge of their Superiors? . . . ."[65] The power
of Parliament as the "dernier Resort," he regarded as absolute and unlimited in all things temporal in England. A difficulty presented itself at this point from the fact that the appeals
from law courts had been heard for a long period in the House of
Lords alone. It might appear therefore that "Parliament as a
court" meant only the upper house. But according to Atkyns, the
Lords could not *be* a court if the Commons did not meet at the same
time, for the two houses meet and adjourn together "like the twins
of Hippocrates."[66] Atkyns admitted that a Parliament might err,
"for they are not infallible, but the Law hath provided a remedy
against those errors, and a way to reform them. A subsequent
Parliament may reform the errors of a preceding Parliament. . . .
But to say they will be partial or unjust or corrupt, or do anything
out of malice, is to raise a scandal upon the whole Nation, whose
Representatives they are."[67]

Atkyns' whole argument rests upon the court conception of
Parliament, and upon the theory that its acts are, to a large degree,
of a judicial nature. The law that governs this Highest Court of
the realm is not the *lex terrae*, but the *lex parliamenti*—a law to be
determined in Parliament only, and not to be called in question outside its walls. Even as a legislature, Parliament acts according to
lex parliamenti—if we accept Atkyns' theory. Since *lex parlia-*

[64] Atkyns, *Parliamentary and Political Tracts*, 95.
[65] *Ibid.*, 95.
[66] *Ibid.*, 99.
[67] *Ibid.*, 119

menti cannot be called in question elsewhere than in the two houses, Parliament, acting by that law, practically becomes a sovereign legislature. Atkyns' position shows that even in his time—the close of the seventeenth century—the confusion between the legislative and judicial functions of Parliament still existed, and that Parliament's legislative supremacy was frequently built up on the theory that the "High Court of Parliament" was the highest judicial body in the kingdom, and acted by a law that was supreme over all other laws. In other words, functions and characteristics of Parliament as a court were used to bolster its position as an omnipotent legislative body.

In *Rex and Regina v. Knollys,* we find Justice Holt deciding against a claim of the Lords, grounded upon the *lex parliamenti,* just as on another occasion he had checked the extravagant claims of the lower house.[68] But in this decision, he had the support of his colleagues. A certain Knollys had murdered his brother-in-law. On the ground that his grandfather had been made Earl of Banbury, and that he was his male heir, Knollys pleaded peerage. On December 13, 1693, he petitioned the House of Lords for a trial by his peers. The Lords dismissed the petition, and ordered the case tried by the common law. Two years later, the case came before the King's Bench. The defendant demurred to the order of the Lords and the judges unanimously sustained the demurrer. Holt held that the order of the upper house could not deprive the defendant of his peerage, "because the order was not a judgment of Parliament." Even if it had been, the House of Lords, as the supreme court, could not pass upon an original matter.[69] Peerage Holt regarded as a simple matter of inheritance over which the Lords could have no power to judge unless that power were specifically given them by the king. In other words, the Lords cannot claim a power under the *lex parliamenti* which does not exist as part of the law of the

---

[68] See *ante,* 63 *et seq.*

[69] See Holt's opinion. "The parliament (consists) of the king, the lords spiritual and temporal, and the commons. The judicial power is only in the Lords, but legally and virtually it is the judgment of the king as well as of the lords, and perhaps of the commons too. . . . If the parliament took connusance of original causes, the party would lose his appeal, which the law indulgeth in all cases, for which reason the parliament is kept for the last resort; and causes come not there until they have tried all judicatories. . . ." 1 Lord Raymond, 15. *"Lex Parliamenti,"* in the words of Holt, "is to be regarded as the law of the realm; but supposing it to be a particular law, yet if a question arise, determinable in the king's bench, the King's bench ought to determine it. . . . The common law then does not take notice of any such law of parliament to determine inheritance originally. . . . If inheritance shall be originally determinable in parliament, where the parliament, namely the house of peers, hath no jurisdiction, the peers would have an uncontroullable power." 1 Lord Raymond, 18.

land. Judgment was given for Knollys. Some of the Lords were much displeased, and in 1697, Holt was summoned to the bar of the upper house to state the reasons for his ruling. Holt refused to give them in "so extrajudicial a manner," but expressed his willingness to state them very fully if the case should be removed to the Lords by writ of error. "At which some Lords were so offended, that they would have committed the Chief Justice to the Tower. But notwithstanding, all their endeavors vanished in smoak."[70] Holt had simply applied his old principle in this case—namely, that *lex parliamenti* must cease to be an exception to the ordinary law of the kingdom.

In 1745, the Exchequer Chamber—on an appeal from the King's Bench—was called upon to pass on a question arising from a disputed election to Parliament. The House of Commons had concluded its investigation, and had decided that one Wynne had been elected. The latter then sued the sheriff for £6000 damages, for having made a false return. The Court of King's Bench had awarded damages to the plaintiff, and on the appeal, the judges of the Exchequer Chamber upheld the decision of the lower court. By a statute of 7 and 8 William III c. 7, double damages had been provided for false returns. Judge Willes therefore ruled the action well founded. He based his decision on the statute, and remarked— "We are not bound by law to take notice from time to time of the particular resolutions of the House of Commons, who of themselves cannot make law." "There would be," the Chief Justice continued, "the greatest inconvenience if the doctrine should prevail that there must be a determination in the House of Commons as to the election, before the action for a false return can be brought; for if so, it would be in the power of the house to repeal this act of Parliament, by contriving to put off a petition from time to time for two years, within which time this sort of action must be brought."[71] Judge Willes clearly realized that such a procedure would be nothing less than one-house legislation.[72]

---

[70] 1 Lord Raymond, pp. 10-18.

[71] 1 Wilson, 127.

[72] The remainder of the opinion is worth citing. "I declare for myself, that I will never be bound by any determination of the House of Commons against bringing an action at common law for a false return or double return, and a party injured may proceed in Westminster-hall *notwithstanding any order of the House*, for the members are not upon oath, nor can they administer an oath to witnesses; and it would be very extraordinary to say, that we, who are judges upon oath, should be bound by a determination of persons not upon oath. I would pay great regard to a determination of the House, but yet I would go on." I Wilson, 127, 128.

In 1750, when the gamekeeper of Lord Willoughby de Brooke, under suit for debt, petitioned the King's Bench to discharge him, on the ground that he had business to attend to for his lord, which he could not transact while under arrest, the request was denied because of insufficient evidence. The court was very careful to abstain from expressing an opinion as to whether privilege of Parliament could be claimed by the defendant or not. The decision was expressly based on an order of the House of Lords of 1715, of which the court took judicial notice. The order "which seems to be a declaration of their privileges," did not claim freedom from arrest for all menial servants of lords, but limited the privilege to "such as are necessarily and properly imployed about their estates, and about their persons."[73] This declaration the judges accepted as law, applied it to the case before them, and disclaimed all intention to pass upon a question of privilege of themselves. This was the customary procedure. It was the exception to find a judge who ventured to express his own views in regard to the claims of either house under the law of privilege. Most judges preferred to take refuge behind the resolutions of the Parliament houses, rather than risk a controversy between Parliament and courts.

The famous case of John Wilkes and the Middlesex election has been widely discussed because of its political and constitutional importance.[74] It involved such momentous and basic questions as freedom of the press, the law of libel, and the validity of general warrants. It also has its place in the history of privilege and ranks in importance with the Aylesbury cases, *Stockdale v. Hansard,* and the well-known Bradlaugh incident.

In 1763, John Wilkes, a member of the House of Commons for Aylesbury, published his famous No. 45 of the *North Briton.* In this number of his paper, Wilkes labeled as false certain statements in the speech from the throne, on the Peace of 1763. This act was the first in a chain of events which resulted in struggles between the Lords and Commons, the Commons and the people, the Comons and the courts and Crown running over nearly a score of years. By skillful manipulation, public opinion was aroused, and Wilkes— profligate and demagogue—became a popular hero. The king chose to regard the publication in the *North Briton* as a personal insult, and throwing all notions of ministerial responsibility to the winds,

---

[73] 1 Wilson, 278.

[74] For a good discussion of freedom of the press, libel, general warrants, etc., see May's *Constitutional History of England,* (Standard Ed., 1882) Chapters IX, X, XI.

decided to prosecute the author in a most arbitrary fashion. A general warrant for the arrest of all persons suspected of some connection with the libel was accordingly issued and a number of seizures were made as a result. The warrant named no specific offender; it was directed against all suspects. Wilkes was brought in with the rest, and sent to the Tower. At once he applied to the Court of King's Bench for a writ of habeas corpus. It was granted, and when Wilkes appeared before the judges, he claimed his privilege of freedom from arrest as a member of Parliament. In addition, he protested the illegality of general warrants. The judges allowed the plea of privilege, and declared general warrants illegal, and Wilkes, already followed about as a hero, was discharged amid the plaudits of the mob.[75]

Thwarted in their attempt to prosecute Wilkes in the courts, the ministry turned to its obsequious majority in both houses of Parliament for support. Another issue was soon found, and it was decided to prosecute Wilkes for another of his scurrilous publications. The attack was launched in the upper house. Lord Sandwich, who had a character "of which holiness and virtue were not constituents," and who was hardly on a sufficiently high moral plane to pose as a champion of purity, brought in a complaint against Wilkes' so-called *"Essay on Woman,"* an obscene parody on Pope's *Essay on Man.*[76] It was a case of Satan rebuking sin. To the notes, published with the essay, Wilkes had affixed the name of the Bishop of Warburton, a member of the House of Lords. This furnished an additional reason for the action of the Lords, for was not the honor and good name of one of their members involved? Still another work from the pen and brain of Wilkes—the *"Veni Creator paraphrased"*—received the condemnation of the peers. The author was declared to be guilty of a breach of privilege, for reflecting on a member, and publishing "a most scandalous, obscene, and impious libel; a gross profanation of the Holy Scripture; and a most wicked and blasphemous attempt to ridicule and vilify the Person of our Blessed Saviour."[77] Wilkes was ordered into the custody of Black Rod. Thus, the upper house, under a plea of privi-

---

[75] 13 Howell, *St. Tr.*, 982 *et seq.* Also 2 Wilson, 151. Chief Justice Pratt held: "We are bound to take notice of their privileges, as being part of the law of the land. . . . We are all of opinion that a libel is not a breach of the peace: it tends to the breach of the peace, and that is the utmost. . . ." 2 Wilson, 157.

[76] See Cobbett, *Parl. Hist.*, XV, 1346 *et seq.*

[77] 30 *Lords J.*, 415.

lege, was assuming to apply the law of libel and through this power, to rid the government of a hated foe and most unsparing critic.

Meanwhile, the Chancellor had informed the House of Commons of Wilkes' arrest. That body was also informed that their member had suceeded in gaining his freedom on a claim of privilege in the King's Bench. The obedient, royally-controlled majority of the lower house thereupon promptly resolved that *North Briton No. 45* was a scandalous libel, and that privilege of Parliament "does not extend" to the case of seditious libel, nor ought it "to be allowed to obstruct the ordinary course of the laws, in the speedy and effectual prosecution of so heinous and dangerous an offence." [78] The publication was ordered to be burned by the common hangman. Pitt, although suffering severely from one of his frequent attacks of the gout, vigorously opposed this surrender of privilege in one of his best efforts, but with no success. [79] The Lords concurred in this resolution, but not until several members had voiced a strong protest against such a limitation of the privilege of freedom from arrest. [80]

Wilkes, meanwhile, had other troubles because of his publications. The *North Briton* brought him a challenge to a duel. The duel was fought, Wilkes was injured, and then retired to Paris. When the libellous publication was burned by the hangman, a general riot ensued. The constables were pelted with stones, and the mob, frantically shouting for "Wilkes and Liberty," attacked the City Marshall. But the burning was duly completed, and the sheriffs of London received a vote of thanks from both houses for their devotion to duty. An attempt in the Commons by the opposition to declare general warrants illegal, was defeated. [81]

On January 19, 1764, Wilkes was to attend the House. Instead, he sent letters and a doctor's statement from Paris to the effect that he was ill and could not attend. He refused to be examined however by a physician designated by the House. He was then

---

[78] 29 *Com. J.*, 667, 675.

[79] Cobb. *Parl. Deb.*, XV, 1363-1364.

[80] The Lords declared: "We are at a Loss to conceive with what View such a Sacrifice should be proposed, unless to amplify, in Effect, the Jurisdiction of the inferior, by annihilating the ancient Immunities of this Superior Court. . . . This Method of relaxing the Rule of Privilege, Case by Case, is pregnant with this farther Inconvenience, that it renders the Rule precarious and uncertain. Who can foretell where the House will stop?" Rogers' *Lords' Protests* (1767), II, 261-272. Also 13 Howell, *St. Tr.*, 993-999. In the debates in the upper house, Lord Lyttleton observed: "Privilege against law, in matters of high concernment, to the public, is oppression, is tyranny, wheresoever it exists." *Parl. Deb.*, XV, 1371.

[81] *Parl. Deb.*, XV, 1393. 29 *Com. J.*, 846.

voted guilty of contempt. Witnesses were summoned and examined in regard to the authorship of the *North Briton;* Wilkes was declared guilty of libel; and was expelled from the House.[82] The Speaker was instructed to issue a new writ for the election of a member from Aylesbury.

The case now assumed new proportions. To the populace, it appeared like an attempt on the part of the king to abolish ministerial responsibility, since the speech from the throne was represented as the personal utterance of an absolute and irresponsible ruler. Further, it seemed as though the king had determined to interpret the law of libel and what constitutes libel to suit his own particular fancy, and then to enforce that interpretation by general warrants of arrest and search, and by the resolutions of a royally-controlled majority in Parliament. Wilkes' cause was represented, with all the noisy publicity his friends could give it, as the cause of the people, as indeed it was. The contest became eventually a contest between the electors of England and the Crown—the latter acting through a controlled and bought House of Commons. Under guise of privilege, the Parliament houses infringed more and more upon the fundamental rights of the electorate of England. And in the words of Burke, "It was precisely the same, whether the ministers of the Crown can disqualify by a dependent House of Commons, or by a dependent Court of Star Chamber, or by a dependent Court of King's Bench."[83]

As the battle went on in the legal tribunals, it seemed for a time as though a great clash between Parliament and the courts was imminent. In the King's Bench, Wilkes was sued on two informations for libel. He was found guilty on both counts, and writs of *capias* were issued against him. Wilkes was in Paris, and so ignored the proceedings. After the fifth failure to present himself, he was outlawed. It was April 27, 1768, when Wilkes finally surrendered to the sheriff, and was brought before the court on a writ of habeas corpus. His objections to technical errors in the proceedings were overruled, and he was sentenced to a fine of £1000, and twenty-two months' imprisonment, and was ordered to give £2000 surety. The case was appealed to the House of Lords on a writ of error, and there the judgment of the King's Bench was affirmed.[84]

---

[82] 29 *Com. J.,* 723; *Parl. Deb.,* XV, 1393.
[83] *Works of Burke* (Boston, 1865), I, 507.
[84] 13 Howell, *St. Tr.,* 1075-1183.

Wilkes had also instituted a number of suits for damages. He sued Robert Wood, Under-secretary of State, for trespass, alleging that he had entered his house, broken the locks, and seized and carried off a number of papers. The case of course turned on the validity of the general warrants issued by the Secretary of State at the time the attempt was made to locate the publisher of *North Briton No. 45.* Wood had entered Wilkes' residence on mere suspicion. The jury gave a verdict for the plaintiff, and awarded £1000 damages.[85] Then Wilkes tried for bigger game. He sued Lord Halifax, on substantially the same grounds, trespass under an illegal general warrant, and recovered damages amounting to £4000 from the Secretary of State.[86] The printer of the *North Briton* then sued one of the king's messengers who had executed a general warrant against him for false imprisonment and breaking into his house, and obtained an award of £400.[87] In *Entick v. Carrington,* the plaintiff also secured a verdict, on the ground that general warrants were illegal, and therefore Carrington, the king's messenger, could not plead his warrant from the Secretary of State in defence of his act of trespass.[88] Wilkes' uncompromising attitude toward what he regarded as the illegal action of the Crown and his ministers resulted in a great victory for the public press and for personal liberty, for it secured the judicial condemnation of general warrants.

As already indicated, Wilkes was expelled from the House of Commons in 1764, and went to Paris. There he remained until after the dissolution of Parliament in 1768. In that year he returned, petitioned the king for pardon, and offered himself as a candidate for Parliament from London. Defeated here, he succeeded in having himself triumphantly elected for Middlesex. Almost immediately, he was in trouble again with the courts. He decided to surrender to his outlawries, and for that purpose went to the Court of King's Bench. He was promptly committed on a *capias utlagatum.* A mob surrounded his prison and demanded his release so that he might attend the opening session of Parliament. A riot followed, the soldiers fired into the crowd and several were killed. Eventually Wilkes succeeded in getting his outlawry reversed on technicalities. But when he appeared in the House of

[85] 13 Howell, *St. Tr.,* 1154-1176; 1382.
[86] 19 Howell, *St. Tr.,* 1406.
[87] *Leach v. Money,* 19 Howell, *St. Tr.,* 1154.
[88] *Ibid.,* 1154.

Commons to take his seat as the duly elected representative of the voters of Middlesex, the Commons declared him incapable of being elected to their body because of his former misconduct. On February 3, 1769, a new writ was issued and Wilkes was reelected. Again he was declared unfit to have a seat in the Commons; new election writs were issued, and once more, Wilkes was returned by the voters of Middlesex. March 17, 1769, the process was repeated for the third time, with Wilkes again carrying the election. April 14, 1769, the House of Commons declared the election null and void, and on the ground that Henry Lawes Luttrell "ought to have been returned," gave the latter the contested seat in the House—in spite of the fact that he had received but 296 votes, while Wilkes had 1143.[89] This action of the lower house was a crude violation of the principles of the *lex terrae*, and it was justified by the law and custom of Parliament. The Commons, by the *lex parliamenti*, were undoubtedly the sole judges of their disputed elections; moreover, they had a right to expel an unruly member. These privileges were essential to preserve the power and effectiveness of the House as a representative body. In the Wilkes case, however, the House of Commons, out of sheer vindictiveness, created a disability hitherto unknown to the law. Furthermore, by expelling Wilkes and barring him from membership, the Commons were interfering with the franchise rights and the rights of representation, guaranteed by law, to the voters of Middlesex. A great majority of them had expressed their preference for John Wilkes; they had a right under the law to express that preference. Why should they be deprived of the services of their duly elected representative? Not content with expelling Wilkes, the House had deliberately given the seat in Parliament to one whose votes represented only a very small minority of those who enjoyed the franchise in Middlesex. *Lex parliamenti* was thus reconstructing some of the most basic principles of the common law, and was substituting minority for majority rule. Worst of all, it had become the tool of the Crown, intent upon establishing its absolutism, and carrying out its purposes through a submissive majority in the House of Commons.

Wilkes, whatever his other failings—and they were many—never lacked courage. For almost a score of years he was at war with Crown, Parliament, and courts, and in the end, he won. He knew how to rally public opinion to his support, and "Wilkes and

---

[89] See *Parl. Deb.*, XVI, 437, 532 *et seq.*

Liberty" became the watchword of the party of constitutional government. The voters of Middlesex remained loyal; Wilkes was expelled and reelected, time after time; and in the end, the House of Commons had to submit in the contest between privilege and the people. Many of the leaders of political opinion, and a large portion of the electorate, became conscious of the real issues involved. In one of its phases, the Wilkes' affair was a battle over privilege, in which Wilkes and the electorate, arrayed on one side, as the champions of the fundamental guarantees of the law, opposed the Crown and the royally-controlled majority in the Commons, who took refuge behind an unjustifiable extension of the principles of the *lex parliamenti.*

The majority of the Commons who had declared Luttrell elected argued that they "were acting in a judicial capacity," and therefore their resolutions were equal in effect "to a law." [90] "The House of Commons is the sole court of judicature in all cases of election;" it has "exclusive jurisdiction," and is the "dernier resort." [91] In a debate of January 25, 1770, on a resolution that in election matters the House of Commons is bound to judge by the law of the land, some made the sweeping assertion that the people of England had no rights whatever, except those that exist within the walls of the House of Commons; in short, the House can make any rules or orders it deems necessary. [92] On February 19, the Commons adopted this same resolution, but stripped it of part of its significance by adding that they *had* followed the law of the land in the decision of the Middlesex election. The Lords concurred, although a number warned against the dangers of one-house legislation, and advised the upper house to take up the defence of the people's rights. [93]

May 1, 1770, the Earl of Chatham introduced a bill in the Lords to reverse the judgment of the Commons' house in the Wilkes' case as illegal—as "cutting off the subject from his indubitable birthright, by a vote of one house of Parliament, exercising discretionary power and legislative authority, under colour of a jurisdiction in elections." Chatham made an excellent argument for his measure, but it failed to pass. [94] Seven months later, he moved that a resolution be adopted, declaring the capacity to be chosen a mem-

[90] *Parl. Deb.*, XVI, 585.
[91] *Ibid.*, 594.
[92] *Ibid.*, 785.
[93] *Ibid.*, 813, 820-830.
[94] *Ibid.*, 955, 957.

ber of Parliament an inherent right of the subject. In a two hours' speech, he endeavored to show that such cases as the Wilkes incident were cognizable in the courts of law, and that the House of Commons could not, and ought not, be the final judge. Adjournment came before any action could be taken.[95] April 30, 1771, the Lords refused to expunge their record of the Middlesex election dispute.[96] April 26, 1773, Wilkes demanded that he be sworn in by the House as the member for Middlesex. The ministry always proved able to control a sufficient number of votes in the Commons to keep him out. Bills dealing with the case and designed to help Wilkes to his seat were introduced, debated—and always defeated.[97] It was 1774 before he finally gained admission. He came in on a wave of popular support. Sixty thousand had petitioned the Crown on his behalf. Popular pressure finally became so great that there was no other alternative than to admit Wilkes to the House. He came in "scorched, but not consumed," to use his own phrase. In a speech teeming with stinging sarcasm and bitter defiance, Wilkes flayed the Commons for their vindictiveness. He accused them of an attempt to set up one-house legislation and overturn the laws of the land. He moved that all records of the case be immediately expunged from the Journal. A number of expunging resolutions were brought in in every session from 1774 to 1782, Wilkes insisting that "While the resolution . . . . is suffered to continue on our Journals, I shall believe . . . . that the elective rights of the nation lie at the mercy of the minister, that is, in fact, of the Crown."[98] Finally, May 3, 1782, Wilkes was successful. By a vote of 115 to 47, all records of the case were ordered erased from the Journal. Wilkes saw to it that it was done with due ceremony. He had won a great fight for constitutional government and personal liberty. He had been instrumental in defeating the dangerous practice of general warrants. He had won a victory for freedom of the press. He had directed popular attention to the royally-controlled House of Commons, and pointed out its unrepresentative character, and had shown how easily a claim of privilege might be used to sanction the arbitrary proceedings of ministers and Parliament, even when a fundamental right of the subject was concerned. It was one of life's little ironies that work of such magnitude had

---

[95] *Parl Deb.*, XVI, 1302 *et seq.*
[96] *Ibid.*, XVII, 214-219.
[97] *Ibid.*, XVII, 838; 1054.
[98] *Parl. Deb.*, XIX, 197.

been reserved for one of the worst libertines and demagogues of all time.[99]

In 1771, as part of the general plan on the part of George III's government to enforce the law of libel and to stop the disrespectful reports of debates in the Commons that were being circulated, the House of Commons made one of its spasmodic efforts to enforce the standing order that prohibited the publication of accounts of its proceedings. A number of printers were ordered to the bar. Alderman Wilkes encouraged the publishers to defy the authority of the House, and he himself devised means to oppose the execution of its orders. A crisis was reached when a messenger of the Commons, sent to arrest a printer, was in turn arrested by a city constable of London and taken before Brass Crosby, the Lord Mayor, and Aldermen Oliver and Wilkes. These officials freed the printer, and put the messenger of the House under arrest and bail, and thus precipitated another conflict with the lower house, just as had been hoped. Wilkes was spoiling for another fight, but the Commons decided to concentrate on Oliver and Crosby. Crosby, after a hearing at the bar, where he justified his course by claiming that his oath of office required him to protect the rights and liberties of the citizens, was committed to the Tower for a breach of the privileges of the lower house. The journey to the Tower was a triumphal procession—a large and friendly mob had been provided by the circulation of handbills. The Lord Mayor immediately asked for a writ of habeas corpus, and obtained a hearing in the Court of Common Pleas. Serjeant Glynn acted as his counsel, and argued that the judges of the court must decide whether the fact charged was *by law* a contempt or breach of privilege. The argument proceeded on the principle that the actions of a Parliament house, even under *lex parliamenti*, must conform to the rules of the common law. The House of Commons, it was urged, "has a certain limited jurisdiction; and this court must judge whether it has not trans-

---

[99] See *Parl. Deb.*, XVII, 214, 219, 838, 1054; XVIII, 359-374, 376, 1336; XIX, 193-197; XX, 144 etc.; XXII, 99, 1407, 1410. It is interesting to note that such a pronounced liberal as Fox opposed the expunging resolutions on the ground that the power of the House to expel was for the ultimate good of the people. See *Parl. Deb.*, XXII, 1410. For additional references on this famous case, see Fitzgerald, *Life of Wilkes* (2 Vols.); Thomas Wright, *Caricature History of the Georges*, Ch. 8; W. F. Rae, *Wilkes, Sheridan and Fox*, pp. 1-138; Tonybee, *Letters of Horace Walpole*, V, 315, 316, 398, 412; May's *Constitutional History of England* (1882 Ed.), I, chapter 7. See also, A. von Ruville, *William Pitt, Earl of Chatham* (3 Vols.); III, Section 2, pp. 105 *et seq.*; Basil Williams, *The Life of William Pitt* (2 Vols.), II, 155-159; 249-277, *passim;* Winstanley, *Lord Chatham and the Whig Opposition* (1912), pp. 219-414, *passim;* R. Lucas, *Lord North* (2 Vols.).

gressed and gone beyond the bounds of its jurisdiction, and must pronounce upon it. . . . ."[100] Glynn denied that the Commons' house was a court of record. Much of his reasoning was based directly upon Holt's decisions in the Aylesbury cases.

The opinion of the court was unanimous in favor of remanding Crosby to the Tower. It was a long and unqualified endorsement of the law of privilege. Lord Chief Justice de Grey began with a quotation from Coke's *Fourth Institute*, on the judicial nature and power of Parliaments. The analogy between the House of Commons and a court of law was closely adhered to throughout. De Grey believed that the power to commit was inherent in the House of Commons from its very nature, and so, part of the law of the land. Since all contempts, he argued, must be punishable either in the court contemned, or in some higher court, the contempts against either house must be punishable by them alone, since Parliament has no superior court.[101] Further, Crosby was committed by the law of Parliament; he could not, therefore, get redress from the common law, for "the law of Parliament is only known to parliament-men, by experience in the house. . . . The House of Commons only know how to act within their own limits; we are not a court of appeal, we do not know certainly the jurisdiction of the House of Commons; we cannot judge of the laws and privileges of the house, because we have no knowledge of those laws and privileges. . . . . I wish we had some code of the law of parliament, but till we have such a code, it is impossible we should be able to judge of it."[102] De Grey was convinced that *lex parliamenti* was superior to *lex terrae* in all cases of the nature of the one before him. In his opinion, "the laws (could) never be a prohibition to the Houses of Parliament, because, by law, there is nothing superior to them." If Parliament should abuse its power, there could be no remedy—"it would be a public grievance."[103] The opinions of the other members of the court were substantially in accord with that of the Chief Justice. Only Blackstone's needs special mention. He believed that "The House of Commons is a supreme court," and judge of its privileges and contempts. "All courts," he continued,

---

[100] 3 Wilson, 188-198, for the case.

[101] "When the House of Commons adjudge any thing to be a contempt, or a breach of privilege, their adjudication is a conviction, and their commitment in consequence is execution; and no court can discharge or bail a person that is in execution by the judgment of any other court." 3 Wilson, 199.

[102] *Ibid.*, 200.

[103] *Ibid.*, 202.

"by which I mean to include the two houses of Parliament, and the courts of Westminster-hall, can have no controul in matters of contempts. The sole adjudication of contempts, and the punishment thereof, in any manner, belongs exclusively, and without interfering, to each respective court. Infinite confusion and disorder would follow, if courts could by writs of habeas corpus, examine and determine the contempts of others. . . . . It is our duty to presume the orders of that house (the Commons) and their execution, are according to the law. . . ."[104] Blackstone undoubtedly regarded Parliament's power to commit for contempt as analogous to the power enjoyed by every law court, and explained Parliament's immunity from interference from other ordinary courts by the judicial supremacy of the High Court of Parliament.[105]

In *Rex v. Wright*, a case based on the conflict between the ordinary law of libel and the privilege of free speech in Parliament, Lord Kenyon ruled: "This is a proceeding by one branch of the legislature, and therefore we cannot inquire into it. I do not say that cases may not be put in which we would not inquire whether or not the House of Commons were justified in any particular measure; if for instance, they were to send their Serjeant-at-arms to arrest a Counsel here who was arguing a case between two individuals, or to grant an injunction to stop proceedings here in a common action, undoubtedly, we should pay no attention to it." Justice Lawrence seems to have justified the privilege of publishing the proceedings of Parliament on the ground that "proceedings of courts of justice are daily published," some of which contain serious reflections on individuals, but nevertheless, the publishers are immune from action for libel.[106]

In the case of *Walker v. Earl of Grosvenor* (1797) the Court of King's Bench held that no attachment could be granted against the defendant, for non-payment of a sum, pursuant to an award under a rule of *nisi prius*, because the defendant was a "peer of the realm."[107] In November of the same year, the court denied an

---

[104] 3 Wilson, 240.   Also 9 Adolph & Ellis, 120.

[105] Palgrave's statement is interesting in this connection. He points out that in the era of Charles I, Parliament "could not claim the prerogative rights included in the word privilege, as a legislative body; privilege answered to its call because Parliament was also High Court of Justice; there lay the secret of that possession: by no possibility could the highest judicial tribunal in the land be denied the power, enjoyed by every petty law court, of punishing disobedience, or insult." Reg. F. D. Palgrave, *The House of Commons* (1878), p. 71.

[106] 8 Durnf. & East, 293-299.   The case of *King v. Lord Abingdon* and its application to the law of libel and privilege was discussed earlier.   See *ante*, 31, and 1 Maule & Selwyn, 275 *et seq.*

[107] 7 Durnf. & East, 171.

attachment against a member of the House of Commons, under similar circumstances.[108]

In *Bernal v. The Marquis of Donegal* (1805) the court refused a writ of *ne exeat regno* to restrain a member of Parliament from going to Ireland. The member owed the plaintiff in the case £21,000, and apparently wanted to leave the kingdom to escape payment. But his legal advisers insisted that such a writ would hinder him "from performing his duty to his constituents by going occasionally among them, to advise with them." The Marquis represented an Irish borough. Bernal maintained that privilege was limited to the purpose of attending Parliament, and did not protect the intermediate time between the two periods of forty days, if the prorogation extended beyond eighty days. The court recognized the claim of privilege, and refused to restrain the member from leaving England.[109]

---

[108] See *Catmur v. Sir. E. Knatchbull, Bart, et al.*, 7 Durnf. & East, 448.
[109] Vesey (Senior) *Repts.*, Vol. II, p. 43.

CHAPTER VI

LEX PARLIAMENTI VERSUS LEX TERRAE *(Concluded)*

The discussion of cases in the preceding chapter has brought us to the opening of the nineteenth century. By that time, a great many of England's political institutions seemed to have completed their development, and to have assumed something like their present-day forms, although there were of course some notable exceptions to this statement. A great many of the basic principles of English law had been established and the functions, powers, and forms of many of the institutions of the English government had been clearly defined, and with the appearance of absolute finality. But not so with privilege. Parliamentary privilege remained the one great problem that seemed to defy solution. At the opening of the nineteenth century, the solution of the troublesome questions of the relation between Parliament and the courts, and between privilege and the law of the land, was hardly nearer than it had been centuries ago, and certainly the definition of the proper sphere for the exercise of privilege was no more accurate. The High Court of Parliament still regarded its privileges as part of the *lex parliamenti;* the interference of the ordinary "inferior" common law courts was as bitterly resented as before; and the courts and Parliament still found it impossible to work out a satisfactory solution for the conflict between their jurisdictions. As a matter of fact, the struggles between Parliament and the courts, and *lex parliamenti* and *lex terrae,* were at no time more prolonged and severe than in the nineteenth century. There are no more important cases in the whole history of privilege than those of Sir Francis Burdett, Stockdale v. Hansard, and Charles Bradlaugh, and all occurred in comparatively recent times. To our own time, many judges and parliamentarians were influenced by the notion of Parliament's judicial supremacy, and believed that its acts, when grounded upon the *lex parliamenti*, had a peculiar sanctity. The Commons, through at least part of the nineteenth century, still had reasons to fear the appellate jurisdiction of the House of Lords, and therefore persevered in their efforts to keep questions of privilege out of the ordinary courts. And there were some who were

127

still unable to distinguish between the remnants of Parliament's judicial characteristics and Parliament's now fully developed legislative sovereignty.

The case of Sir Francis Burdett ranks with the great landmarks in the history of privilege. In its various ramifications, it covered a period of seven years. It involved not only the two houses of Parliament, but passed through various stages of litigation in the Court of King's Bench, the Exchequer Chamber, and finally the Lords. The case showed in what hopeless confusion many of the questions of parliamentary privilege still were at the opening of the nineteenth century.

The case began in 1810. The Commons had committed a publisher of a placard which advertised the conduct of two members of Parliament as the subject for debate in a debating society. Sir Francis Burdett, a member of the lower house, denied the power of the House of Commons to commit for such an offence, and presented his reasons fully in a public address to his constituents. On March 27, 1810, a complaint was lodged in the House of Commons to the effect that a letter had appeared in Cobbett's *Weekly Register*, entitled "Sir Francis Burdett to his Constituents, denying the power of the House of Commons to imprison the People of England." The House viewed the publication as injurious to its dignity and honor. Burdett was present when the charge was made. He arose in his place, and promptly acknowledged the authorship of the letter.[1] After several days of debate on the subject, it was resolved that Burdett's letter was a "libellous and scandalous paper, reflecting on the just rights and privileges of this house," and Burdett was voted guilty of a breach of privilege, and ordered to the Tower.[2] The Serjeant of the Commons found the execution of the order exceedingly difficult. From his report to the House, it appears that he called at Burdett's home on several occasions to make the arrest, but each time found him absent. Finally, with the aid of the military and police, the Serjeant succeeded in effecting an entry and arresting the offender. It was reported that Burdett was found busily engaged in teaching his infant son to read and translate Magna Charta. Burdett steadfastly maintained that the arrest was unjustified, disputed the legality of the Speaker's warrant, and submitted only after the most vehement protest. After many diffi-

---

[1] 65 *Com. J.*, 224, 228. This was not the first time Burdett caused trouble. See 60 *Com. J.*, 13..

[2] 65 *Com. J.*, 252.

culties, some of which will be recounted later, Burdett was finally safely lodged in the Tower.[3] Four days after the arrest, the prisoner notified Speaker Abbott, in a carefully drawn letter, that he would bring suit against him in the Court of King's Bench, for trespass and false imprisonment, and for having "forcibly broke and entered" his house.[4] The Speaker read the letter to the Commons, but that body took no immediate action. Several days later, a second letter, similar to the first in content, arrived. Again, the House refused to take action.[5] Finally, on May 7, the House appointed a committee to examine and report on the two letters and on the general issues involved.[6] Several reports of the select committee were printed. They upheld the "inherent right" of the Commons to "commit generally for all contempts," according to the decision of the Lord Chief Justice De Grey in Brass Crosby's case.[7] The power to commit for libel of the House or its members was considered essential to the freedom of debate, the independence of Parliament, and the general safety of the state. The committee believed this power to be "in truth part of the fundamental law of Parliament," and the "Law of Parliament is the Law of the Land."[8] Parliament possessed the power to commit as much as any court of justice in Westminster, and this power was regarded as having been "established and confirmed as clearly and incontrovertibly as any part of the Law of the Land," and as "one of the most important safeguards of the Rights and Liberties of the People."

On June 8, 1810, the House of Commons seriously debated several plans for dealing with the Burdett case. A motion was made to the effect that all persons who should presume to prosecute any one for acts done in obedience to the orders of the House should be declared guilty of a high breach of the privileges of the Commons. Another motion applied the principle directly to the actions Burdett had by this time commenced against Charles Abbott, Speaker of the House, under whose warrant the arrest had been made, and John Coleman, the Serjeant-at-arms who had executed the order. Still another demanded that a proper officer of the Court of King's Bench attend the House with all records of the proceedings in the

---

[3] 65 *Com. J.*, 262-271.
[4] *Ibid.*, 285.
[5] *Ibid.*, 294.
[6] *Ibid.*, 339.
[7] See *ante*, 123.
[8] See Committee Repts., May 11, June 15, 1810. The second contains an appendix giving a list of libel cases against the House from 1559-1805 ; and the names of offenders and the disposition of their cases. See also 1 Hatsell, 294-298 ; 8 Howell, *St. Tr.*, 23.

Burdett litigation. All three motions were defeated by moving the previous question, and the House, instead of forcibly resisting the prosecution of its officers in the courts—as precedents would have abundantly justified—decided to direct its Speaker and Serjeant to plead in court, and instructed the Attorney-general to act as their counsel. Fortunately, the courts upheld the claims of the lower house; what might have happened if the ruling had been otherwise, may be inferred from what actually did take place in the later Stockdale-Hansard cases.

Analysis of the arguments and decisions in the extended litigation carried on by Burdett will prove most profitable and illuminating. In 1811, Burdett brought an action in the Court of King's Bench against Charles Abbott, Speaker of the House of Commons, charging him with trespass, forcibly breaking into the plaintiff's home, and illegally imprisoning him in the Tower. Burdett asserted that his confinement had been contrary to law; Abbott, of course, pleaded parliamentary privilege in justification of his acts. The Speaker appeared in court, and explained his position very carefully to the judges. Parliament, he asserted, was sitting at the time of the alleged trespass, and the House had declared the plaintiff's publication libellous and had ordered his arrest for breach of privilege. The Speaker therefore, acting solely in his official capacity, and according to ancient usage, had drawn up the warrants for the arrest and confinement. One warrant had been given to the Serjeant-at-arms, another to the Lieutenant of the Tower, asking him to receive and detain the prisoner when he should arrive.[9] Serjeant Coleman had repaired to Burdett's house, and "with a loud and audible voice," had stated the purpose of his visit, and had demanded admission. The outer door was found closed and barricaded, and Burdett refused to surrender himself. Thereupon, the Serjeant had procured an opinion from the Attorney-general, as to how much force he might legally and properly employ in effecting an entry. He had then returned to the scene, with some cavalry, infantry, and thirty police, to make the arrest. The door had been broken down, Burdett had been seized, and the imposing cavalcade, followed by a jeering mob, had then proceeded to the Tower, where the prisoner had been safely deposited. Abbott completed this detailed account of the facts in the case, and then withdrew without making any plea.

---

[9] See 14 East, 1-7.

Holroyd appeared for the plaintiff and made an able argument. He presented the case in a manner which left but one question to be decided, namely, did this court of King's Bench have the power to inquire into, and decide upon, the law and custom of Parliament when it came incidentally before them, in order to determine whether the particular case in judgment was or was not governed by that law and custom? Holroyd, of course, contended that the court had that right. In a country where the king's prerogative, and the rights and liberties of the people are defined and limited by law, Holroyd believed it absurd to allow parliamentary privilege alone to remain vague and confused. Without some clearly-drawn limitations, people would constantly incur the liability of being punished for offences against a law which it was impossible for them to know or learn. Lord Hale's *History of the Common Law* was cited to prove that *lex et consuetudo parliamenti* is not to be considered as opposed to the common law, but as a part of it.[10] Burdett's contention was grounded upon the conception that *lex parliamenti* was part of the *lex terrae*, namely, that part which applied especially to the rights and privileges of Parliament, and so, *lex parliamenti* could not supersede *lex terrae*, of which it was but a part. Therefore the judges, who sat in the common law courts and administered the common law, must be acquainted with, and were bound to pass upon cases arising under the law of Parliament, a special branch of the common law. In trying to establish this point, Holroyd reviewed most of the great cases that have been discussed in the preceding pages. Naturally, he laid greatest stress upon Holt's decisions in the Aylesbury cases, and in *Rex and Regina v. Knollys*. Holroyd also tried to explain the history of privilege of Parliament. In the earliest times, he maintained, recourse was had to the law, to ascertain and confirm the privileges of Parliament. The process was by suing out a writ of privilege, issuing out of Chancery, and under the great seal. Then, privilege was claimed as the privilege of the whole Parliament, not of one house alone, and therefore "no danger resulted from the courts of common law tak-

---

[10] Hale, in treating the *lex non scripta*, "includes under that term not only the general customs, or the *common law* properly so called, but even those more particular laws and customs applicable to certain courts and persons. Therefore, though the law of parliament be sometimes contrasted with the common law, that is only where the common law is used in a narrow sense, as applying only to a particular branch of it; in the same manner as it may be contrasted with the *lex prerogativae*, or the *lex forestae*, or the *lex mercatoria*, all of which Lord Hale stated to be branches of the common law used in its large and general significance." 14 East, 14.

ing cognizance of it, from whose decision a writ of error lay to one branch of the Parliament, the lords; because they had an equal interest in protecting the privilege, if by law it existed, for themselves, as well as for the House of Commons."[11]   Holroyd either failed to see or purposely passed over, the real difficulty this state of affairs raised, namely, that by the English legal system, the Lords were the highest court of the realm, and so became the ultimate judges of the privileges of the lower house, should questions of privilege be left to the ordinary courts of the realm for determination.   Burdett's counsel maintained that "the judges have a right, and indeed are bound to determine all cases of privilege, brought judicially before them, except when they arise in the lords' house of parliament, where they are no parties to the determination: but where the question comes before them in a legal way in their own courts, they are bound to take cognizance of the existence and extent of the privilege, and to decide upon it. . . ."[12] The argument denied that the Commons were a court of record, and took exception to the form of the warrant under which the arrest had been made, on the ground that it should show good cause for commitment, and what the contempt and breach of privilege was, in addition to the resolution of the House declaring it so.[13] A great deal of emphasis was laid upon the fact that Burdett's door had been broken open, an action that had never before been regarded as lawful except for some crime, and upon process at the suit of the king for that crime.   Holroyd concluded his argument with a brilliant summary—"By laying the basis of parliamentary privilege in the law of the land, and subjecting them to the examination and control of the courts of law, no arbitrary and despotic power can be exercised, and no person can be deprived of his liberty without ultimate redress, except by a law made or recognized by the whole body of Parliament; whereby the one house may operate as a check upon the other, agreeably to the general principle of the constitution, which is composed of checks and balancing power."[14]

The Attorney-general appeared for Abbott. He argued that the defendant had acted in his capacity as an officer of a court

---

[11] 14 East, 53.

[12] "Any subject of the realm, when imprisoned, has a right to appeal to the law against any other who procured or aided that trespass and imprisonment, in order to ascertain whether he was rightly arrested and imprisoned or no." 14 East, 74.

[13] 14 East, 53.

[14] 14 East, 78.

of competent jurisdiction, and a suit of trespass against an official
for obeying the orders and issuing the process of the court he
serves, must be dismissed as absurd. The analogy between Parliament's power to commit for contempt, and that of other courts of
Westminster-hall, was consistently preserved. In the case before
the court, the Attorney-general maintained that the House of Commons had already rendered a decision, and therefore, their judgment must be regarded as final and unimpeachable in any other
court. To the technical objections which Burdett had made to the
form of the resolutions of the House, Abbott's defender replied:
"The House of Commons is not bound by nor tied down to technical
forms: it is enough that the court see in substance what the plain
meaning of the resolution is, of which there can be no doubt. . . ."[15]
In regard to breaking in the door of the plaintiff's house, the Attorney-general sought to establish a distinction between the process
issued at the instance of a private person, in the maintenance of a
private right, and one issued at the instance of a public authority,
for a public right.[16]

Holroyd, in rebuttal, argued that the "House of Commons cannot, by their single resolution, without the rest of parliament, either
make, or declare the law: that they cannot themselves make a privilege; for that would in effect be making a law: and that this had
been declared both by the courts of law and by the conduct of parliament itself; because in several cases the Commons had claimed
privileges which were questioned in the courts of law, and disallowed by Parliament."[17] In claiming that the *lex parliamenti* must
conform to the *lex terrae* and that no extension of privilege which
could result in an infringement or violation of the guarantees of the
common law, should be tolerated, Burdett's counsel was substantially in agreement with the modern solution of the relation of
Parliament's privileges to the rights of the subject. In trying to
prove however that in this particular case the House was endeavoring to create a new privilege, by virtually one-house legislation, he
was wrong. The action of the House had the sanction of ancient
custom, and the right of the House to commit for contempt was
well established. Further, it never had been the practice to sum-

---

[15] 14 East, 85.
[16] *Ibid.*, 81-116.
[17] *Ibid.*, 121.

mon officials of the House personally before the courts to answer for their official acts executed by order of the House.[18]

The ruling of the judges was unanimously in favor of the defendant, on every point raised in the argument. It was based on the court theory of Parliament, and rested upon the assumption that Parliament's peculiar rights arise from the fact that it is the highest court in the kingdom. Lord Ellenborough pointed out that the right to commit for contempt was an essential right of self-protection. ". . . . Can the High Court of Parliament, or either of the two houses of which it consists, be deemed not to possess intrinsically that authority of punishing summarily for contempts, which is acknowledged to belong, and is daily exercised as belonging to every superior court of law, of less dignity undoubtedly than itself? . . ."[19] The learned judge held that any commitment for contempt, by the House of Commons, was not to be inquired into further. Such an act of a Parliament house—"or any other of the superior courts"— must be recognized as valid and sufficient. But, should the commitment appear to be not professedly for a contempt, but for some matter appearing on the return, which could not reasonably be interpreted as a contempt, but on the contrary constituted an arbitrary or unjust proceeding, contrary "to every principle of positive law," then, and then only, according to Lord Ellenborough, the judges "must look at it and act upon it as justice may require, from whatever court it may profess to have proceeded. . . . ."[20] In the Burdett case, the matter was one which the House was competent to decide, both as to the fact and the effect of the publication. "Then," Lord Ellenborough concluded, "by analogy to the judgment of a Court of law (and the judgments of either House of Parliament cannot with propriety be put upon a footing less authoritative than those of the ordinary Courts of law) the House must be considered as having decided both, as far as respects any question thereupon which may arise in other Courts."[21] The objections raised to the breaking of the door were dismissed with the observation that the

---

[18] Lord Ellenborough, early in the trial, observed, "The question in all cases would be, whether the House of Commons were a court of competent jurisdiction for the purpose of issuing a warrant to do the act. . . . It is not pretended that the exercise of a general criminal jurisdiction is any part of their privileges. When that case occurs, which it never will, the question would be whether they had general jurisdiction to issue such an order ; and no doubt, the Courts of justice would do their duty. . . ." 14 East, 128.

[19] 14 East, 138.

[20] *Ibid.*, 151.

[21] *Ibid.*, 153.

personal good of an individual must yield to the public weal. The opinions of the other judges were in complete agreement with that of the Lord Chief Justice. They followed the same analogy between the commiting power of the House and that of the ordinary courts of law, and need not be discussed further.[22]

Burdett thus lost his suit against the Speaker. But this was not the only action he had begun. On June 19, 1811, he filed an action against John Coleman, Serjeant-at-arms of the House of Commons, charging him with assault and false imprisonment. Burdett maintained that Coleman, in using a large military force against him, in an unreasonably violent manner, had exceeded the authority of his warrant. The defendant pleaded that he had employed only sufficient force to make the arrest and prevent a riot. Witnesses for the Serjeant testified that there was a mob near by when the arrest was made, and that without military aid, Burdett could never have been conducted to the Tower. Lord Ellenborough in his charge to the jury, made it clear that no question of the privileges or the rights of the Commons was involved (that issue had been settled in the first case), and that the only question to be decided was whether Coleman had used excessive and improper military force. The jury gave a verdict for the Serjeant.[23]

Burdett refused to admit his defeat and took the case to a higher court. On April 22, 1812, the case of *Burdett v. Abbott* came before the Exchequer Chamber on a writ of error to reverse the judgment of the King's Bench. The argument for the plaintiff followed the same line of reasoning used earlier in the Court of King's Bench. Exceptions were taken to the form of the house resolution, to the order-providing for Burdett's arrest, and to the methods employed by the Serjeant in executing the warrant.[24] The court overruled the objections and the Chief Justice upheld the power of the House of Commons to commit for contempt. The argument that the House had in former times acted only with the Lords, and therefore could not now commit alone, the judge dismissed by declaring it a speculation fit only for antiquarians, since the House of Commons had committed alone ever since the days of Elizabeth, if not earlier. The technical objections to the Speaker's

---

[22] 14 East, 158-160.

[23] 14 East, 163-196.

[24] Burdett's counsel tried to prove that "It was not made out, either upon the ground of reason or necessity, or by the evidence of usage and practice, by any legislative recognition, or by any well-established precedents and authorities, of the judgments of the Courts of Law, that the House of Commons had power to commit for contempts as this." 4 Taunton, 402.

warrant were also ignored, because "the House of Commons have ruled it to be a contempt, and the Judges of Westminster-hall are bound by that. If it were not so, the Courts could never go on; for if one Court committed for a contempt, another Court could review and annul their proceedings, the Court would be in perpetual war."[25] Underlying all this reasoning, was the notion that Parliament was a court, whose privileges arose from its character as a judicial body. The judgment of the King's Bench was affirmed.

Burdett took the last possible step to get a reversal of the judgments against him. July 27, 1817, the cases of *Burdett v. Abbott,* and *Burdett v. Coleman,* came before the Lords from the Exchequer Chamber, on a writ of error.[26] Only the plaintiff's counsel was heard, and his arguments were not new. The judgment of the lower court was affirmed, and the case ended in a complete victory for the claims of the House of Commons. Lord Erskine, in giving the opinion in the Lords in affirmation of the judgments of the lower courts, held that "Privileges are part of the law of the land, and upon this record there is nothing more than the ordinary proceedings; the Speaker of the House of Commons, like any other subject putting himself on the country as to the fact, and pleading a justification in law; for this was not a plea to the jurisdiction, but a plea in bar." He remarked that "This course of proceeding gave me (him) the most heartfelt satisfaction; for if the judgment had been adverse to the defendants, the house would no doubt have submitted. It would be a libel upon the House of Commons to suppose that it would not. Therefore, by this judgment, it appears that it is the law which protects the just privileges of the House of Commons, as well as the rights of the subject."[27] Lord Erskine's opinion contained the true solution for the conflict between the privileges of Parliament and the ordinary law of the land, but a number of years elapsed before a court of law definitely announced the principles on which a final settlement was based—and what is more important—was able to put them into effect, even against a hostile House of Commons.[28]

---

[25] 4 Taunton, 444-448.

[26] 5 Dow, 165.

[27] 5 Dow, 200.

[28] The extended litigation in the Burdett cases attracted considerable public attention, and elicited some expressions of opinion on the case that reveal the general conceptions of parliamentary privileges which existed at that time. One of the interesting pamphlets of the time was that of Charles Watkin Williams Wynne, M. P. *Lex parliamenti* he regarded as a branch of the common law. Parliament he believed to be a high court. "The authority of this high court is supreme, and paramount to that of every other within this kingdom." "Each House

In 1820, John Hobhouse was confined in Newgate under a warrant from the Speaker of the House of Commons, for seditious libel. His case is much like that of Burdett. Hobhouse's counsel moved for a writ of habeas corpus in the Court of King's Bench. The court instructed him to point out what objections he intended to raise to the warrant under which his client had been committed. He refused, maintaining that a writ of habeas corpus was grantable in the first instance as of course, and that the time for presenting defects in the warrant would be on the return of the writ. Apparently the court came to agree with this view of the law, for a writ was granted, and the prisoner was brought before the judges. All objections that were raised to the Speaker's warrant were overruled, and the prisoner was remanded to Newgate. Hobhouse's plea that the commitment was illegal was based upon the contention that the House of Commons was not a court of judicature, competent to pass judgment upon the alleged offence. Even if it were a court of judicature, it was insisted, the offence was an offence at common law, and not a contempt of the House, to be judged by the *lex parliamenti*. Hobhouse complained that he had received no opportunity to defend himself, and asserted that the House, even if it were a court, and could take cognizance of libels, could not condemn an Englishman to prison. He contended that the Court of King's Bench had the power and the right to liberate by writ of habeas corpus any English subject, committed by the Commons' House, and that privilege must be brought into agreement with the rules of the common law.

The judges, in the decision, upheld the ancient right of the Commons to commit offenders, and defended the time-worn principles that made the House of Commons sole judge of its privileges.

---

is a Chamber of the King's High Court of Parliament." "The House of Commons is an original and permanent part of the highest judicature in the country, and as a Chamber of Parliament, combines the magisterial and judicial functions with those of a permanent and universal inquest." The writer frequently employs the analogy between a Parliament house and the courts of the kingdom. "It is difficult to imagine" (he writes) "what reason can be urged, why the House of Commons should not be entrusted with a power (i.e. to commit) which it has been found necessary to grant to every court of record in the kingdom." It is impossible to accept all the argument made by Mr. Wynne in this pamphlet. Nevertheless, I have cited it here as further evidence to show that the notion that Parliament was a court, the highest in the land, and exercised some of its important powers because of its judicial nature and characteristics, still existed in the nineteenth century, and was a vital force in supporting Parliament's supremacy in matters of privilege. For the extracts given above, see the pamphlet—Charles Watkin Williams Wynne, M. P.—"*Argument upon the Jurisdiction of the House of Commons to Commit in Cases of Breach of Privilege.*"—1810. In support of the power of the House to commit, Mr. Wynne claims to have made an actual count of all commitments recorded from 1547 to 1810, and he finds the total to be a "little less than a thousand."

Here again, their reasoning seems to have been based on the judicial nature of Parliament. "The power of commitment for contempt is incident to every court of justice, and more especially it belongs to the High Court of Parliament. . . . . We cannot enquire into the form of commitment, even supposing it is open to objection on the ground of informality."[29] The judges ruled that the habeas corpus act did not apply to the case before the court, "because it is confined wholly to the cases of Commitment for *crime*, with the exception of treason and felony, or the suspicion thereof."[30]

In *Phillips v. Wellesley* (1830) the court decided that an unprivileged person in custody in execution, and elected a member of Parliament, is entitled to his discharge on motion. The defendant had become a member of Parliament for St. Ives, between the perfecting of bail and obtaining final judgment. The bail was discharged from his responsibility.[31]

In 1831, parliamentary privilege became involved in the action of *Wellesley v. the Duke of Beaufort*, in the Chancery. Wellesley "the father of several infants," had received an order from the Chancery Court not to interfere with, or disturb his children, who were in the care of guardians. Disregarding the order of the court, Wellesley drove to the home of the guardians, and carried off his children. For this action, he was committed by the court for contempt. Being a member of Parliament, Wellesley claimed that the court had infringed upon his privileges, and wrote a letter to the Speaker of the House of Commons, setting forth the facts and demanding the protection of privilege. It appears that the Lord Chancellor also addressed a communication to the Speaker, informing him of the arrest, and explaining the reasons for the confinement.[32] A committee of the Commons was directed to investigate. On July 27 it made its report. It deserves some attention, for it reflects a new spirit on the part of the Commons in the matter of privilege. If an identical case had occurred several centuries

---

[29] 2 Chitty's *Repts.*, 210.

[30] *Ibid.*, 211. The court believed that a writ of habeas corpus was not grantable in the first instance as of course. Chief Justice Abbot observed on this point, "It seems to me that the Court are not bound as of course and without any cause shown, to grant this writ in the first instance." The other judges concurred and added that an applicant for a writ should first be compelled to state some reason for granting the writ; if the judges knew beforehand that the prisoner must be remanded, it would be folly to issue it. See 3 Barneswell & Alderson, 420-425.

[31] 1 Dowling's *Practice Cases*, 9-15. A few years earlier, an interesting situation developed in the Lords. Strangers were really prohibited below the bar, but officers let them in if they left all sticks and umbrellas outside. A person left his umbrella behind, and it was stolen. Thereupon he sued the officers of the Lords. He was declared guilty of a breach of privilege. Hans. *Parl. Deb.* New Series, XVII, 34-5.

[32] 2 Russell & Mylne, 639.

earlier, when the position of the lower house had not yet been so firmly established, in all probability the House would have upheld the claim of the arrested member. As it was, privilege was denied. It appears that the Lord Chancellor had issued an order to prohibit Wellesley from attending the sessions of the House. While the committee was making its investigations, the Chancellor decided that Wellesley should be permitted to attend, and informed the Commons to that effect. Thus he cleared himself of any possible suspicion of desiring to violate the privileges of the lower house, and the sole question left for the committee to decide, was whether Wellesley was entitled, by privilege of Parliament, to his discharge.[33] The committee of the House of Commons concluded that "The same principle on which it has been resolved by the House of Lords (1757) that Privilege shall not prevent the Courts of Law from enforcing obedience to a Writ of Habeas Corpus, seems to require, by analogy, that the Lord Chancellor should possess equal powers for the protection of Wards of the Crown, committed to his charge, and should be enabled to exercise the most prompt and effectual means to prevent them from being withdrawn out of his jurisdiction." The committee adhered to Blackstone and Hawkins' view that courts of law may commit privileged persons for some highly criminal contempts, and on the ground that "the present case falls within the principle under which persons committing indictable offences have been considered not to be entitled to privilege," the report recommended that Wellesley be not discharged.[34] The committee report was printed and laid on the table, and the Commons did nothing to aid their imprisoned member. But a motion to discharge the order of the court was made in the Chancery. Wellesley's counsel raised a plea to the jurisdiction of the court, and tried to fortify his argument by citing a great array of authorities and cases from the earlier history of privilege—Coke, the Wilkes case, *Hodges v. Moor*, and others that have been discussed in the preceding pages. From these precedents, he sought to prove that the person of a member of Parliament cannot be touched under any circumstances. The plea was an excellent exposition of the old

[33] 86 *Com. J.*, 699 *et seq.* The committee report reviews the precedents of 1641, 1726, 1757, 1763, etc., and cites the acts passed to restrain privilege in civil suits, 1 James I, c. 13; 12 and 13 Will. III, c. 3; 11 George II, c. 24; and 10 George III, c. 50.

[34] 86 *Com. J.*, 699 *et seq.* The committee, in its search for precedents, unearthed a record of 1641, when the Commons, in conference with the upper house, declared, "That Privilege cannot be pleaded against an indictment for anything done out of Parliament, because all indictments are *contra pacem Domini Regis*, and that privilege is "not to be used to the danger of the Commonwealth." '

theory of privilege, but the Chancellor refused to follow it. He pointed out that in the old days parliamentary privilege had a much wider application, but times and conditions had changed radically, and therefore the old precedents must necessarily lose much of their force. He cited the famous fishery case—the commitment of an offender for fishing in a member's pond as a breach of privilege— to show how absurd it was to rely wholly on precedent. Moreover, he cautioned the courts to be on the watch for new extensions of privilege. "Against all civil process, privilege protects; but . . . . against contempt for not obeying civil process, if that contempt is in its nature or by its incidents criminal, privilege protects not." [35] The Chancellor believed that "he who has privilege of Parliament in civil matters, matters which whatever be the form, are in substance of a civil nature, may plead it with success, but that he can in no criminal matter be heard to urge such privilege; that members of Parliament are privileged against commitment, *qua* process, to compel them to do an act; against commitment for breach of an order of a personal description, if the breach be not accompanied by criminal incidents, and provided the commitment be not in the nature of punishment, but rather in the nature of process to compel a performance; but that they are no more protected than the rest of the king's subjects from commitment in execution of a sentence, where the sentence is that of a court of competent jurisdiction, and has been duly and regularly pronounced." [36] This opinion reveals no trace of the old conception of privilege that derived its sanction from the *lex parliamenti,* a code separate from the *lex terrae,* and one which the ordinary courts might not only not interpret, but could not even be supposed to understand. On the contrary, the reconciliation between the two bodies of law is accomplished by merging the *lex parliamenti* in the *lex terrae*—abolishing it as a separate code, and making it a part of the law of the land. *Lex parliamenti* no longer protects against the legitimate punishments of the common law. "Privilege never extends," the Lord Chancellor concluded, "to protect from punishment, though it may extend to protect from civil process; and . . . . privilege never extends to protect even from civil process where the object of the process is the delivery of the person wrongfully detained by a party." [37]

---

[35] 2 Russell & Mylne, 655.
[36] 2 Russell & Mylne, 665 *et seq.*
[37] *Ibid.,* 673.

In 1836, the Chancery had to pass upon another claim of privilege, in the case of the Ludlow Charities. A barrister, Lechmere Charlton, who was the member for Ludlow, appeared before a Master, as counsel in support of a petition presented by himself and others, in regard to the administration of the Ludlow Charities. Charlton, it appears, addressed a letter to the Master in charge of the case after the hearing had been concluded, in which he used violent language and tried to induce the Master to change the opinion he was believed to have formed.

The Chancellor issued a warrant to the warden of the Fleet prison, instructing him to find Charlton, and to keep him in custody until further notice. Charlton succeeded in escaping arrest until Parliament met. The Chancellor at once addressed a communication to the Speaker of the Commons, informing him that the member for Ludlow was to be committed for contempt, on the charge of having written a threatening letter designed to influence the judgment of the court. The Chancellor made this notification "for the purpose of accounting for the probable absence of the Honourable Member, and of testifying my (his) profound respect for the Honourable House." On the same day, Charlton also wrote to the Speaker. He informed him of the plans for his arrest, and asked for the protection of the House, to enable him to take his seat, and present his version of the case. The letter was referred to the Committee on Privileges.[38] February 3, 1837, Charlton was arrested. The committee did not report for almost two weeks. On February 16, it decided that the letter written by the prisoner to the Master had been intemperate and immoderate, and recommended that Charlton be kept in confinement and his privilege disallowed, on the ground that parliamentary privilege did not extend to cases of contempt of the Court of Chancery. Charlton apparently remained in prison for another week. After several petitions, praying for release, he was finally discharged by order of the Chancellor.[39]

---

[38] Charlton wrote—"I have just reason to believe that Mr. Wm. Pell (a messenger of the Chancery Court) and others . . . are determined, under directions of the Lord Chancellor, to interrupt me in my progress to the House of Commons this day, and I humbly request, therefore, . . . that you will vouchsafe to extend to me your protection. I seek not to withdraw myself from the criminal jurisdiction of the realm, well knowing that privilege of Parliament, which is allowed in cases of public service for the commonwealth, must not be used to he danger of the commonwealth. To be protected however from 'any violence of the Crown or its ministers' is, I apprehend, the established and undoubted privilege of a Member of Parliament. . . . I ask for no more than to be allowed, without molestation, to take my seat, that I may state what I do know of the matter to the House, and then bow, with respect, to their decision. , . ." 2 Mylne & Craig, 345.

[39] 2 Mylne & Craig, 348.

In 1817, Lord Erskine, in giving his opinion in the Lords, affirming the judgments of the lower courts against Sir Francis Burdett, pointed with great satisfaction to the course of procedure followed by the Commons in that case. He was happy to see the Speaker, "like any other subject, putting himself on the country as to the fact, and pleading a justification in law." He rejoiced that the time had at last come when privilege was regarded as simply a part of the law of the land. In the Burdett case, of course, the decision of the courts had completely upheld the claims of the Commons, but Lord Erskine believed that even in case of an adverse ruling, the House would have submitted—"It would be a libel on the House of Commons to suppose that it would not."

The famous actions of *Stockdale v. Hansard,* begun just twenty years later, sadly disillusioned all those who had heralded the procedure of the Commons in the Burdett case as the dawn of a new era in the history of privilege and its relation to the courts and to the law of the land. In *Stockdale v. Hansard,* the decision was unfavorable to the claims of the lower house, and the latter showed no intention to abide by it. On the contrary, mustering all the ancient precedents and powers at its command, the House of Commons entered upon a conflict with the courts, whose violence had been seldom exceeded. It is well to remember that this controversy occurred in almost the middle of the nineteenth century. It was not until then that the question of privilege was settled with some hope of finality. The case of *Stockdale v. Hansard* is one of the greatest in the history of privilege because of the magnitude of the issues involved, the extremely complicated litigation that ensued, and its final settlement which at last seemed to give some hope of finding a basis for the reconciliation of claims of privilege with those of the law of the land. That it occurred so late is the best possible proof that it was extremely difficult to reconcile *lex terrae* and *lex parliamenti.*

The case began in February, 1837. Stockdale was the publisher of various learned and scientific works, among them a book on the generative system, printed for a certain physician. The work was amply—not to say boldly—illustrated by a series of plates and drawings. In a printed report of the Inspectors of the British Prisons, published by the order of the House of Commons, Stockdale's book was described as a publication "of the most disgusting nature," containing plates "obscene and indecent in the extreme." The report of the prison inspectors had been printed by order of the House, by the regular House printer, Hansard, and copies were on sale at the latter's shop in Pall Mall. Stockdale decided to sue Hansard for the publication of a libel. Hansard, of course—and the Commons with him—regarded the publication by order of the House as privileged, and he made his plea accordingly. The Attorney-general was instructed to defend Hansard. He briefly explained the obscene character of Stockdale's publication, and showed that the statements in the published report of the inspectors could not be a libel, because in absolute agreement with the facts. The Attorney-general argued that publishing reports had always been considered a part of the legitimate proceedings of the House of Commons, and was therefore privileged. The defendant, in offering the report for sale, had acted under authority of the House Resolution of August 13, 1836, providing "That the parliamentary papers and reports printed for the use of the House should be rendered accessible to the public, by purchase at the lowest price they can be furnished, and that a sufficient number of extra copies shall be printed for that purpose." The committee of the Commons' House on printing had fixed the selling price of this report at one-half penny per sheet, and a fixed additional charge for charts and drawings, and had designated Messrs. Hansard, the House printers, to manage the sale.[40] Hansard had therefore committed no offence, since he had only printed and sold the report on the order of his employers, the House of Commons, whose acts were sanctioned under the law of privilege. This, in substance, was the Attorney-general's plea.

Lord Chief Justice Denman instructed the jury. He pointed out that the first questions to be decided were those dealing with the publication itself, whether it was really injurious to the plaintiff or not. If the book was obscene, the jury was to return a verdict for the defendant. Lord Denman then proceeded to explain his views on privilege. "I am not aware," he began, "of the existence in this country of any body whatever, which can privilege any servant of theirs to publish libels on any individual. Whatever arrangements may be made between the House of Commons and any publishers whom they may employ, I am of opinion that the person who published that in his shop, and especially for money, which can be injurious, and possibly ruinous to any one of His Majesty's subjects, must answer in a court of justice to that subject, if he chal-

---

[40] 2 Moody & Robinson, 10.

lenges him for that libel." Any other view, Lord Denman correctly maintained, would result in "a destruction of the liberties of his country, and expose every individual in it to a tyranny no man ought to submit to."[41] In short, an order of the House of Commons could no longer furnish special exemptions under a separate body of *lex parliamenti*. All acts—be they the acts of individuals or of a Parliament house—must henceforth be in accordance with one body of common law which protects alike all the subjects of England. Lord Denman's opinion pointed the way toward that settlement of the questions of privilege which was in the end adopted, but the ruling obviously put the printers in an unfortunate position. They had obeyed the orders of the House that employed them, and much like the English soldier who obeys the orders of his military superior, and then may be summoned before an ordinary court to answer for those same acts which he was compelled to perform by military law, they found themselves liable in a civil suit for acts they had considered to be privileged. On the other hand, any other ruling would have enabled the House of Commons to open a veritable "libel shop" under the protection of a claim of privilege. The jury gave a verdict for the plaintiff in the first issue, namely as to the fact of the publication, and for the defendant in the second, i. e., that the book was really obscene and indecent, and therefore the statements concerning it were not libellous.

The case was carried through several of the higher courts, and precipitated a lively controversy with the Commons. The arguments of both sides, and the issues involved, became more complicated as the struggle progressed, for both sides had set to work "the revivers of dead ink, the hunters after precedents."[42]

In 1839, undoubtedly encouraged by Lord Denman's ruling in regard to privilege of Parliament, Stockdale brought another suit against Hansard in the Court of Queen's Bench. The circum-

---

[41] 2 Moody & Robinson, *Nisi Prius Cases,* 12.

[42] In 1837, Pemberton, a member of the lower house, wrote an interesting letter to Lord Langdale, giving his opinion of this litigation. The letter was written before the close of the Stockdale-Hansard actions. Pemberton opposed granting privilege to Hansard. He wrote, "There appears no countenance whatever in the authorities for the dangerous assertion, that the order of the House of Commons justifies the act of publishing, without reference to the nature of the publication. If such an order can justify the publication of libels. . . it can, by parity of reasoning, justify the violation of Copyright,—it may, in fact, justify any act or wrong whatever." Pemberton held that the privileges of Parliament were examinable in court, and that the courts need not decide the case in strict obedience to the orders or resolutions of the House. The letter gives a summary of notable cases of privilege, and concludes that the worst period of abuse was from 1689 to 1768. Pemberton, M. P., *Letter to Lord Langdale* (1837), pp. 34 and 89. A reprint of the letter is in the Harvard Law Library.

stances that gave rise to the action were much like those brought out in the first suit, but this time, the arguments of counsel were much more elaborate and extended.

Curwood opened for Stockdale. He insisted that any view of privilege that makes the privilege of either house of Parliament constitute the law of Parliament, is false; and he ridiculed that view by citing some of the extensions and abuses that had occurred under that interpretation of privilege, especially during the years from the Restoration to 1760. To argue from precedent alone, in a case occurring under the altered conditions of the nineteenth century, would be obviously foolish.[43] In his recital of earlier cases, Stockdale's counsel could not escape Thorpe's.[44] The way he disposed of it is exceedingly interesting. He denied that it could be employed in a nineteenth century argument to support a claim of privilege, for "it must be referred to a period when the King, Lords, and Commons constituted *the supreme court of judicature,* and the distinction of Houses was imperfectly marked. At this day the functions of each branch of the legislature are defined, and it is clear that neither the King alone, nor either House separately can make or declare law. . . . . Each House might make contradictory declaration of law, and each declaration would equally be the 'Law of Parliament' . . . ."[45]

The Attorney-general again represented the defendants. In his opinion, the case involved nothing less than an attempt to call the House of Commons "before an inferior tribunal," for having authorized a publication which it considered "beneficial to the community, and essential to the discharge of its legislative functions."[46] The House had acted in accordance with an ancient privilege, based on the principle that there must be free intercourse between members and their constituents—a privilege designed solely for the public benefit. The Attorney-general explained to the court that the House of Commons, in directing Hansard to appear and plead, did in no way mean to submit its privileges to the adjudication of this or any other court; the defendant appeared for the sole purpose of informing the court in the regular manner that what had been done was done by order of the Commons, under "a legitimate use of privilege."[47] It was admitted that the publication in question was

---

[43] See 9 Adolphus & Ellis, pp. 12-15 and footnote.
[44] See *ante,* 34 and 91.
[45] 9 Adolph & Ellis, 9.
[46] *Ibid.,* 15.
[47] *Ibid.,* 15, 16.

criminatory, but not that it was a libel, since "a libel is a criminatory writing published without just occasion or authority." In
the case before the court, the occasion justified the publication, it
was urged, and therefore any loss to the party was simply*"damnum
absque injuria."* The old plea to the jurisdiction of an inferior
court was revived, and the Attorney-general expounded an interesting, but far from satisfactory view of the relation between *lex
terrae* and *lex parliamenti.* He said, in part—"It is objected that
the house cannot alone supersede, suspend, or alter the law of the
land. No such power is claimed. The house only claims a right to
declare and explain the law of the land respecting its own privileges.
In doing so, it no more alters or makes law than this court does
when it declares the common law in the ordinary course. The
House does not claim the power to create a new privilege by its
own authority."[48]   The alleged grievance—so argued Hansard's
counsel—arose from an act of the Commons, in the exercise of a
privilege which they claimed, and therefore, the question of privilege arose *directly,* and no court could inquire into its existence,
but must give judgment for the defendants. The argument proceeded a step farther by maintaining that even though the question
of privilege should arise incidentally, the court would still be power-
less. But in spite of this flat denial of the court's jurisdiction,
Hansard's defender took great care to prove that the privilege
claimed really existed. He compared the action of the House with
the power to commit, and represented the right to print and publish
its proceedings as as much a part of the procedure of the House as a
vote of commitment. In the case before the court, an adjudication
had already been made on the particular privilege at issue, "by a
court of exclusive jurisdiction," and that judgment must bind all
other courts. Each house, it was insisted, enjoys all the privileges Parliament had previous to its separation into two bodies,
and "whatever was done by either in the exercise of its privileges,
was the act of the whole Parliament." *Lex parliamenti* was regarded as a separate body of law, "not known to the judges of the
common law courts," who have "no means of arriving judicially
at any information on the subject of privilege."[49]   The same reasoning could be found in the speeches of parliamentarians and in
the decisions of the courts, several hundred years earlier, and very
little progress had been made in the suggestions for a satisfactory

---

[48] 9 Adolph & Ellis, 17.
[49] *Ibid.,* 31.

solution of the problems privilege raised. The majority were fully conscious of the fact that an interpretation of the *lex parliamenti*, such as the Attorney-general supported in the argument just outlined, had led to serious abuses in time past, and might do so again. But while admitting this in theory, they did not suppose that a real abuse from the use of privilege would actually arise. Some of the defenders of this view were content to point out remedies for extreme situations, such as petitioning the House for relief, conferences between the two houses to settle a disputed privilege, or even a dissolution of Parliament. Few were ready to admit that the courts were the proper agencies to give relief, when a house of Parliament abused its privileges.

The Attorney-general, in his argument for Hansard, had Coke, the decisions in Thorpe's, Ferrer's, Crosby's cases, and many other precedents to support his contentions. Furthermore, since the first trial of their printers, the House of Commons had accepted the report of one of its committees, to the effect that Hansard should be granted the protection of the House. That was regarded as sufficient to settle the issue. "The Court has here a declaration of the House of Commons, not upon a matter of general law, of which the court itself is a proper judge, but upon parliamentary privilege. That declaration is evidence of the law, which the Court is bound to receive as authority. . . . . It is a general rule that judgments of Courts of exclusive jurisdiction are conclusive against all the world, and their decisions bind Courts in which the questions decided arise incidentally."[50] No argument could be simpler or more logical than this, founded as it was on the accepted practice of all judicial bodies. And yet, if privilege were allowed in this case, nothing could prevent the House from publishing and distributing among the general public, material that was defamatory and a libel on the character of individuals, if the House should ever believe such a procedure necessary. The individual would be without a remedy.

The reply of Stockdale's counsel was an able bit of argumentation, designed to prove that no solution of the troublesome problems of privilege could be secured until *lex parliamenti* should become merged in the general body of the common law, bringing questions of privilege, like all other matters, under the general jurisdiction of the ordinary courts. It was argued that the House

---

[50] From the Attorney-general's argument, see 9 Adolph. & Ellis, 62.

of Commons had none of the attributes of a modern court of justice,
and that while professing to declare and apply the law of Parliament, it was virtually depriving the subject of his right of action.
Further, suppose that each house should make contradictory declarations of the *lex parliamenti*—as actually happened in the Shirley-
Fagg controversy[51]—whose law should the subject regard as authentic? "These absurdities and mischiefs," the plaintiff's counsel
declared, "are to be remedied only by declaring the law of Parliament subject to the general law of the land, and holding the privileges of the house to be (as the prerogative of the Crown has ever
been) within the cognizance of the ordinary Courts." Then, "if
privilege be part of the law, this Court not only may notice, but is
bound to know it."[52]

The court gave judgment for Stockdale. In the opinion of the
judges we get a clear statement of the legal basis on which the
question of privilege could be settled with a fair prospect of finality.
Holt had suggested the same solution a century and a half earlier.
Lord Denman ruled out a plea that based the claim of privilege
upon the supremacy of Parliament, on the ground that the House
of Commons was only a coordinate and component part of Parliament, and not the Parliament itself. Each house's privileges are of
course, in a sense, the privileges of Parliament, "because whatever
impedes the proper action of either impedes the functions which
are necessary for the performance of their joint duties;" but it
does not follow, Denman rightly observed, "that the *opinion* that
either house may entertain of the extent of its own privileges is
correct, or its declaration of them binding."[53] It is for the court,
the Chief Justice held, to determine, in every instance, whether the
House is declaring a matter of privilege, or is endeavoring to make
a general law. The latter would obviously be in excess of its powers. The Chief Justice admitted that the courts were without a
rule to determine when cases involved privilege directly or only
incidentally, and that where the subject matter falls within the
jurisdiction of a house of Parliament, the court cannot question
its judgment. Nevertheless, in the present case, the court must
inquire "whether the subject matter *does* fall within the jurisdiction of the House of Commons."[54] One thing the court regarded

---

[51] See *ante*, 81.
[52] 9 Adolph. & Ellis, 103, 106.
[53] 9 Adolph. & Ellis, 107.
[54] *Ibid.*, 147, 148.

as absolutely certain, namely, neither house could *bring* a matter within its jurisdiction by *declaring* it so. The privilege of publication Lord Denman viewed as unnecessary and unsupported by early usage. The scheme to sell these reports, with a fixed discount for wholesale purchasers, was preposterous and abusive. Since the defamatory matter had absolutely no bearing on any question in Parliament, the plea of the defendants could not be considered as a proper legal defence. "The mere order of the house"—to quote from the opinion again, "will not justify an act otherwise illegal, and . . . . the simple declaration that the order is made in exercise of a privilege does not prove the privilege."[55] It must be remembered that the resolution of the House, attempting to justify the libellous publication, was passed after Stockdale had instituted his action against Hansard.

The other judges were in substantial agreement with Lord Denman. All gave evidence of the same determination to bring parliamentary privilege under the general principles of the common law. Justice Littledale believed that parliamentary privilege must be confined strictly to the proceedings within the walls of Parliament. This might include the right to print documents for the use of members, "but a publication sent out to the world, founded on and in pursuance of an order of the house . . . becomes separated from the house; it is no longer any matter of the house, but of the agents they employ to distribute the papers; those agents are not the house, but . . . . they are individuals acting on their own responsibility. . . . ."[56] The judge denied the Commons "the power to declare what their privileges are, so as to preclude enquiry whether what they declare are part of their privileges."[57] Any inferior court, "if the law be so," might inquire into such a declaration.[58] Judge Patterson arrived at the same general conclusion by a somewhat different argument. He admitted that no action could be maintained for anything said or done in the House, and that the members composing the House of Commons—"whether it be a court of record or not"—may, like other members of a court of record, be free from personal liability on account of the orders issued by them as such members. But if the orders themselves be illegal, and not merely erroneous, upon no principle known to the

---

[55] 9 Adolph. & Ellis, 148.
[56] *Ibid.*, 184, 185.
[57] *Ibid.*, 162.
[58] *Ibid.*, 185.

laws of this country can those who carry them into effect justify under them.[59]   Patteson conceded that the ordinary courts were inferior to the High Court of Parliament, but insisted that one house alone could not be that High Court, and so no resolution of the Commons could bind a court of law.   Throughout the opinions of the judges the new idea of privilege is apparent.   Privilege is stripped of its ancient sanctity, and *lex et consuetudo parliamenti* is no longer a separate, mysterious body of laws unknown to all but members of Parliament.   Under the new order the judge must learn the principles of the *lex parliamenti*, and interpret and apply them as he does all law.   In making this interpretation, proper respect must be shown to the resolutions of the houses of Parliament, but nevertheless it might become the duty of a law court to give an adverse ruling, according to the law of the land.   Especially would this be true whenever Parliament or one house tried, under a claim of privilege, to authorize an act which would injure an individual who had in no way obstructed the procedure of the House, and was in no way amenable to its authority.[60]   Justice Coleridge endeavored to cast some light upon the distinction between cases involving privilege directly and those involving it only indirectly. "The question of privilege arises directly," in his opinion, "wherever the House has adjudicated upon the very fact between the parties, and there only; wherever this course, and the case may be one of privileges, no court ought to enquire whether the House has adjudicated properly or not; but whether directly arising, or not, a court of law . . . . must take notice of the distinction between privilege and power; and where the act has not been done within the House (for no act there done can any tribunal . . . . take cognizance but the House itself) and is clearly of a nature transcending the legal limits of privilege, it will proceed against the doer as a transgressor of the law."[61]   Coleridge also had an interesting comment to make upon the judicial character of Parliament.   "Vastly inferior as this court is to the House of Commons, considered as a body in the state, and amenable as its members may be for ill conduct in their office to its animadversions, and certainly are to its impeachment before the Lords, yet, as a Court of Law, we know no superior but those courts which revise our judgments for error; and in this respect there is no common term of comparison between

[59] 9 Adolph. & Ellis, 189.
[60] See the opinion, *Ibid.*, 210.
[61] *Ibid.*, 227, 228.

this Court and the House. In truth, the House is not a court of law at all, in the sense in which the term alone can be properly applied here; neither originally, nor by appeal, can it decide a matter in litigation between two parties; it has no means of doing so; it claims no such powers: powers of inquiry and accusation it has, but it decides nothing judicially, except where it is itself a party, in the case of contempts." [62]

Judgment was given for the plaintiff, as has been stated. The jury assessed damages amounting to £600, and a writ of inquiry was issued to the sheriff of Middlesex. The sheriff delayed in making his return of the writ, and the court therefore definitely ruled him to do so. A *fieri facias* was issued, and on November 29, it was returned by the sheriff with the endorsement that he had seized the property of the defendants, Messrs. Hansard, preparatory to collecting the £600 damages for Stockdale. The sheriff notified the court that the property was still in his possession for want of a buyer. Stockdale subsequently lodged a writ of *venditioni exponas* with the sheriff to levy the damages, with costs, etc., and the sheriff was ordered to return the writ. December 19, 1839, he reported that Hansard's goods had been sold, in accordance with the court order, and that the proceeds were ready to be delivered to the plaintiff, as the writ commanded. But at this point, a new complication arose. The House of Commons was much disturbed by the judgment of the Court of Queen's Bench, and viewed it as a direct violation of their specifically declared privileges. The lower house might have instructed the defendant to carry the case on appeal or writ of error to a higher court for final adjudication, but such a procedure might have ended in an appeal to the Lords, and the House wished to avoid creating the impression that it was content to leave the adjudication of its privileges to the upper house. So the Commons determined to enforce their claim in another way, namely, by ordering the sheriff not to pay the damages awarded, and holding him for contempt if he did.[63]

When Stockdale appeared at the sheriff's office, he was informed by a deputy that instructions had been given not to pay out the money. Thereupon Stockdale procured a summons, calling upon the sheriff to show cause why the sum awarded should not be paid. December 22, Judge Patteson heard both parties, and refused to

---

[62] 9 Adolph. & Ellis, 223.

[63] Spencer Walpole has pointed out why the Commons would not let the case go to the higher courts, and eventually to the Lords, in his *History of England* (1880) III, 502-510.

make an order, because he believed a judge on summons had no such authority. January 11, Stockdale reappeared at the sheriff's office, to get his money. The deputy again informed him that the money was there for him, but that he would not pay it out. On the same day, Stockdale's counsel obtained a court ruling, calling on the sheriff to show cause why he delayed the payment.[64] In the hearing, it became evident that the sheriff—on January 5—had been served with an order from the Insolvent Debtors' Court, instructing him to hold the funds in his possession. The order was issued on petition of Stockdale, who was insolvent, and an affidavit of one of his creditors, who apparently was pressing him to pay off his debts. The court set January 22, for hearing Stockdale and the sheriff, and ordered them to show cause why the money should not be paid to Stockdale's creditors.[65] At the hearing, the counsel for the sheriff presented to the judges, as matter relevant to the case before the court, a record of proceedings in the House of Commons on January 21, relating to the Stockdale-Hansard litigation. This introduced one more complication and served to reopen the whole contest over privilege between courts and Parliament. The Commons had adopted resolutions, declaring the damages levied by the sale of Hansard's property a contempt of the privileges of the House and had ordered the sheriff of Middlesex to refund the money. The sheriff was voted into the custody of the Serjeant-at-arms for breach of privilege. In fact, while the case was being heard in court, the sheriff was in confinement, under a warrant of the Speaker of the House of Commons.[66] The extremely embarrassing position in which the sheriff found himself is not difficult to understand. Should he refuse to carry out the order of the Court of Queen's Bench, to levy damages on Hansard and pay them to Stockdale, he would be held for contempt of court. Should he execute the order, he would incur further punishment from the Commons, and he had already received some indication of how far the House was determined to go to vindicate its claim of privilege. Should he refund the money to Hansard, he might be held on an attachment in the debtor's court, from which he could escape only by paying the money a second time to Stockdale's creditors. Counsel for the Sheriff took great pains to explain these distressing circumstances to the court. He argued that "the House of Commons have voted

---

[64] 11 Adolph. & Ellis, 254.
[65] *Ibid.*, 255.
[66] *Ibid.*, 256.

that the levy was a contempt of their privileges; and that is a judgment, which, when brought before this court, is not to be inquired into, even according to the decision in *Stockdale v. Hansard*. It is enough for the present argument if the levy could by possibility be a contempt of the House; as if the Sheriff had entered the house and seized goods in the presence of the members while sitting." In short, the sheriff had been prevented from obeying the rule of the court by an "incontestable assertion of privilege." [67]

In rebutting this argument, it was maintained that there are supposable instances when an inquiry must be made into the validity of the resolutions of the House of Commons. For example— if the sheriff, when committed, had killed the officer making the arrest, a criminal court would have been obliged to examine into the legality of the warrant of commitment. Moreover, it was argued that the House had no right to pass a resolution ordering a sum of money, awarded by a court decision, to be withheld from the proper legal claimant. [68]

Lord Chief Justice Denman delivered the opinion of the court. He lamented the fact that the lower house apparently disapproved of the court's previous judgment, but stood firm in his opinion that the decision of the House on a legal point, "in whatever manner communicated," could be no reason for "arresting the course of the law, or preventing the operation of the Queen's writs in behalf of every one of her subjects who sued in her courts." [69] Lord Denman regarded the reason of the House for trying to arrest the enforcement of the court's decision on the simple ground of "contempt of privilege," as insufficient. The order of the court must be executed, no matter how sympathetic the court might be with the sheriff in his dilemma. All the judges based their decisions on the simple rule of practice, and refused absolutely to discuss "the more delicate topics" that might be raised. [70] In accordance with this ruling, another order was served on the sheriff, demanding that he pay out the money. The sheriff refused to obey it, and on January 27, Stockdale's counsel obtained an attachment against him for non-payment. In answer, the sheriff made affidavit stating the history of the proceedings in the Commons' House, relative to the case, and officially informed the court that he was at the time in the Serjeant's

[67] 11 Adolph. & Ellis, 259.
[68] *Ibid.*, 261, 262.
[69] *Ibid.*, 262.
[70] *Ibid.*, 264.

custody, and that the House was keeping him in confinement to compel him to restore the funds involved to Hansard. Therefore, it was a physical impossibility to get the money and pay it to the claimant. The sheriff refused to send an order to his subordinates, lest they too should become liable to punishment for contempt of the House. Lord Denman ruled that the plaintiff was entitled to his money, in spite of every difficulty.[71]

Meanwhile, another action had been begun in the Court of Queen's Bench. On January 23, 1840, counsel for the imprisoned sheriff of Middlesex moved for a writ of habeas corpus, to order Sir William Gossett, Serjeant-at-arms of the House of Commons to bring his prisoner into court and show cause for his detention. The Serjeant brought in the sheriff, and notified the court that he was being held under a Speaker's warrant, for contempt and breach of privilege. A motion was made to discharge the prisoner, on the ground that there had been no legal cause for the commitment; that the court ought to inquire into the truth of the facts alleged; and that the sheriff had been committed for having attempted to execute the legal order of a court, in a decision which, until reversed, must be considered the law of the land. Furthermore, it was pointed out that the House of Commons had failed to make clear what privileges had been violated—"If the house may declare its own privileges, as the common law courts declare the law, it should at least, when it punishes for a breach of privilege, point out the privilege violated, so that the law on that subject may be known in the future."[72]

The court, at the very outset, dismissed from serious consideration the technical criticisms of the warrant[73], and the ruling in the earlier case of *Stockdale v. Hansard* was upheld in principle. But in the present case, the Speaker's warrant was regarded as a sufficient return—"it would be unseemly to suspect that a body, acting under such sanctions as a house of parliament, would, in making its warrant, suppress facts, which, if discussed, might entitle the person committed to his liberty."[74] Justice Littleton concurred in upholding the court's previous decision, especially since it had not

---

[71] 11 Adolph. & Ellis, 270. "Whatever the consequences may be, this is a mere civil process to enable a party to a cause tried by this Court to obtain his rights; the Court has no discretionary power; and the rule must be made absolute."

[72] *Ibid.*, 273-277.

[73] "We must presume that what any court, much more either house of parliament, acting on great legal authority, takes upon it to pronounce a contempt, is so." *Ibid.*, 291.

[74] *Ibid.*, 291.

been appealed to a higher tribunal, and all the other judges agreed with him in holding that the House of Commons has the power to commit and that it must be supposed to have adjudicated with sufficient reason. The prisoner was remanded into the custody of the Serjeant.[75] The decision thus recognized the old right of the Commons to commit for contempts, and established the rule that no court will release persons so committed because the warrant of commitment fails to specify the reasons for which they had been voted guilty of contempt, and no court can, in such a case, inquire into the merits of the commitment.

On April 14, 1840, Parliament passed "an act giving summary protection to persons employed in the publication of parliamentary papers." By this statute, all criminal and civil proceedings against persons for publication of papers printed by order of a house of Parliament, must be stayed by the courts, upon delivery of a certificate or affidavit, stating that such publication is by order of either house of Parliament.[76] April 20, the Speaker of the Commons, following the process described in the statute, signed a certificate to the effect that the report of the prison inspectors (in which Stockdale had found his cause for action) had been printed by Messrs. Hansard, "by order and under authority of the House of Commons." On April 25, Hansard's counsel moved to stay further proceedings in the Queen's Bench. He based his argument entirely upon the statute just passed. The judges ruled that the act of Parliament on the case must be regarded as imperative. Its provisions had been carefully observed, and therefore the court unanimously ruled to stay all proceedings. Similar action was taken in Middlesex where another suit was in progress.[77] The House discharged the sheriff of Middlesex on April 15, and with him Stockdale's attorneys

---

[75] 11 Adolph. & Ellis, 292.

[76] 3 and 4 Vict. c. 9.

[77] The case of *Mangena v. Wright* (1909) resulted in a further interpretation of the Parliamentary Papers Act of 1840. The suit arose because of an alleged libel in "*The Times*." The court held that a person who *bona fide* and without malice prints and publishes an extract from or an abstract of a parliamentary paper, though in doing so he does not act by authority of either house, is protected by the Parliamentary Papers Act of 1840, in an action for libel. A communication from a public servant, in a matter within his own province concerning another public character, about whose actions the public is entitled to information, may be published in the press as a privileged publication. *King's Bench Reports*, (1909) II, 976. In *Wason v. Walter* (1868) it was held that "a faithful report in a newspaper of a debate in a Parliament house, containing matter spoken in the debate which is disparaging to an individual," is not actionable. The publication is privileged on the same principle that an accurate report of proceedings in a court of justice is privileged, namely, because the advantage to the community at large is greater than any private injury that may come from the publication. 4 *Queen's Bench* (1868) 73-96.

and all others who had incurred the enmity of the Commons by disputing the claims of privilege.[78] Thus ended this phase of this memorable conflict between the Commons and the courts.[79]

The principles announced by the judges, during this litigation, in regard to the relation of privilege to the law of the land, remained as the basis for later cases, even though it may seem, on superficial examination, that the House of Commons gained its point in the controversy. In fact, the courts emerged as victors. Whatever victory the lower house can claim, it gained through the passage of an act of Parliament, and not by a mere declaration of privilege by one house. This act became part of the law of the land, and the judges recognized and applied it as such. Privilege was thus no longer claimed as part of a special law of Parliament. It had become a real part of the law of the land, enacted by both houses of Parliament, as a piece of legislation.

Several other actions arose from the Stockdale-Hansard trouble. One was the action of *Howard v. Gossett*, December, 1842. Howard had acted as Stockdale's legal advisor; Gossett was the Serjeant of the lower house. On February 4, 1840, the latter had broken into the plaintiff's house, "broke open and injured divers doors and locks," and had remained on guard on the premises for twenty-four hours. Some time later, the procedure had been repeated, the Serjeant again lying in wait for his victim, who was wanted by the House on a charge of contempt, because he had defended Stockdale in his various suits. Howard was finally seized and sent to Newgate for over a month. He now brought suit for damages against the Serjeant of the Commons. The latter was

---

[78] See 9 Adolphus & Ellis, 297; and *Hans. Deb.* (3d Series), for April 15, 1840.

[79] *The Greville Memoirs* (A Journal of the Reigns of George IV, William IV and Queen Victoria), contain a number of interesting comments on the Stockdale-Hansard proceedings, especially its later phases. For 1840, the following entries are noteworthy. January 24, 1840: "The Privilege question occupies everybody's thoughts, and there is much interest and curiosity to the sequel of it. The state of the House of Commons upon it is curious; all the Whigs for Privilege, and the chiefs of the Tories with them; with some of the lawyers (except Sugden) the same way; . . . On the other side, are the great bulk of the Tories and all the second-rate lawyers." IV, 266, 267. Feb. 21. "I heard . . . this morning that the Duke (Wellington) has set his face resolutely against any Bill in the House of Lords to settle the Privilege question. . . . The Duke in fact, goes as far as any of the opponents of the Privilege, for he not only thinks that the dicta of the Judges are not to be questioned, but that the House of Commons ought not to have the Privilege at all—that is, that their papers ought not to be sold, and that they ought not to be circulated without anything being previously weeded out of them which the law would consider libellous." *Ibid.*, 280. March 5. " He (Wellington) has consented to waive his objections to the settlement by Bill of the Privilege question, so it probably will be settled; and high time that it should be. It is curious to see how little interest the public takes in it, not caring a straw for the House of Commons, or the sheriffs, and regarding the squabble with extreme apathy." IV, 282.

defended by the Attorney-general. The court justified the breaking of the doors and locks, but ruled for the plaintiff because the
Serjeant had remained on guard in his house longer than was necessary; £100 damages were awarded.[80] The House of Commons
had permitted its officer to plead, perhaps because it was felt that
the right of committal had not been directly raised or disputed, and
that it was merely a suit to determine whether an act of their Serjeant had been in excess of his authority. In the decision of the
court itself, the jurisdiction of the House was not questioned, and
therefore the case caused no serious difficulties. Howard was not
satisfied with his victory. He instituted other actions against Gossett and officers of the House, for having confined him in Newgate.
This provoked a long and heated debate in the Commons. Defenders of the old view of privilege were not lacking, and many uttered
grave warnings of what disasters might befall the liberties of the
Commons, should they grant the courts even the slightest jurisdiction in matters of privilege. It was finally decided to allow the
defendants to plead in this action also, and the Attorney-general
was instructed by the lower house to appear in defence of its
officers.[81]

In the second action of *Howard v. Gossett* (1844) the following
facts came to light. Howard had been reprimanded by the Speaker
and then discharged, for having acted as counsel for Stockdale in
his third suit against Hansard. In spite of the warning, Howard
had filed another suit for his client. Ordered to attend the Commons, he evaded the summons and kept himself concealed from the
officers of the lower house for a considerable time. Finally, he was
brought in under the Speaker's warrant. Thereupon he brought
suit for trespass against those who had made the arrest. His
counsel made the usual objections to the insufficiency of the warrant
in authorizing the committal, and pointed out technical irregularities in the proceedings. The main contention however was that the
Commons had ordered Howard arrested before having passed a
resolution judging him guilty of contempt. The imprisonment was
therefore represented as an arrest upon a mere charge, and not
upon a conviction. Howard obtained a judgment, but not upon
these grounds. One judge found technical defects in the warrant,
another objected because it failed to show cause for sending for the
offender, Lord Denman found still other irregularities. All the

---

[80] Carrington and Marsham, 380 *et seq.*
[81] See *Hans. Parl. Deb.* (3d S.) Vol. 67, pp. 22 *et seq.*, also 975-1070.

judges agreed however that no question of parliamentary privilege was involved, and that the form of the Speaker's warrant might be declared technically bad without in any way raising the question of the privilege of the House of Commons.[82]

The Commons were not entirely satisfied with this view of the matter, but resolved not to exercise their own powers at once, but to take the case to a higher court on a writ of error. This was done, and the Court of Exchequer Chamber completely reversed the ruling of the judges of the Queen's Bench, and held the warrant valid. The court believed that the warrant should not be examined with all the strictness applied in examining warrants of magistrates, for this was a writ of a superior court, namely the High Court of Parliament.[83]

The debates in the House of Commons while this litigation was in progress, literally cover hundreds and hundreds of pages of Hansard. Stockdale brought no less than five petitions to the House. The sheriff was repeatedly arrested and committed, the Serjeant brought in Stockdale's attorneys every few days, and numerous orders as to how the money involved should be disposed of, were debated by the House from time to time. Some of the members

---

[82] 10 *Queen's Bench Repts.*, 359 *et seq.* The opinions of the judges reflect the new tendency to bring privilege under the *lex terrae.* Justice Coleridge observed, "The law of Parliament is parcel of the law of England, of the same authority as any other parcel." *Ibid.,* 382. Lord Denman remarked, "I apprehend that the goodness of a warrant in respect of its contents is wholly independent of the authority from which it proceeds. However dignified and powerful the body which sends forth the process, that process must be consistent with itself and with the law, in order to defend the officer who acts upon it." *Ibid.,* 409.

[83] Extracts from the judgment given in the Exchequer Chamber—" . . . The answer to the question as to the validity of the warrant depends mainly upon a preliminary point: on what principle is the instrument to be construed? Is it to be examined with the strictness with which we look at warrants of magistrates or others acting by special statutory authority, and out of the course of the common law, or is it to be regarded as the mandate or writ of a superior Court, acting according to the course of the common law?. . . The difference between the opinion of this Court and that of the majority of the Queen's Bench is only this: that they construe the warrant as they would that of a magistrate, we construe it as a writ of a superior Court. The authorities relied upon by them relate to the warrants and commitments of magistrates; they do not apply to the writs and mandates of superior Courts, still less to those of either branch of the High Court of Parliament. . . ." 10 *Queen's Bench Repts.,* 452, 459.

The debates on the Stockdale-Hansard proceedings in the House of Commons are scattered through Volumes 51, 52, 53 of Hansard (3d Series). See the index in Volume 55 under "Privilege." As one example of the new view of privilege that was developing in this modern period, see the speech by Mr. Fitz Roy Kelly. "He held that the privileges of that House were part and parcel of the law of Parliament, and that the law of Parliament was part and parcel of the law of the land. It was a confusion of terms, and was erroneous to suppose that the law of Parliament was superior to the common law of England. The law of Parliament, the law administered in the Courts of Equity, and in the Ecclesiastical and Admiralty Courts, as well as the common law and the statute law, were all comprised in the great body of law called the law of England, which the judges of the land were bound to administer. . . ." *Hans. Parl. Deb.,* Vol. 51, 267, 268.

defended views of privilege that were centuries old. Some foresaw an ultimate appeal to the Lords, if the Commons should allow the courts to review their privileges. It must be remembered that O'Connell's Case, in which the Lords as a body tried for the last time to exercise their appellate jurisdiction, had not yet occurred, and that the first act that definitely provided for a supreme court of legally-trained Law Lords was not passed until 1876.

The principles laid down by Lord Denman in the Stockdale-Hansard cases seemed to furnish the legal basis upon which future cases of privilege could be grounded and determined, but it by no means prevented new cases from arising. Although as time went on, the House of Commons found it less and less necessary to vindicate its authority, as now limited and defined by law, and gradually became content to leave cases to the Attorney-general and the courts, or to inflict no penalty more serious than a reprimand, cases involving privilege came before the courts constantly down to our own time. Some of these were of minor significance, one at least ranks with the greatest struggles over the privilege of Parliament.

In *Cassidy v. Steuart* (1841) the plaintiff obtained a judgment on a promissory note against Steuart, a member of Parliament, and the sheriff was directed to carry out the order of the court. Before any definite action could be taken, the defendant obtained a summons to set aside the proceedings against him for irregularity, and as contrary to the privilege of a member of the lower house. Judge Erskine accordingly directed that all proceedings against the defendant be set aside. Several months had elapsed when counsel for the plaintiff moved for a rule, calling on the defendant to show cause why Judge Erskine's order should not be cancelled. Cassidy argued that the judge knew nothing of Steuart's membership in the Commons, or whether he was entitled to privilege, and therefore ought to allow the writ to be issued against him, so that the sheriff might execute it. The latter would find out whether privilege applied or not when he tried to execute the order. The plaintiff denied that he had any intention of interfering with the person of the defendant; he simply wanted the writ issued so that it might be enforced as soon as the time of privilege expired. The defendant pleaded freedom from arrest, and "from being made the subject of a command to arrest." The court ruled that the arrest of a member of Parliament being clearly illegal, the order permitting it must necessarily be illegal also. In other words, the court must not place in the hands of an individual suitor a process whose execution would be illegal.[84]

In 1865, the European and American Finance Corporation brought action against a member of Parliament, to compel him to appear in court, and submit to an examination to determine his ability to pay a debt of £8000. Counsel for the company maintained that privilege of freedom from arrest, while a "matter of public convenience," to the particular member, could not be extended to exempt him from paying a just debt. The court gave judgment for the defendant on the ground that a judgment debtor summons under the Bankruptcy Act of 1861 could not properly be issued against a member of the House of Commons.[85] A similar case came before the Lords in 1870, on appeal. A certain Norris had petitioned for an adjudication of bankruptcy against the Duke of Newcastle. The latter's legal advisors insisted that parliamentary privilege prohibited such actions, and maintained that every statute passed to that time which provided for the liability of persons having privilege of Parliament to adjudication in bankruptcy, had expressly stated that the ancient privilege of freedom from arrest should remain unaffected. No such clause, however, had been inserted in the Act of 1861. So the court ruled that the Duke, a non-trader, yet a peer entitled to privilege, was liable to an adjudication in bankruptcy under the Act of 1861.[86]

The Bradlaugh case, beginning in 1880, and extending over almost six years of litigation in the courts and conflict in the House of Commons, ranks with the Wilkes case—with which it has so many features in common—in public importance. Unlike some of the great cases which preceded it, the Bradlaugh incident failed to arouse a great conflict between the courts and Parliament and most of the scenes were enacted wholly within the walls of the lower house. But some of the opinions expressed in the debates there were curiously like the defences of privilege made by parliamentarians several centuries earlier. The old notions of Parliament's special law and custom still survived, and in spite of the recent decisions of the courts, the problems of privilege seemed as confusing and their solution as difficult, to some who lived in the last quarter of the nineteenth century, as they had been to their predecessors in Parliament several hundred years before them. If some great ques-

---

[84] 2 Manning & Granger, 437 et seq.
[85] 14 Weekly Reporter, 135 et seq.
[86] Duke of Newcastle v. Morris, 19 Weekly Reporter, 26-31.

tion of privilege should arise today—in the twentieth century— especially if it should appear likely to result in conflicting interpretations of privilege by the courts and a Parliament house, it is highly probable that the same arguments for parliamentary privilege as a part of the separate body of law, the *lex parliamenti*, would crop out somewhere in the speech of some member of Parliament whose historical and antiquarian instincts had led him to delve into the musty records of centuries gone by, or in the plea of some learned advocate at the bar who had joined the hunters after precedent. The amazing thing is that even after the relation between courts and Parliament, and the relation of the privileges of the lower house to the appellate jurisdiction of the upper, had been worked out to the apparent satisfaction of all parties concerned, some were still unable to rid their minds of the notion that Parliament had once been the High Court of Parliament, with judicial characteristics and powers that were not yet totally extinct. Such conceptions, to endure through so many centuries, must have had their roots deep down in the very origins and groundwork of English institutions.

Charles Bradlaugh, whose atheistic writings were well known throughout England, had the good fortune to be elected a member of the House of Commons for Northampton. On May 3, 1880, he appeared at the bar of the lower house and asked permission to affirm rather than swear to the oath for members. He based his request on the Evidence Amendment Acts of 1869 and 1870, which permitted persons holding certain religious views to affirm instead of swear, when summoned before the courts of law. Bradlaugh informed the House that he had affirmed before the law courts for the past nine years, and now requested the same privilege of the Commons.[87] Immediately some of the members—whether for reasons founded on real piety or to raise a troublesome issue and heckle the government—manifested grave concern as to the advisability of allowing such a person to take his seat; to an atheist and infidel not even an affirmation could have much binding force. A select committee was appointed to investigate the legal phases of the question. While the committee was deliberating, Bradlaugh reappeared in the House, advanced to the Table, and declared a willingness to take and subscribe to the oath. A clerk proceeded to

---

[87] See *Hans. Parl. Deb.* (3d Series) Vol. 252, p. 20.

administer it, when another member again raised strenuous objections.[88]   A long debate followed. Bradlaugh's opponents argued
that "by the Common Law of England," no atheist was entitled to
take an oath, and the select committee also reported unfavorably on
Bradlaugh's claim. Gladstone then moved that the matter be referred to another select committee, in order to get more legal information for the use of the House in settling the trouble. The proposal precipitated a heated discussion, in which Bradlaugh's publications were rather thoroughly examined and sharply criticized.
One member ventured the suggestion that the House of Commons
was not a fit tribunal to pass an unbiased judgment on the case,
and provoked the retort that "the House, a branch of the Supreme
Tribunal of this country," was certainly able to judge in so simple
an issue.[89] The court theory of Parliament was called upon to render valuable aid in bolstering up the House's claim of privilege to
determine who are fit persons to take the oath. One member observed—"A Country Court Judge had (has) the power to prevent a
witness being sworn who did not believe in the validity of an oath;
and was that House, the highest tribunal in the land, without the
power which the Judge of a Country Court possessed?"[90] The case
was finally submitted to a select committee of twenty-three for
further investigation.[91] On June 16, its report was ordered to be
printed, and was then laid on the table.[92] Five days later, Mr.
Labouchere, Bradlaugh's colleague and untiring defender, moved
that Bradlaugh be permitted to affirm or declare, instead of taking
the oath. It appears that the second commitee had recommended
such a course.[93] Again a long and bitter debate resulted. Bradlaugh's friends argued that the House had no right to dictate the
particular pattern of men constituencies should select to represent
them. The perfect similarity with the Wilkes' case in this respect,
was repeatedly pointed out. Bradlaugh had a legal right and a
legal duty to take the oath or to affirm, and with what a statute pro-
vides, one house of Parliament has no right to interfere.[94] Arguments of this sort brought a sharp retort from Arthur O'Connor,
a devout member, who maintained that "There were laws above any

---

[88] *Hans. Parl. Deb.*, Vol. 252, p. 187.
[89] *Ibid.*, 379, 383. See speeches of Mr. Trevelyan and Mr. Newdegate.
[90] *Ibid.*, 393. Speech of Mr. Gorst.
[91] *Ibid.*, 450, 667.
[92] *Ibid.*, Vol. 253, p. 163.
[93] *Ibid.*, Vol. 253, p. 443.
[94] *Ibid.*, Vol. 253, p. 463.

rules of the House of Commons, and there were commandments higher than any Act of Parliament."[95] The Attorney-general urged that the case was of such a nature that only a court of law could decide it properly. The second committee had reported that "the common law right of every member to take his seat ought not to be taken away from Mr. Bradlaugh," and so had suggested that he affirm, since he could not swear, and then leave the question of penalties, if any should arise, to the determination of the law courts.[96] But such suggestions were very displeasing to certain members of the Commons. They gave rise to some of those vigorous defences of parliamentary privilege, free from all encroachments of courts and the common law, that one would expect to find in the sixteenth and seventeenth centuries, but hardly in the nineteenth. One member was struck with terror by the argument that the House should denude itself of its power, "by delegating it to the Courts of Law." "A Judge might take on himself to allow children or lunatics to affirm; but no man could come into that House and seek to affirm merely because a Court of Law had allowed him to affirm." The member pointed out what disastrous results might spring from a conflict between the courts and the House of Commons.[97] Spencer Walpole, himself an able student and writer on English historical and constitutional subjects, called the attention of the Commons to the possible collision between the law courts and a Parliament house. Walpole put the query—"Are we to bring ourselves into collision with the Courts of Law; or are we so incapable of determining what is the true construction to be put upon this Act of Parliament that we are to hand it over to the Courts of Justice which may take any view irrespective of the point upon which we want to have a decision. . . . ."[98] Sir H. Drummond Wolff expressed the fear that the case might come before the Lords on appeal, if the courts were allowed to examine it. Mr. Newdegate insisted that the question was one in which no court of justice could have jurisdiction. If Bradlaugh should be allowed to take his seat and vote, he argued, an application might be made in the Court of Exchequer, not to support, but to contravene, the decision of the House of Commons, and "as Parliament was considered the highest court existing in this country, the inferior court would be asked to

---

[95] *Hans. Parl. Deb.* (3d Series), Vol. 253, p. 483.
[96] *Ibid.*, 488.
[97] *Ibid.*, pp. 490, 491. Speech of Mr. Grantham.
[98] *Ibid.*, 494.

contravene the decision of a superior."[99] Gladstone, in reply, maintained that the House had no jurisdiction at all, in the sense of the law and the constitution. While no court action could be brought against the House of Commons, there was always the opportunity to sue a servant of the House, carrying out its orders; and the Premier called attention to the unhappy results of previous attempts of the House to assume powers which had never belonged to it as a single branch of the legislature. Gladstone pointed out that the final judge in all such cases was always the public outside, and he warned against a repetition of the Wilkes' incident, when the House had been compelled to retreat so ignominiously before the demands of an infuriated public opinion.[100] The prime minister's able argument failed to influence the majority of the Commons, and when the vote was taken, the House resolved not to allow Bradlaugh to affirm or take the oath.[101]

Not in the least discouraged by the resolutions passed against him, Bradlaugh presented himself again, and asked permission to take the oath. He claimed his right to sit as a member, and pointed out that the House by its action had "deprived a citizen of his constitutional right of appeal to a Court of Law to make out what the statute means in dealing with him." Until he should be received on the floor of the House, Bradlaugh insisted that the Commons had no right to expel him or declare his constituency vacant. With a threat to resign and appeal to public opinion, he withdrew. He was recalled, and forced to listen to the resolution excluding him. This

---

[99] *Hans. Parl. Deb.* (3d S.), 555-557.

[100] *Ibid.*, 566-579.

[101] I cannot refrain from quoting extracts from the remarks of two other members. They reflect so well the old idea of privilege, and are based on the theories I have been trying to establish. These are speeches from the year 1880, not the sixteenth or seventeenth century. *Mr.* Synan—"Was the High Court of Justice to be asked to decide this question adversely to the Resolution of the House? When did that House permit a Court of Law to decide upon the validity of its proceedings? Were they to establish a supreme jurisdiction in the highest Courts of the land to decide upon the law of Parliament, as in America? If we are not, the House must restrain the High Court of Justice from proceeding." *Hans. Parl. Deb.*, 3d Series, Vol. 253, pp. 608, 609. Sir H. Drummond Wolff—". . . As decisions of the Courts at Westminster were subject to appeal to the House of Lords, a reference of the question to the Courts of Law would result in this anomaly,—that, as it was certain to be pursued to the bitter end, if taken up at all, it would go to the Highest Court of Appeal, and the House of Lords would have to decide upon the right of a member of the House of Commons to take his seat. . . ."—*Ibid.*, 612. This argument expresses the same fear of the Lords' judicature, stated in the Commons' resolutions in the Shirley-Fagg case, two centuries before. In 1880, conditions were greatly altered, and there was no longer real cause for alarm. The highest judicial tribunal was no longer the whole upper house, but a small, legally-trained corps of Law Lords, in whose decisions the rest of the Lords could no longer participate. In O'Connell's Case of 1844, the Lay Lords tried to assert their jurisdiction for the last time. See *Queen v. O'Connell (State Trials)* New Edition, Vol. V, entire volume, and especially pages 911-914.

time Bradlaugh refused to retire, and a scuffle with the Serjeant-at-arms was the outcome. As a result, on June 23, 1880, Bradlaugh, "having disobeyed the Order, and resisted the authority" of the House, was ordered into the custody of the Serjeant, where he remained for twenty-four hours, before he was able to secure his release.[102] Some of the members of the lower house doubted the wisdom of this commitment. They feared that the prisoner might procure a writ of habeas corpus and thus bring the whole matter before the judges and precipitate a conflict between Parliament and the law courts. One member believed that "They were undoubtedly on the eve of a contention between the house and the courts of law, and there ought to be no backwardness on the part of the house in facing the consequences of its own action."[103] July 1, 1880, Gladstone presented a resolution permitting Bradlaugh to affirm according to the Parliamentary Oaths Act of 1868 and the Promissory Oaths Act of 1868, "subject to any liability by statute." After extended debate, the resolution was made a standing order of the House.[104] Bradlaugh complied with the terms of the resolution and made the affirmation.

But now new difficulties arose. Legal proceedings had been instituted, and in the case of *Clarke v. Bradlaugh*, the court held that Bradlaugh was not a person entitled to affirm.[105] This simply led Bradlaugh to the conclusion that he must take the oath. The House interpreted the decision of the court differently. It declared the seat for Northampton vacant, and issued a writ for a new election. The electorate remained loyal, and Bradlaugh was reelected. On April 26, 1881, he appeared at the bar and demanded his right to take the oath. The usual debate took place, and ended in the passage of the same prohibitive resolutions.[106] The day following, the same performance was enacted, and this time the Serjeant removed Bradlaugh below the bar. After repeated adjournments and postponements, and long and involved debates, a Parliamentary Oaths Bill, permitting affirmation and proposed by the government, was defeated and Bradlaugh was excluded by another resolution. He was reelected the next year by his old constituency, and the Commons again excluded him by resolution.[107] Bradlaugh did not

---

[102] *Hans. Parl. Deb.* (3d Series). Vol. 253, pp. 660, 725.
[103] *Ibid.*, 652.
[104] *Ibid.*, 1346, 1347.
[105] 29 *Weekly Reporter*, 516; and *Hans. Parl. Deb.*, Vol. 260, p. 1186.
[106] *Hans. Parl. Deb.* (3d Series) Vol. 260, pp. 1184-1251.
[107] *Ibid.*, Vol. 267, p. 223. March 6, 1882.

present himself until the next session, May, 1883. He was granted a hearing and made an able defense of his acts, concluding with the defiant exclamation—"While I have my civil rights, I will claim them. If the law cannot give them to me—and perhaps it is better that this House should be above the law—then I can only try to obtain them, and wherever my voice may go, say that you, the High Court of Parliament, greater than the law, have trampled upon law. . . . ."[108] His eloquence was of no avail, the excluding resolution continued to bar him from his seat in the House.

As might have been foreseen, Bradlaugh was not content to let the adjudication of his case entirely to the Commons. He appealed to the courts in the case of *Bradlaugh v. Erskine* (Queen's Bench, 1883), in which he sued Erskine, Deputy-Serjeant-at-arms of the House of Commons, for assault, and charged him with having forcibly prevented him from entering the House to take his seat. Erskine, of course, had no personal interest in the case, and informed the court that he had simply carried out the orders of the House he served. He also pleaded that privilege did not extend to an elected member who had not yet taken his seat. The Attorney-general represented the deputy-serjeant in court, and pleaded the right of the Commons' house to act as the sole judge of a breach of its privileges, and also the mode of prevention or punishment. The House must remain free from the interference of all other courts, for "In fact," said the Attorney-general, "the House of Commons is a portion of the highest court of the realm, and is clothed with all those rights and privileges for the protection of its proceedings which belong to every court of record in the kingdom."[109] The court gave judgment for the defendant, and in general sustained the argument of the Attorney-general. "It is not to be presumed," Justice Field maintained, "that any court, whether it be the High Court of Parliament, or this court, will do that which, in itself, is flagrantly wrong. . . . . The present (case) appears on the face of the pleadings to be for an alleged breach of the privileges of the House, committed within its walls and committed in the face of the House. I have always understood . . . . that it would be highly unjust and contrary to the great advantage which this country possesses, both in the Legislature and in its judicial system, that either Parliament or any other court . . . . should not have in itself the power not only of deciding effectively and immediately upon all questions,

---

[108] *Hans. Parl. Deb.* (3d S.), Vol. 278, p. 1850.
[109] 31 *Weekly Reporter,* 366.

whether its privileges had been broken or contempt had been committed, but also that it should be the sole and final judge of the contempt."[110]

In February, 1884, the case was reopened in the Commons. Bradlaugh, again elected for Northampton, entered the House and without having been called by the Speaker, advanced to the Table. The Speaker called him to order, but he proceeded to read the words of the oath which he had written down and brought in with him, kissed a book he held in his hand, signed the paper and then withdrew. The House was in an uproar. A spirited debate followed, and during its progress, Bradlaugh remained in the room, and on the final vote ordering his withdrawal, he joined those voting in the negative. The House promptly gave orders to expunge his vote,[111] and instructed the Serjeant to exclude Bradlaugh until he should promise to cause no further disturbances. Thereupon the rejected member applied to the Chancellor of the Exchequer for the appointment to the Chiltern Hundreds. The acceptance of this office, of course, automatically vacated his seat in the House and necessitated a new election. The voters of Northampton promptly returned Bradlaugh to his seat. Once more the exclusion resolution was moved and debated. Gladstone and Labouchere advocated obtaining a court decision in the controversy, to serve as a legal guide for the House. "I cannot imagine," said Bradlaugh's colleague from Northampton, "that the House would still be determined to set up its own judgment against what is laid down by the Courts of Law as the law of England."[112] The majority were unshaken in their conviction that Bradlaugh ought to be excluded, and another resolution to that effect was passed. Bradlaugh brought another action in the courts, and was granted leave to enter and use the library of the House to procure the necessary records for the prosecution of the case.[113]

The case of *Bradlaugh v. Gossett*—the latter the new Serjeant of the House—was similar to the earlier action against Erskine. Bradlaugh argued that the exclusion resolutions of the Commons were contrary to the Parliamentary Oaths Act, and therefore illegal, since one house could not alter the law of the land by mere resolution. The judges admitted the correctness of his logic, but

---

[110] 31 *Weekly Reporter*, 368.
[111] *Hans. Parl. Deb.*, 3d Series, Vol. 284, p. 449.
[112] *Ibid.*, 1580. See also 1567-1580.
[113] *Ibid.*, Vol. 286, p. 1137.

held that the House must be supposed to be acting in accordance with its own view of the law, which the court does not know. In substance, the decision was practically this—the House of Commons has the power to regulate its own proceedings; each house has the exclusive power to interpret the provisions of a statute, so far as the regulation of proceedings within its own walls is concerned; and even though the resolution in question be inconsistent with an act of Parliament, the court cannot interfere. The decision was a startling and dangerous assertion of the power of privilege. This extraordinary authority was to be strictly confined within the walls of Parliament, to be sure, and therefore, by inference, could not apply outside.[114] In other words, matters arising in Parliament depend upon the resolutions of Parliament, and if the courts should interfere, they might, in the language of one of the judges, "provoke a conflict between the House of Commons and this court, which in itself, would be a great evil, and even upon the most improbable supposition of their acquiesence in our adverse decision, an appeal would lie from that decision to the Court of Appeal, and thence to the House of Lords, which would thus become the judges in the last resort of the powers and privileges of the House of Commons."[115] The fear of the Lords' judicature might have been used with telling effect several decades earlier. In 1880, the whole House of Lords no longer constituted the English Supreme Court.

In February, 1884, Bradlaugh was for the fourth time reelected to represent Northampton in the Commons. It seems that during the winter of 1884, and the adjourned session of 1885, Bradlaugh repeatedly attended the sessions of the lower house, remaining during its divisions as an unsworn member. In 1885, a change of government occurred.[116] Bradlaugh apparently waited until the elections had taken place, and then on July 6, 1885, he came to the Table to take the oath. In the preceding January, the Court of Appeal, in *Attorney-general v. Bradlaugh*, had declared Bradlaugh incapable, by the law of England, of taking an oath.[117] Con-

---

[114] 32 *Weekly Reporter*, 552 *et seq.* The judges admitted that Northampton had a legal right to be represented in Parliament, and that Bradlaugh had a legal right to sit and vote in the lower house. However, some of the rights are to be exercised in Parliament, and some outside. Those that are exercised out of Parliament "are under the protection of this court, which . . . will apply proper remedies if they are in any way invaded, and will in so doing be bound, not by the resolutions of either House of Parliament, but by its own judgment as to the law of the land, of which the privileges of Parliament form a part." *Ibid.*, 555.

[115] *Ibid.*, 556.

[116] See *Hans. Parl. Deb.*, 3d Series, Vol. 298, p. 1601.

[117] *Ibid.*, 1672, 1676.

sequently, the Chancellor of the Exchequer, Sir Michael Hicks-Beach, moved the reenactment of the resolutions prohibiting Bradlaugh from taking his seat. A suggestion to settle the question by legislation was disregarded, and the excluding resolutions were re-enacted. Bradlaugh appeared to protest, but was ordered to withdraw. January 13, 1886, a new Parliament assembled. The Speaker read a letter from Sir Michael Hicks-Beach, giving a complete account of the Bradlaugh trouble, and urging that the atheist be prohibited from taking the oath, at least until the House could express its opinion on the matter. Several other communications of a similar nature reached the Speaker, but he correctly declined to follow the suggestions offered. He ruled that this was a new Parliament; he knew nothing of past resolutions, and any member had the right to present himself to be sworn in, in performance of his legal duty. So, after almost six years of opposition in the House, and a number of suits in the law courts, Bradlaugh was at last admitted and allowed to exercise his legal rights. All this time, the electors of Northampton had been deprived of their constitutional right to be fully represented in Parliament.[118]

In 1887, the case of *Dillon v. Balfour* came before the courts for adjudication. The plaintiff was certainly poorly advised—a most superficial examination of the preceding decisions in similar cases would have proved that the action would be unsuccessful. The case arose in Ireland. The plaintiff was a midwife and "monthly nurse in large practice and considerable repute" in the County of Galway. The defendant was Chief Secretary for Ireland, and a nephew of the English Prime Minister. The plaintiff was offended by certain statements which had been made by Balfour in the House of Commons, and had been published in the papers. It was alleged that the member had attacked the midwife for refusing to attend a woman because her husband had worked for a boycotted person. This attack in the Commons, she claimed, had injured her professional reputation, to the extent of £500 damages. It soon became apparent that the statements complained of were part of a speech made by Balfour on the Criminal Procedure Act of Ireland. The remarks were published, it was true, but the defendant was unacquainted with the plaintiff, and had obtained his information and her name from the official reports. The case was dismissed on the

---

[118] *Hans. Parl. Deb.*, Vol. 302, pp. 21-29. For contemporary accounts, see Justin McCarthy, *History of Our Own Times*, III, 167, 168; and W. S. Churchill, *Lord Randolph Churchill*, I, 122-131, 209-211.

ground that words spoken by a member of Parliament, in Parliament, are absolutely privileged, and the court has no jurisdiction.[119]

In the suit, *In re Gent, Gent-Davis v. Harris*, (1888), the claim of privilege was disallowed. The action was brought against Gent-Davis, a member of Parliament, for default. The defendant had acted as receiver in a case and had failed to pay in to the court certain sums which had become due. It was argued that default was a criminal act and that for that reason privilege could not apply. The court, following the ruling in Wellesley's case[120] held that process to enforce civil obligations was subject to privilege, "but process for acts in the nature of offences is not."[121] The same distinction was observed in *Ex parte Lindsay, in re Armstrong* (1891), where the claim of privilege was allowed, the application being in the nature of civil process to compel performance of a court order, and not in the nature of a punishment. As long as no element of personal contempt or offence for which imprisonment might be the punishment, is involved, the claim of privilege is allowed.[122]

The action of *Chaffers v. Goldsmid* (1894), arose from the refusal of the defendant, a member of Parliament, to present a petition to the House of Commons. The plaintiff, Chaffers, was a voter in Goldsmid's district. In 1891, he sent a petition to the defendant, which the latter presented to the House, and had returned to him by the clerk of the committee on petitions as a petition not proper for the House to receive. In 1892, Goldsmid rejected a similar petition. Later, he presented it, and it was again refused. Chaffers claimed his right as an English subject to petition Parliament had been interefered with, and insisted that the defendant was bound by both the common law and the law of Parliament to present a proper petition to the House of Commons.[123] He demanded £500 damages, and a mandamus to compel Goldsmid to present his petition. The court ruled that there was no cause for action; that the right of petition exists, but that there is no common law right to compel the presentation of a petition by an individual member of Parliament.[124]

---

[119] 20 *Law Repts.* (Ireland), 600-615.
[120] See *ante*, 138.
[121] 37 *Weekly Reporter*, 151-153.
[122] 40 *Weekly Reporter*, 159-160.
[123] "This right is recognized by the law of Parliament, which forms part of the common law." 42 *Weekly Reporter*, 289.
[124] *Ibid.*, 239, *et seq.*

Cases involving claims of privilege came before the courts for settlement down to our own time. At present, it seems that the difficult problem of the application of privilege and its relation to the common law, has been settled. Courts and Parliament are today in practical agreement that the law of Parliament is part of the law of the land, and that there can be no privilege of which the courts cannot take cognizance. But as champions of a supreme High Court of Parliament, and a separate *lex parliamenti*, were not wanting throughout the whole of the nineteenth century, it would be surprising if none could be found in the twentieth, should another crisis arise. It took centuries to evolve the conception of an all-embracing *lex terrae* of which even the law and custom of Parliament was but a part. So long have the judicial characteristics of the High Court of Parliament endured and colored its activities.

CHAPTER VII.

PROCEDURE IN THE DEPENDENCIES.

The procedure in the colonies of Great Britain is worthy of some examination. Most of the institutions of the colonies were modelled on those of the mother country, and their fundamental legal conceptions were inherited from the same source. Procedure in the colonies should therefore cast considerable light upon the procedure and privileges of Parliament.

When legislative bodies were established in the self-governing dependencies, how much of the law of privilege as understood and applied in the Parliament and courts of the mother country did they inherit? Did a colonial assembly receive all those privileges the *lex et consuetudo parliamenti* gave to the High Court of Parliament, or only such as were absolutely necessary for its protection and existence as a legislative body? Could a colonial legislature commit an offender for contempt, on the analogy of the power exercised by judicial tribunals and by the High Court of Parliament? These are some of the questions which naturally suggest themselves. To the cases following, I would direct special attention, for the examination of procedure in the dependencies throws much light upon the origin of the privileges of "the Mother of Parliaments," and upon the nature of Parliament's peculiar law of privilege and its relation to the *lex terrae*.

If we believe that the common law of England was transplanted to the new soil with the creation of new colonies, we would logically suppose that the legislature in the new settlements would also inherit the *lex parliamenti*, if the latter were part of the *lex terrae*, as Englishmen finally decided it was. Under this view, a colonial legislative body might exercise all the privileges and punitive powers enjoyed by the British House of Commons. Such was not the case, as the following cases will show. From them we may conclude that in the minds of judges in the colonies, and members of the English Privy Council—to say nothing of a host of legislators and lawyers, both in the dependencies and at home—there was a clear distinction between a simple legislative body and the High Court of Parliament. The latter, from its original nature, possessed attributes

172

which no colonial legislature could ever inherit, and therefore it
possessed privileges and powers which no legislative assembly could
hope to claim or exercise. My discussion is necessarily limited to
but a few of the most important cases, but I believe it would prove
a very profitable undertaking to make an exhaustive study of the
history of parliamentary privilege as administered and applied in
the colonies.

In 1832, an action which had its counterpart in many of the
English cases cited in the preceding pages, came before the King's
Bench of Quebec. A certain Daniel Tracey of Montreal had been
committed to jail by order of the clerk of the Legislative Council,
for publishing a libel against that house, and the prisoner now attempted to regain his liberty by habeas corpus proceedings. Tracey's
counsel tried to establish the principle that the provincial assembly
could only commit for an actual obstruction of its proceedings, but
not for libel; and that it by no means enjoyed those general powers
of commitment conceded to belong to the houses of the English
Parliament. The origin of Parliament's powers he found in that
"remote antiquity" when the two houses formed a part of the *Aula
Regis*, and claimed to have all those judicial powers which had
not been transferred to the king's courts after the breaking up of
the *Aula Regis*.[1] The provincial legislature, he maintained, had
no inherent powers, and none of the judicial functions which the
British Parliament had retained. For that reason, he believed the
commitment of his client had been without legal warrant, and so
sought his release. The court did not accept his reasoning, and on
the ground that the power to commit for libel was necessary for
the self-protection of the assembly, and that a court, on habeas
corpus proceedings, had no right to judge of a legislature's privileges, remanded the prisoner. One of the judges believed that the
privilege in question did not depend upon the judicial powers vested
in the body which had ordered the arrest, but upon the "principle
of self-defence," as essential to a simple colonial legislative body as
to the houses of Parliament.[2]

Four years after the adjudication of this case, the English
Privy Council received an opportunity to pass on a case of privilege
coming up from a dependency. In 1836, the case of *Beaumont v.
Barrett,* came up on appeal from the Court of Errors of Jamaica.
The suit was for trespass and assault, alleged to have been com-

---

[1] *Stuart's Repts.* (Lower Canada), 488.
[2] For entire case, see *Ibid.,* 478 *et seq.*

mitted by Barrett, the Speaker of the House of Jamaica. The plaintiff endeavored to prove that there was a wide difference between the powers and privileges of the Jamaica Legislature and those of the "High Court of Parliament," and therefore questioned the Speaker's authority. The Privy Council sustained Barrett's claim of privilege, thus upholding the judgment of the Jamaica court, on the ground that the power to punish contempts was inherent in every assembly possessing supreme legislative authority, and since the House of Assembly had supreme authority in Jamaica, it could commit a party guilty of publishing a libellous paragraph which the house regarded as a breach of privilege.[3] The decision had little effect, for the Privy Council in the very next case coming before it saw fit to reverse this ruling, and then made its new interpretation the basis for later decisions.

This new view was expounded in the case of *Kielley v. Carson*, which came before the Privy Council in 1843. As it became the basis for so many of the later judgments, it deserves somewhat more extended discussion. Carson, a member of the House of Assembly of Newfoundland, in a speech before that body, cast certain reflections upon the management of a hospital in which the plaintiff was district surgeon. A bitter controversy between the two men followed, and the Newfoundland Assembly finally ordered the plaintiff to be brought in to the bar of the House. This led to an action for assault, battery, and false imprisonment against the officers of the house, and the Supreme Court of Newfoundland gave judgment for the defendants. The case then came before the English Privy Council for final determination. Counsel for the plaintiff argued that since the Legislative Assembly in Newfoundland had been created by Letters Patent from the Crown, it could have no such privileges as the British Commons' House enjoyed, for the latter's privileges exist under the *lex et consuetudo parliamenti*. A colonial assembly, by its very nature, could have no such body of ancient precedents. Further, Kielley's counsel maintained—the House of Commons possesses this power 'as a Court of Judicature . . . . as part of the High Court of Parliament, the aula regia."[4] The Newfoundland Assembly never was such a court, and since the Crown had no such judicial power either, it could not be conferred upon a legislature in the colonies by letters patent. The defendant's

[3] Moore, *Privy Council Cases*, 59-71.
[4] Moore, *Privy Council Cases*, 69.

counsel maintained that the power to commit for a violation of privileges was inherent in every legislative assembly, and that the British House of Commons was no more a court of justice than any colonial assembly. The Privy Council, in giving judgment for the plaintiff, reversed the decision of the Supreme Court in the colony. In the opinion of the Privy Council, the colonial House of Assembly did not possess the power to arrest with a view to adjudicate, on a complaint of contempt committed outside its doors. Since the statute law was silent on this question, common law must be applied. Therefore it was held that all steps necessary to protect itself from impediments to the free exercise of its legislative functions might be taken by an assembly, "but the power of punishing any one for misconduct as a contempt of its authority, and adjudicating upon the fact of such contempt, and the measure of punishment as a judicial body, irresponsible to the party accused, is not essential to the exercise of its legislative functions."[5] Then followed a striking sentence which seems to indicate that in the opinion of the Council, Parliament enjoys its peculiar rights under the *lex parliamenti*, and by virtue of its earlier functions as a court. "The reason why the House of Commons has this power, is not because it is a representative body with legislative functions, but by virtue of ancient usage and prescription; the *lex et consuetudo Parliamenti*, which forms a part of the Common Law of the land, and according to which the High Court of Parliament, before its division, and the Houses of Lords and Commons since, are invested with peculiar privileges, that of punishment for contempt being one."[6]

In *Cuvillier v. Munro* (1848) a Canadian case coming before the Queen's Bench at Montreal, the court held that privilege of members of the Canadian Legislature from arrest upon civil process, was based entirely upon the ground of necessity, and not upon an analogy with the English Parliament and therefore could not be extended beyond such necessity. The judges followed the decision of the Privy Council in *Kielley v. Carson* throughout.[7]

In *ex parte Louis Lavoie* (1855) another Canadian case turning upon the question of what power the House of Assembly had in election cases, Lavoie's counsel contended that the provincial legislature could not possess the power to determine judicially matters affecting the election of members, unless it were admitted that

[5] 4 Moore, *Privy Council Cases*, 88.
[6] *Ibid.*, 89.
[7] *Lower Canada Repts.*, IV, 146.

it possessed 'the same judicial character as the House of Commons," which he regarded as a "Court of Judicature." "The House of Assembly," he concluded, "is not a Court of Judicature, and consequently cannot exercise such power." The court decided that the power in question was vested in the Assembly, because it was "necessary to its existence." The strict rule of necessity became the guide for settling most of these cases. Courts as a rule made no attempt to clothe colonial legislatures with those general powers of commitment and punishment which the High Court of Parliament enjoyed because of its peculiar nature and ancient usage.[8]

In *Fenton v. Hampton,* a case coming from the Supreme Court of Van Diemen's Land, to the Privy Council in 1858, the ruling in *Beaumont v. Barrett* was again disregarded. The Privy Council decided that colonial legislatures, whether deriving their authority from the Crown or from a statute of the Imperial Parliament, do not possess the same authority to punish for contempt which the House of Commons enjoys in England. The *lex et consuetudo parliamenti* was held to apply only to the Lords and Commons of England, and not to extend to the supreme legislature of a colony simply because the common law had been introduced there.[9] The opinion obviously proceeded on the assumption that *lex parliamenti* was not a part of the common law.

In 1864, the action of *Dill v. Murphy* was appealed to the Privy Council from Victoria. By Act of Parliament of 1855, the Victoria Legislature had been permitted to make a definition of its privileges, by acts and otherwise, provided the privileges assumed did not exceed those claimed and at the time enjoyed by the English House of Commons. Two years thereafter, the Victoria Assembly had passed an act taking over all the privileges of the House of Commons, enjoyed "by custom, Statute, or otherwise," and making the Journals of the British lower house *prima facie* evidence in disputes over privileges. In the case at bar, Dill, a newspaper publisher,

---

[8] *Ibid.,* V, 99 *et seq..* In 1815, the question of the extent of the privileges of a colonial legislature and especially those of the Lower Canadian Assembly was referred to the British law officers. It was ruled that ". . . . a colonial legislature was not entitled to all the privileges belonging by the *Lex Parliamentaria* to the House of Commons. The king by his charter could not grant such powers." See A. Shortt and Arthur G. Dougherty (General Editors)—*Canada and Its Provinces,* IV, 474. Duncan McArthur, who writes the article in this volume on Canadian Constitutional History from 1763 to 1840, adds, "The granting to the assembly of Lower Canada of the entire privileges of the imperial House of Commons, when followed to its logical conclusion, would have conferred on the legislative council judicial powers which would have conflicted with certain clauses of the Constitutional Act." *Ibid.,* 475. For entire discussion of privilege in Canada, see *Ibid.,* 474-482.

[9] 6 *Weekly Rept.,* 341.

had been committed for one month by the Victoria Legislature because he had refused to appear at the bar when ordered to present himself and answer for an article which had been offensive to a member. Dill instituted a suit against Murphy, Speaker of the Victoria Legislature, for assault and false imprisonment. The defendant pleaded privilege, and based his plea on precedents from the records of the English House of Commons. Dill maintained that the colonial legislature had "no judicial or inquisitorial functions analogous to those of the High Court of Parliament," and therefore could have none of the latter's powers of commitment or punishment for contempt.[10] Elaborate arguments had been advanced in the courts of the colony. The plaintiff's counsel had insisted that "The power for committing for contempt was confined to Courts of Justice, and that all commitments by the House of Lords and the House of Commons respectively depended for their validity on the fact that Parliament is a Court."[11] Certainly no colonial legislature could claim such a judicial origin. To clinch his point, Dill's counsel maintained that "The House of Lords, in dealing with appeals and writs of error, without the presence of the House of Commons, adjudicates as the Parliament, and not as the House of Lords, so likewise a commitment by the House of Commons for contempt is substantially a commitment by the High Court of Parliament."[12] "Although commitments for contempt of the House of Commons in its Legislative character are constantly made . . . they are recognized only by the other Superior Courts as committments by a Court of Justice for contempt of such a Court." [13] The argument is another indication of how long the view existed that Parliament was a court and exercised its privileges as such. The Supreme Court of Victoria, in 1862, had given judgment for the defendant, on the ground that the privileges of the House of Commons applied to the case and were ascertainable, because the "privileges of the House of Commons are part of the Common Law." [14]

---

[10] 1 Moore *Privy Council Cases* (New Series) 493.

[11] *Ibid.*, 494.

[12] *Ibid.*, 494.

[13] *Ibid.*, 498.

[14] Mr. Justice Williams seems to have entertained some doubt on this point at the outset. In his opinion, he says: "Although at first I was inclined to the opinion that the Imperial Parliament, in giving power to the House of Assembly in Victoria to specify its privileges and immunities, provided they were not in excess of those of the House of Commons, merely purposed to clothe the Assembly with privileges incidental to a deliberative body to protect the Members during the progress of debate, and to permit them to assemble together and depart

In the argument before the Privy Council, one additional point was brought out. It was insisted that the colonial assembly, in the act asserting its privileges, instead of assuming in bulk, as it were, all the privileges of the English House of Commons, should have specified what particular powers and privileges it intended to claim. It was claimed that *lex et consuetudo parliamenti* applied to the British Parliament only, and that the introduction of the common law of England into a colony did not confer the *lex parliamenti* upon a supreme colonial legislative assembly. The Privy Council upheld the claims of the Victoria Legislature, and the appeal was dismissed without much discussion.[15]

In the same year (1864) the Court of Queen's Bench ruled that a legislative body, like the House of Keys in the Isle of Man, could not claim the power to commit for contempt simply because it had been endowed with legislative functions.[16]

Doyle v. Falconer (1866) was a case coming up on appeal to the Privy Council from the Common Pleas Court of Dominica. Doyle was Speaker of the House of Assembly of Dominica; Falconer was one of its members. During a debate, the Speaker had called Falconer to order, and the latter had retorted, "Who the devil are you to call me to order." For such disrespectful language, the member was declared guilty of contempt and breach of privilege. He refused to apologize, and continued to disturb the proceedings of the house. Finally, he was forcibly removed and held in confinement for three days by the Serjeant-at-arms. Falconer then sued the Speaker for assault and imprisonment, and received damages in the lower court. The case was appealed to the Privy Council. Doyle's counsel tried to show that the case was different from that of *Kielley v. Carson*, and *Fenton v. Hampton*, in that here the contempt was not committed outside the legislative body, but by a member, in the house itself. Over such contempts he claimed the House of Assembly had full punishing powers. Falconer's plea was that the Dominican House of Asembly was not a "Court of Record,"

without fear of arrest or molestation, and that it was not the intention of the Imperial Parliament to confer on the House of Assembly the powers that the House of Commons enjoys as a component part of the highest court in the realm; nevertheless, on closer investigation . . . I am led to the conclusion that my first impression was wrong, and that the powers and privileges of the Commons House of Parliament, whether obtained by the *lex et consuetudo Parliamenti* or not; whether enjoyed as a deliberative Assembly or as a component part of the highest Court in the realm, are claimable by the Legislative Assembly in this colony. . . ." I Moore, *Privy Council Cases*, New Series, 505 and 506.

[15] 1 Moore *Privy Council Cases*, N. S., 511 and 512.
[16] *In re Brown*, 33 *Law Journal* (Q. B.) 193 *et seq.*

and had no "judicial functions whatever," but was "simply a Legislative Assembly;" and that "to punish by imprisonment . . . can only be done by a Court of Record, or by the Imperial Parliament, by the *Lex Parliamenti*."[17] The Privy Council affirmed the judgment of the lower court. Sir James W. Colville agreed to the proposition that "The privileges of the House of Commons . . . belong to it by virtue of the *lex et consuetudo Parliamenti*, which is a law peculiar to and inherent in the two Houses of Parliament of the United Kingdom. It cannot . . . be inferred . . . that like powers belong to Legislative Assemblies of comparatively recent creation in the dependencies of the Crown."[18] The members of the Privy Council giving the decision clearly distinguished between such privileges as are necessary to the self-protection of a legislature, which colonial legislatures enjoyed, and the power to punish for contempt, "which is a judicial power," and which colonial assemblies do not possess. The advice was given to resort to the ordinary courts whenever obstructions of procedure amounted to breaches of the peace.[19]

In 1871, it was maintained that the Constitution Act and the Colonial Act for Victoria (giving the assembly power to commit for contempt and breach of privilege by general warrant) could not give the assembly the same privileges and powers the House of Commons enjoyed, but the Privy Council refused to sustain the argument. Nothing more significant than the interpretation of these particular statutes seems to have been involved, and the Privy Council simply applied them as the language prescribed.[20]

The case of *Ex parte Dansereau* arose from the refusal of a witness, summoned by the Provincial Legislature of Quebec, to attend the house. He was consequently arrested by the Serjeant-at-arms for contempt. Thereupon Dansereau asked for a writ of habeas corpus, in the court of Queen's Bench at Montreal.[21] He argued that the English House of Commons acted by the *lex parliamenti*, which did not extend to local assemblies, and that the House of Com-

---

[17] 4 Moore *Privy Council Cases* (New Series), 214.

[18] *Ibid.*, 218.

[19] 4 Moore, *Privy Council Cases* (New Series) 203-222. In 1869, in a communication from the Canadian Department of Justice, we find the following opinion of the Attorney-general: "It is clear, from the current of judicial decision in England, that neither of the branches of a Colonial Legislature have any inherent right to the privileges of the Imperial Parliament." *Canada Sess. Papers* (1877) No. 89, p. 202.

[20] 7 Moore, *Privy Council Cases*, N. S., 449-468. *Speaker of Legis. Assembly of Victoria v. Glass.*

[21] *Lower Canada Jurist*, XIX, 210-248.

mons could compel witnesses to attend because it is a court of record, while the Quebec Legislature, on the other hand, possessed "no
inherent powers or judicial functions such as could be assigned to
or exercised by a Court of Record." The judges upheld the right of
the Quebec Legislative Assembly to summon witnesses and to commit them if they refused to testify; quashed the writ of habeas corpus, and refused to allow an appeal to the English Privy Council.
Justice Ramsay alone dissented. He believed that the real basis for
the exercise of the British House of Commons' power to commit
witnesses was "immemorial usage; perhaps founded on the fact
that in early times the House of Commons had judicial functions as
part of the High Court of Parliament."[22]

In 1878, the Canadian Supreme Court reaffirmed the judgments handed down in *Doyle v. Falconer,* and *Kielley v. Carson,* in
an action which came before the court on appeal from the Supreme
Court of Nova Scotia. A certain Woodworth, a member of the
House of Assembly of Nova Scotia, had charged a provincial secretary with falsifying a record. As a result, a committee investigated
the charges and found them to be untrue. Woodworth was declared
to be guilty of a breach of privilege and was ordered to apologize.
When he refused, he was voted guilty of contempt. He finally had
to be removed by the Serjeant-at-arms. Woodworth then sued the
Speaker and certain other members for trespass, and obtained a
verdict of £500. The Canadian Supreme Court upheld the judgment
of the lower court, on the ground that the provincial assembly, in
the absence of an express grant, had no power to remove a member
for contempt, unless he actually obstructed the procedure of the
house. Woodworth had been removed not for obstruction, but because he had refused to apologize. Judge Ritchie of the supreme
bench strictly limited the punishing power of the Nova Scotia Assembly to actual obstructions of its proceedings, and held that
"without prescription or statute, local legislatures have not the
privileges which belong to the House of Commons of Great Britain
by the *Lex et consuetudo Parliamenti.*"[23] His colleague, Judge
Henry, believed that "the House of Commons has jurisdiction as a
court only from the law and custom of Parliament, and the right to
commit for contempt is held to rest solely thereon. . . ."[24] He
was unable to see "how any Provincial Assembly could obtain any

---

22 7 Moore *Privy Council Cases,* N. S., 214.
23 *Canadian Supreme Court Rept.,* II, 201 and 202.
24 *Ibid.,* 210.

right to exercise judicial functions, unless by legislation; for there are no laws or customs peculiar to each which would give the right by which an alleged contempt could be tried. . . ." [25]

Substantially the same reasoning was followed by the judges of the New South Wales Supreme Court in 1886. A certain Taylor, a member of the New South Wales Assembly, was under suspension, and when he entered the legislative chamber some time later, he was removed by force by the Serjeant-at-arms. Taylor then brought suit for trespass. The court once more asserted the old doctrine that only such powers are incident to and inherent in a colonial legislature as are "necessary to the existence of such a body, and the proper exercise" of its functions. This did not include a general punitive power, or the right to suspend a member unconditionally and at pleasure. The attorneys in the case endeavored to point out an analogy between the legislature's powers and those enjoyed by the English Parliament, but the judges advised them to take their analogies from "other assemblies, (not legislative) whose incidental powers of self-protection are implied by the common law . . . ." and not "from the British Parliament, which has its own peculiar law and custom. . . ." [26] In *Norton v. Crick*, a New South Wales case occurring eight years later, the Chief Justice held that "the Legislature of this colony does not enjoy all the privileges which the House of Commons, by virtue of ancient usage and prescription, does enjoy; nor can it be inferred from the possession of certain privileges of the House of Commons by virtue of that ancient usage and prescription that the like privileges belong to, or are inherent in, a colonial Legislature." [27] Under the powers of the Constitution Act of 1902, the Legislative Assembly of New South Wales passed a standing order, allowing the house to suspend a member charged with an offence until a verdict could be obtained or further orders should be given, and the Privy Council upheld the right of the house to pass such an order, and refused to dispute its validity. Here again, the members of the Privy Council simply applied the statute of Parliament. [28]

---

[25] *Canadian Supreme Court Rept.*, II, 212.

[26] *Law Repts., Appeal Cases*, XI, 203. Entire case, 197-208.

[27] 15 *New South Wales Law Repts.*, 176.

[28] *Harnett v. Crick, Law Repts., Appeal Cases*, (1908) 470-477. For other references on this subject, see Forsyth, *Cases and Opinions on Constitutional Law* (1869), 25; Fennings Taylor, *Are Legislatures Parliaments?* (1879); Keith, A. B., *Responsible Government in the Dominions* (London, 1909), 95-102; Alpheus Todd, *Parliamentary Government in the British Colonies* (2d Edition), pp. 682-695; *Gipps v. McElhone, N. S. Wales Law Repts.*, II, 18; *Ex Parte S. W. Monk, Stuart's Repts.* (Lower Canada) 120; *Toohey v. Melville, N. S. Wales Law Repts.*, XIII, 132, *et seq.*

It may not be amiss to conclude this chapter with a few words on procedure and privilege in the United States. In the United States, many of the notions of law, forms of government, and methods of procedure have been modelled upon English precedents, and the practice in regard to the ordinary privileges of Congress is no exception. In the Constitution, the ordinary privileges of freedom of speech and freedom from arrest are guaranteed to all members of Congress. Both houses of Congress have in the past punished for cases of libel upon Congress or its membership, for bribery, for assaults upon individual members, and for misconduct in the halls of Congress, by members themselves. The Serjeant-at-arms has exercised practically the same powers as his prototype in the British Parliament. The Speaker of the House of Representatives has, on many occasions, called members and non-members to the bar, and administered a public rebuke, following almost exactly, in these cases, the procedure in the English House of Commons. A number of cases have come before the courts for adjudication, and the judges have often passed upon the privileges of Congress. No conflicts arose between courts and Congress because the American Congress could never claim such supreme judicial powers and functions as the High Court of Parliament exercised for centuries, and because the relations and functions of the Senate and House of Representatives are not those of the Lords and Commons in England. The privileges of the two houses of Congress have, much like those of the legislatures of the dependencies of Great Britain, been strictly limited to those absolutely necessary and indispensable for carrying on the business of legislation and for preventing obstructions of proceedings.

Congress has never claimed the general punitive powers and the judicial functions exercised for centuries by the British Parliament, simply because it would have no basis for such a claim. Congress is a legislative body, and was so from the beginning. What few judicial functions it has and exercises, have been specifically conferred upon it by the Constitution. Congress cannot claim judicial powers and attributes as an inheritance from earlier centuries, as the British Parliament houses can and have claimed their judicial functions as inherent in them by virtue of their earlier existence as the High Court of Parliament.

This difference between Congress and Parliament was clearly recognized by the United States Supreme Court in 1880, in the case of *Kilbourn v. Thompson*, and the decision in that case has been made the basis for later actions and opinions. In this case, Kilbourn had been confined for forty-five days in the District of Columbia jail, for refusing to answer certain questions put to him during an investigation conducted by the House of Representatives. He thereupon sued the Serjeant-at-arms for damages, and lost his case in the lower court. The Supreme Court reversed this judgment, on the ground that the House of Representatives had usurped the functions of a court, in a case that was clearly judicial in its nature. Justice Miller wrote the opinion. He applied the Constitution, and found that no clause in it conferred upon Congress a general punishing power for contempts. The Justice then reviewed the practice of England. He believed that there was little agreement of opinion to be found in the judgments of the English courts on questions of privilege, but on one point he was very positive. He found no difference of opinion in regard to the *origin* of the power of Parliament to punish for contempt. "This," he wrote, "goes back to the period when the bishops, the lords, and the knights and burgesses met in one body, and were, when so assembled, called the high court of Parliament. They were not only called so, but the assembled Parliament exercised the highest functions of a court of judicature, representing in that respect the judicial authority of the king in his court of Parliament. While this body enacted laws, it also rendered judgments in matters of private right, which, when approved by the king, were recognized as valid. Upon the separation of the Lords and Commons, into two separate bodies, . . . the judicial function of reviewing by appeal the decisions of the courts of Westminster Hall passed to the House of Lords. . . . . To the Commons was left the power of impeachment, and perhaps, others of a judicial character, and jointly they exercised, until a very recent period, the power of passing bills of attainder for treason, and other high crimes which are in their nature punishment for crime declared judicially by the high court of Parliament of the Kingdom of England. It is upon this idea that the two houses of Parliament were each courts of judicature originally, which, though divested by usage, and by statute, probably, of many of their judicial functions, have yet retained so much of that power as enables them, like any other court, to punish for a contempt of these privileges and authority—that the power rests."[29] After a careful an-

[29] *Kilbourn v. Thompson*, in *Digest of Decisions and Precedents of the Senate and House of Representatives of the United States relating to their Powers and Privileges &c.*, compiled by Henry H. Smith—1894—*Senate Misc. Doc.* No. 278 (53d Cong. 2d Sess.) pp. 716 and 717.

alysis of some of the great cases on privilege argued and decided in the English courts, Justice Miller concluded "that the powers and privileges of the House of Commons of England, on the subject of punishment for contempts, rest on principles which have no application to other legislative bodies, and certainly can have none to the House of Representatives of the United States—a body which is in no sense a court, which exercises no functions derived from its once having been a part of the highest court of the realm, and whose functions, so far as they partake in any degree of that character, are limited to punishing its own members and determining their election. . . . ."[30]

The opinion shows a rare understanding of the nature and functions of the British Parliament. Justice Miller did not find the origin of the privileges of Parliament in "the political exigencies" of a supreme legislative body. If he had, Congress might easily have laid claim to identical powers. On the contrary, he clearly understood the difference that existed in the very nature of Congress and Parliament; the first was a legislative body, pure and simple, the second had *developed into* a legislative body, but had not always been primarily such. In the beginning, it had been the High Court of Parliament, with a great number of functions of an administrative, judicial, and to an extent, legislative character, and without a clear distinction between its various functions. In the judicial attributes of Parliament, that is, in the powers of the High Court of Parliament, was found the basis for its claims of privilege. Congress had never been a court, and therefore its privileges and its punishing powers were strictly limited to those absolutely necessary for its existence and protection.

---

[30] *Ibid.* For other references on procedure in the United States see the entire volume. The chief cases heard in the courts are discussed at the end of the volume. See also De Alva Stanwood Alexander, *History and Procedure of the House of Representatives* (1916), Chapter VIII. The account is brief, general, and makes no comparison with English procedure.

CHAPTER VIII

CONCLUSIONS

In the preceding chapters, it has been impossible to do more than enumerate and analyze, frequently in chronological order, some of the important incidents and controversies in the history of parliamentary privilege. Such an arrangement was unavoidable in presenting the evidence, but it necessitates a special chapter to summarize the conclusions of this investigation.

The evidence presented seems to prove that underlying all of Parliament's claims of privilege, from the earliest centuries to modern times, was the notion that Parliament was a court, "the antientest," "most authentical," "highest," and "honourablest" of all the courts of England. As such, it was entitled to peculiar protection, was endowed with special and transcendent powers, and was invested with a dignity that must be preserved on all occasions. And so, its membership came to be protected from all molestation, from whatever source the interference might come. In the opinions of the judges and in the statements of members of Parliament dealing with privilege, one finds that the emphasis is always upon the judicial nature and characteristics of Parliament.

To-day we think of Parliament as a purely legislative body, the supreme power in the state. We have forgotten that Parliament's legislative functions developed very gradually. Indeed, Parliament seems to have become fully conscious of its legislative powers only during the period of the Stuart monarchs. But ever before and after this time, Parliament has been spoken of, and has been regarded as, the "High Court of Parliament." Its power and authority was defended, interpreted, and applied on the assumption that it was a "transcendent court," a "Court of exclusive jurisdiction." Such statements of the nature of Parliament were not limited to any particular period of English history, or to any special political crisis or emergency in the life of Parliament. They occur again and again in the speeches of members, in the resolutions of the Parliament houses, in the decisions of courts, and even in addresses from the throne, from the time before Coke gave classic expression to the court theory of Parliament in his famous *Institutes*, to the very close of the nineteenth century. Indeed, some of the best and most illuminating statements of this view came latest in the history of privilege. It would seem illogical to conclude that they were mere words, used to conceal a truer or more fundamental interpretation of Parliament's origin, nature, and functions, or to enable a legislative assembly to meet the various political crises that it had to face from time to time. They must rather be regarded as truthful expressions of a constitutional theory actually held by the men who made them. Their persistency to our own times only serves to prove how deep-rooted these conceptions of Parliament really were. One cannot admit, as any reader of the sources apparently must admit, that such a theory was for centuries expounded and vigorously defended, and yet believe it to be a deliberate misrepresentation of the facts. The zealous parliamentarians of the Stuart and later periods may have found the judicial theory of Parliament a convenient aid in supporting their new ideas and claims of Parliament's legislative supremacy in their struggle with the Crown and the royal courts, but they did not invent this theory concerning Parliament's origin and early functions. The transition to the idea of a sovereign legislature could not have been made more smoothly than under the guise of Parliament's admitted judicial supremacy, but the notion that Parliament was a court, and "the most honorable and highest court" of the realm, and as such, was superior to all others, existed before the time of the opponents of Stuart absolutism, and persisted long after the storm and stress of that particular period of English history had been safely passed and Parliament had emerged from the struggle as the triumphant victor.

It is in the conception of Parliament as the highest court of the realm that the writer believes the explanation for its claims of privilege can be found. It is needless to repeat the abundant evidence presented in the preceding pages. To recall a few of the most important statements of this view will be sufficient. In Thorpe's case, as early as 1453, Parliament was described as "this high court of Parliament—for it is so high and so mighty . . . . that it may make lawe and that that is lawe it may make noo lawe," and still earlier evidence of this judicial nature of Parliament can be found in the preceding chapters.[1] Thorpe's case is interesting for another reason, in that it shows the confusion that existed be-

---

[1] See *ante*, 91.

tween Parliament's legislative and judicial functions. "Confusion" is the only word that will describe the situation, for there certainly was no accurate differentiation between the two spheres of its activity. Very often Parliament's legislative supremacy was defended by an appeal to Parliament's admitted judicial supremacy. It took centuries to bring out a clear distinction between Parliament's activities as a court and its activities as a legislature. Men were unable to determine exactly when an act of Parliament was legislation, and when Parliament was acting in its ancient judicial capacity. Gradually Parliament's legislative functions became predominant, and Parliament became a sovereign legislative assembly. Its ancient judicial functions and its supremacy as the "High Court of Parliament" faded more and more into the background, but they were not forgotten. Precedents, and the records of Parliament's original status and powers were always available and they could be called up at any time to render service. The cases cited in the preceding chapters show what excellent services they rendered. It was always possible for a single house to justify its acts by appealing to the idea that it had once been a part of the High Court of Parliament, whose judgments were supreme. Nowhere was this argument more frequently used than in the history of privilege. Claims of privilege had their origin and basis in the fundamental character of Parliament as a court. In a real sense, the history of privilege is a continuous comment on the "High Court of Parliament" and the judicial characteristics it preserved through so many centuries down to our own time. A Parliament house, acting in its old judicial capacity in matters of privilege, really legislated, at times. There was no clear-cut division between the two functions, and in this confusion, which lasted for several hundred years, is to be found one of the reasons why the law of privilege defied satisfactory solution for so long.

Members of the houses of Parliament naturally enjoyed a special protection from arrest, interference, and molestation, due to the transcendent dignity of this "High Court" of which they formed a part. Coke believed that "every member hath a judicial place." Even Prynne, uncompromising opponent of what he considered to be unwarranted extensions of privilege, preserved throughout his discussions the analogy between members of the houses of Parliament, and "members of the King's other Courts."[2] From this view,

---

[2] Prynne, *Brief Register*, IV, 684, 685.

that members enjoyed a special protection within the walls of Parliament, and that each house had the authority to enforce this privilege, the principle was extended and applied to incidents occurring outside. The right of committal, now so fundamental for the protection of every legislative body, was, I believe, directly based on Parliament's power as a court. Statements of this analogy between the High Court of Parliament's right to commit, and that enjoyed by the other royal courts, can be found again and again in the Journals of Parliament and in the reports of cases argued before the courts.

In 1588, when in a moment of intense excitement, the Commons were on the verge of forgetting their dignity and were all trying to make themselves heard at once, the Speaker called them to order as "judges of a court." He put them "in remembrance, that every Member of this House is a judge of this Court, being the highest Court of all other Courts, and the great Council also of this Realm, and so moveth them in regard thereof, that as in all other Courts, being each of them inferiour to this high Court, such confused courses either of contention, acclamations, or reciprocal bitter and sharp speeches, terms or words are not in any way either used or permitted amongst the Judges of the said Inferior Courts, or the Counsellors admitted in the same Courts, so they would hereafter forbear to attempt the like disorders, as the honour and gravity of this House justly requireth."[3] Hakewell believed that Parliament men enjoyed privilege "in the same Manner, as the Judges and Ministers of other Courts."[4] Sir Mathew Hale regarded Parliament as the "highest and greatest Court, over which none other can have jurisdiction in the Kingdom."[5]

Being the highest court of the realm, it follows that its members must be free from the orders, summonses, and mandates of other courts, all of them of an inferior nature. The claims of members of Parliament to be free from all jury service, and the summons and subpoenas of ordinary courts, and to remain unmolested in their services in the High Court of Parliament, as far as the mandates of all inferior courts were concerned, were all based on the

---

[3] D'Ewes' *Journals*, 434.

[4] Hakewell, *Modus tenendi Parliamentum* (1671), 62.

[5] Hale—*The Original Institution, Power and Jurisdiction of Parliaments*, (1707) 48 and 49. James I, in his speech to Parliament in 1603, observed ". . . The Parliament is the highest Court of Justice, and therefore the fittest Place where divers Natures of Grievances may have their proper Remedy by the Establishment of good and wholesome Laws. . . ." *Harl. Misc.*, I, 12.

judicial conception of Parliament. Hatsell put it well, "As it is an essential part of the constitution of every court of judicature, and absolutely necessary for the execution of its powers, that persons resorting to such courts, whether as judges or as parties, should be entitled to certain privileges to secure them from molestation during their attendance; it is more peculiarly essential to the Court of Parliament, the highest court in this kingdom, that the members who compose it, should not be prevented by trifling interruptions from their attendance on this important duty, but should, for a certain time, be excused from obeying any other call, not so immediately necessary for the greatest services of the nation. . . . ."[6] The king himself, in 1543, and often thereafter, spoke of his "Court of Parliament" as the highest in his kingdom.[7] Citations might be greatly multiplied, and they could be drawn from every period of Parliament's history, down to our own time. In the cases before the Privy Council, coming from the colonial courts, and involving matters of privilege, it was Parliament's character as a court that served as the basis for interpreting its privileges and those of the colonial assemblies. In *Beaumont v. Barrett* (1836) much emphasis was laid on the difference between the privileges of a mere legislature, and those of the "High Court of Parliament."[8] In *Kielley v. Carson* (1843) it was contended that the House of Commons enjoys its peculiar privileges "as a Court of Judicature . . . ., as a part of the High Court of Parliament," and therefore a colonial legislature, deriving its powers from Letters Patent from the Crown, cannot claim similar privileges, since the Crown has no "judicial power" to grant. The Privy Council, in handing down the decision, agreed that "The reason why the House of Commons has this power, is not because it is a representative body with legislative functions, but by virtue of ancient usage and prescription; the *lex et consuetudo parliamenti* . . . according to which the High Court of Parliament before its division, and the Houses of Lords and Commons since, are invested with many peculiar privileges, that of punishment for contempt being one . . . ."[9] In 1858, in *Fenton v. Hampton,* the Privy Council took a similar position.[10] In *Dill v. Murphy,* 1864, counsel for the defendant

---

[6] 1 Hatsell, 1.

[7] See Ferrers' Case, *ante.* Footnote, p. 36.

[8] See *ante,* 174.

[9] 4 Moore, *Privy Council Cases,* 89.

[10] See *ante,* 176.

argued that "Although commitments for contempt of the House of Commons in its Legislative character are constantly made, they are recognized only by the other Superior Courts as commitments by a Court of Justice, for contempt of such a Court. . . ."[11] The procedure in the dependencies and in the United States has been discussed more at length in the preceding chapter and it has been pointed out that there was an inherent and fundamental difference between Parliament and all other legislative bodies. Parliament is not simply a legislature, invested with merely legislative powers. It has peculiar privileges and functions which it has inherited and which it exercises as the High Court of Parliament. It is Parliament's judicial attributes and Parliament's original judicial supremacy that distinguishes it from all other legislative bodies, and gives it special privileges. A theory that persisted so long, and statements of which were almost identical in the nineteenth century with those made four centuries earlier, must certainly be more than a fanciful creation from the fertile imagination of a judge or zealous parliamentarian. It served as a vital force in the struggles of four centuries. The mere fact that it survived intact during all those momentous changes in governments and institutions, proves that it must have been deeply rooted among men's most fundamental conceptions. It seems an inevitable conclusion that parliamentary privilege had its origin in the judicial nature of Parliament, and in its supremacy as the highest court of the realm.

As the supreme court of the kingdom the High Court of Parliament acted and was governed by a peculiar law, the *lex et consuetudo parliamenti*. Under this law, all claims of privilege were included. Privilege of Parliament developed in a time when the notion of separate bodies of law, separate codes, and separate jurisdictions still prevailed. The conception of a great body of common law, including and over all other laws, was still to be evolved. The minds of men were familiar with separate ecclesiastical jurisdictions, admiralty courts, a separate law merchant, a separate forest law, etc.[12] Parliament's special law was the *lex parliamenti*, and

---

[11] 1 Moore *Privy Council Cases*, New Series, 498.

[12] Francis Hargrave, in his *Collection of Tracts Relative to the Law of England* (London, 1787), discusses the jurisdiction of the ecclesiastical courts in such matters as marriage, and points out that judges of the ordinary temporal courts have for centuries given full faith and credit to the decisions of ecclesiastical courts, "however contrary they may be to the reason of our law." pp. 449-487, and especially, 452. The writer also speaks of the separate and exclusive jurisdiction of the admiralty courts, p. 466. In the same way, the law merchant was a "body of rules and principles relating to merchants and mercantile transactions, distinct from the ordinary law of the land." Special penalties protected merchants and markets, and these were

when it acted and adjudicated by that law, it was supreme. It took centuries to establish the principle that the law of Parliament, like all other bodies of law, must be in conformity with the common law. For hundreds of years, the conception that *lex parliamenti* was above *lex terrae* prevailed. Whatever a Parliament house did under the *lex parliamenti* could not be questioned outside, for this was Parliament's special law; the ordinary courts knew nothing about it and could not apply it. The ordinary courts of law applied only the *lex terrae*, of which the *lex parliamenti* was not a part. In fact, it was often regarded as an exception to the common law, and above it.

There is a striking similarity, as has been suggested, between this notion of *lex parliamenti* and the conceptions of the separate codes, the *lex forestae*, the *lex mercatoria*, admiralty law, ecclesiastical law, martial law, etc.[13] All of these laws were, in their time, enforced by separate courts, and were considered as comparable in importance with the common law. Moreover, as long as there was this multiplicity of laws, there was bound to be a contest between them for superiority. *Lex parliamenti*, enforced by all the power of the two houses of Parliament, enjoyed a peculiar advantage in this struggle, and so retained its importance longer than any of the other bodies of law that existed parallel to it.[14] There is an equally striking parallel between the *lex parliamenti* and the *lex prerogativae*. Cowell defined prerogative as "that especiall power, pre-eminence or priviledge that the King hath in any kinde over and above other persons, and above the ordinarie course of the common

---

frequently extended to protect merchants on their journeys to and from the markets and fairs. England duing the middle ages had special courts in the staple towns. See W. Mitchell, *An Essay on the Early History of the Law Merchant* (Yorke Prize Essay, 1903) Cambridge, 1904, especially pp. 10, 25, 75-79. Pollard, in his *Evolution of Parliament* writes, ". . . Down to the Reformation the ecclesiastical courts administered one law of legitimacy and the secular courts another." p. 195.

[13] See the excellent discussion in W. S. Holdsworth's *History of English Law.* Chapter VII of the first volume deals with these special jurisdictions. The law merchant was "a customary law, known to the merchants . . . ," and "with the merchants, his courts, and his law the common law had little concern. . . ." Holdsworth, I, 312. Holdsworth believes that "The complete incorporation of the Law Merchant with the common law was not affected till the time of Lord Mansfield." *Ibid.*, 336. The forest law and the courts to apply it, in the thirteenth century, Holdsworth thinks ". . . were as distinct from the common law and its courts as the law and courts of the merchants or the church." *Ibid.*, 340. "Questions which fell within the scope of that law would not be discussed by the Courts of Common Law. The jurisdiction of the forest courts could be pleaded in bar to proceedings at common law. . . ." *Ibid.*, 345. Curiously enough, the writer says nothing of the *lex parliamenti* in this connection. He might have pointed out many exact parallelisms between its application and the other laws and jurisdictions already mentioned.

[14] In the words of Pollard, "Parliamentary privilege was, in fact, the last of the medieval liberties to be reduced by common law." *The Evolution of Parliament*, 180.

law."[15] Certainly the *lex parliamenti* was also for centuries "above the ordinarie course of the common law." Like the prerogative, it was a kind of inexhaustible reservoir that could be drawn upon at need by the two houses of Parliament. The long accepted theory of the *lex parliamenti* made Parliament and its law supreme in the state, and as much above the ordinary law as the royal prerogative was ever claimed to be. What the results of this "Parliamentáry Omnipotence" were will be pointed out later.[16]

Coke believed that Parliament acted "not by the civill law, nor yet by the common laws of the realm, used in inferior courts." In 1592, during the discussion of Fitzherbert's case in the lower house, a member remarked: "And though the Common Law doth disable the party, yet the privilege of the House being urged, that prevaileth over the law."[17] More striking still was the action of the Court of Common Pleas in the case of *Nevill v. Stroud* (1659).[18] Here the judges, apparently of their own volition, and without pressure from the House, ordered a transcript of the evidence presented in their court to be sent to the House, "this Court doubting whether they have Cognizance of this Cause; being grounded merely upon the Common law; of which they find no Precedent." The judges appeared in person before the Commons to explain the case.

For centuries, the view prevailed that the ordinary courts of the kingdom acted only by the *lex terrae*, and knew nothing, and could learn nothing, of this special *lex parliamenti*, its rules, and its procedure. Many a judge felt that there must be "a particular cunning" in it not known to him, and so, wisely refrained from meddling in a case that might bring upon him the censure or punishment of the High Court of Parliament. Two judges—Jones and Pemberton—were actually called to the bar of the lower house, and

---

[15] See Dr. Cowell's Law Dictionary, *"The Interpreter,"* under "Prerogative" and under "King."

[16] In "An honourable and worthy Speech, spoken in the High Court of Parliament, by Mr. Smith of Middle Temple, Oct. 28, 1641," this conflict between the claims of prerogative and the necessity of protecting the people's liberties, is rather strikingly discussed. What is said of the conflict between prerogative and popular liberties might have been said with equal force concerning the conflict between the *lex parliamenti* and the rights of the people. Smith says in part— "That the King should have a Prerogative, is necessary for his Honour; it differences him from his People; but, if it swells too high, and makes an Inundation upon his Subjects Liberty, it is no longer then to be stiled by that Name: The Privilege of the Subject is likewise for his Majesty's high Honour. . . . Prerogative and Liberty are both necessary to this Kingdom; and like the Sun and Moon, give a Lustre to this benighted Nation, so long as they walk at their equal Distances. . . . What shall be the Compass then, by which these two must steer? *Why, nothing but the same by which they are, the law."* *Harl. Misc.* V, 251. The italics are mine.

[17] See 7 *Com. J.,* 599, and *ante,* 57.

[18] See *ante,* 60.

were punished for a decision unfavorable to Parliament's claims of privilege.[19] In *Regina v. Paty*, Justice Gould specifically recognized the existence of several codes of law in the kingdom, of which the law of Parliament was one.[20] His colleague, Justice Powell, refused to liberate prisoners of a house of Parliament, because "they were committed by another law," and therefore could not be freed by the ordinary courts. "There is a *lex parliamenti*, for the common law is not the only law in this kingdom."[21] The decisions recognized the Commons' power of judicature, "not by the common law, but by the law of Parliament." In 1675, the Commons, driven to extremes by their long quarrel with the Lords over the question of privilege arising in the Shirley case,[22] a quarrel which threatened to bring before the Lords, as the supreme appellate court of England, the ultimate decision of the privileges of the lower house, formulated a most emphatic protest, proclaiming the supremacy of a separate *lex parliamenti* in more sweeping terms than ever before. "As to what your lordships call a transcendent invasion of the right and liberty of the subject, and against Magna Charta, the Petition of Right, and many other laws, the House of Commons presume that your Lordships know, that neither the Great Charter, the Petition of Right, nor many other laws, do take away the law and custom of Parliament, or of either House of Parliament." Never was the supremacy of the law of Parliament more forcefully or unequivocally stated.[23] Not even the right to a writ of habeas corpus—surely one of the best established under the law—has been at all times considered above the law of Parliament. In 1653, when Streater tried to get his release from a commitment for a breach of privilege, by a writ of habeas corpus, the court refused to act, and with simple logic announced, "Mr. Streater, one must be above another, and the inferior must submit to the superior; and in all justice, an inferior court cannot control what the Parliament does."[24] The Earl of Shaftesbury, by the irony of circumstance, found that the Habeas Corpus Act, in whose passage he had been so interested, afforded no relief in case of commitment by Parliament. It was of no avail to plead the guarantee of the law

---

[19] See *ante*, 108.
[20] See *ante* 66.
[21] See *ante*, 66.
[22] *Ante*, 81.
[23] 3 *Com. J.*, 354.
[24] See *ante*, 98.

of the land against the law of Parliament.[25]   The bulwark of English liberty had to yield to the *lex parliamenti.*

No one was so filled with the idea of the judicial character of Parliament and the supremacy of the *lex parliamenti* as Robert Atkyns, himself a judge in later years. His argument in the defence of Sir William Williams was a masterpiece of logic, and a landmark in the exposition of the court theory of Parliament. Atkyns believed Parliament's acts were, on the whole, of a judicial nature. He was a staunch defender of the supremacy of the *lex parliamenti.* In his defence of Williams, before the King's Bench[26] he argued that that court "as all the Courts of Common Law, judges only by the ordinary rules of the Common Law. But the proceedings of Parliament are by quite another rule. The matters in Parliament are to be discussed and determined by the Custom and Usage of Parliament, and the course of Parliament, and neither by the Civil, nor the Common Law, used in other courts."[27] Even when Parliament acted as a legislature, Atkyns believed that it followed the rules of the *lex parliamenti.*[28] It was impossible for him to give up the idea of this fundamental law, governing all the actions of Parliament, even as a legislature. In his opinion, Parliament as a legislature acted by the *lex parliamenti,* a law that could not be disputed or questioned elsewhere, and consequently, Parliament became in effect a sovereign legislative body.

In the eighteenth century, the theory of a supreme Parliament, acting under a separate law, had as many defenders as before. In Brass Crosby's case (1771), Judge De Grey held that "The laws can never be a prohibition to the Houses of Parliament, because, by law, there is nothing superior to them."[29] In Stockdale's case, in the nineteenth century, the plaintiff's counsel referred Thorpe's case to "a period when the King, Lords, and Commons constituted the

---

[25] *Ante,* 101.

[26] See *ante,* 112.

[27] *Ante,* 112.

[28] Frequently, the House of Commons, in determining election cases, insisted that it acted by special rules of law. In a Commons' Resolution on the case of the election for the Borough of Chippenham, during James I's reign, we find—". . . This court, and council of state and justice, is guided by peculiar, more high, and politic rules of law and state, than the ordinary courts of justice are in matters between party and party. . . ." It was maintained that no statute could ". . . abridge, or take, any of the antient and undoubted privilege and power of the said commons in parliament, to examine the validity of elections." Glanville, *Reports of Certain Cases Determined and Adjudged by the Commons in Parliament* (London, 1775) pp. 59 and 60. Very often, the Commons describe their body as a "court of equity and discretion," "a court of law and justice," and "a distinct court of record of itself." See Glanville, 27, 85, 118, 119.

[29] See *ante,* 124.

supreme court of judicature."[30]   The judicial characteristics of
Parliament persisted for centuries and colored all its activities.[31]
From this conception, there constantly arose the confusion between
the legislative and judicial functions of Parliament, and no one
seemed to know just where to draw the dividing line between them.
It was difficult to ascertain when Parliament was acting as a court
—the highest in the land—and when it was a supreme legislative
body.   In the famous Bradlaugh case, almost at the close of the
nineteenth century, the same views of Parliament as a court crop-
ped out in the debates of the Commons, members feared a collision
between courts and Parliament, some solemnly warned against a
practice which would permit a court to interfere in the case lest by
appeal the House of Lords should become the judge of the liberties
of the Commons.   Nothing in English constitutional history is more
striking than the persistence of this old theory through all the years.

That the inevitable result of such an interpretation of the
theory of parliamentary privilege must be a long period of conflict
between the *lex terrae* and the *lex parliamenti*, between the High
Court of Parliament and the courts of the common law, is not difficult to grasp.   Yet the great struggles over privilege did not come
until comparatively late, not until the seventeenth century, in fact.
Before that time, privilege was on the whole not seriously challenged.   With the reign of the Stuarts, a new era began.   It was
then, in the struggle between the Crown and the representatives of
the nation, between royal prerogative and Parliament's growing
powers, that Parliament began to assume a more commanding position in the state, and to insist most stubbornly on its rights and
privileges.   Beginning with James I, Parliament set out to legis-
late on a hitherto unprecedented scale, and each house, but especially the lower, began to enforce and extend its claims of privilege.
No longer would the House of Commons be content to appeal to the
Lords for an interpretation of the law of Parliament and to abide
by their decision, as they had done at least once, in the Thorpe
case of the fifteenth century.   No longer would the Commons ap-

---

[30] 9 Adolphus & Ellis, 9.

[31] There are of course other examples of the judicial nature of Parliament's procedure, for
example, the procedure of the Receivers and Triers of Petitions in the middle ages, the judicial
nature of bills of attainder and pains and penalties, private bill procedure, etc.   The vague distinction between Parliament's judicial and legislative functions is also shown by the controversy
over statutes and ordinances to the sixteenth century, and the contest over proclamations in the
seventeenth century.   To-day the Privy Council, by Orders in Council, legislates without Parliamentary sanction for some parts of the British Empire, and is at the same time an appellate
court.   See McIlwain, *The High Court of Parliament and its Supremacy*, for a full discussion of
Parliament's judicial characteristics.

peal to the King for aid in solving a vexing problem of privilege nor would the Commons wait for an act of Parliament to settle a disputed claim of privilege. In the struggle between the Stuart Kings and Parliament, not a little of the difficulty came from the clash between privilege and prerogative. The clash was inevitable as long as both king and High Court of Parliament claimed to be "above the ordinarie course" of the law. In Parliament's vigorous assertions of its position against the Crown; in the ever-increasing exercise of the legislative power by the Stuart Parliaments; and in the general confusion that existed in men's minds in regard to the ideas of law, privilege, and prerogative, may be found some of the causes for the great conflicts of the seventeenth century over the extent and the application of Parliamentary privilege.

As the highest court of the realm, Parliament could not submit to interference or encroachment by inferior courts. To suppose otherwise, would be illogical, and contrary to all conceptions of legal and judicial procedure. Each house of Parliament claimed for itself the entire body of rights and privileges enjoyed in the old days by the High Court of Parliament as a whole. From the very nature of this conception, it follows that *lex parliamenti* must be inviolable, and that a decision of either house, made in pursuance of the rules prescribed by the law of Parliament, must stand as absolute and unimpeachable. If this were not the case, a house of Parliament might give one interpretation of privilege under the *lex parliamenti*, while a court of law, by the *lex terrae*, might arrive at another and entirely different conclusion. Endless confusion would result, and then things would truly "run round." Further, it was inconceivable, according to all the known rules of law and procedure, that an "inferior" court should be permitted to interfere with, and endeavor to interpret the action of a superior tribunal.

For the Commons, the question assumed vital significance, due to the nature of the English judicial system. The House of Lords constitutes the supreme court of England, and not until O'Connell's Case, well along in the nineteenth century, was judgment in the Lords limited to the specially-trained and legally-expert group of Law Lords. Before that time, the Lords as a body could participate in an adjudication. Let the House of Commons once admit the right of an inferior court to examine into its privileges, and the way lay open for an appeal to the House of Lords. The upper house thus would become the judge of the privileges of the lower. It must

never be forgotten that in the time of the great struggles over
privilege, every member of the Lords could participate in this
judicial decision, whether learned in the law or not. It is conceivable that such serious struggles as those which arose over the
Aylesbury elections and the Shirley-Fagg controversy, might have
been avoided, had there been at that time a separate, legally-trained
body of Law Lords in the upper house, constituting the supreme
court of appeal. In the Aylesbury cases, the Commons insisted
upon their old privileges, even though it became necessary, as a
consequence, to pass judgment upon so fundamental a question as
the exercise of the elective franchise. Rather than let the matter
come before the upper house, it seemed justifiable to deprive an
elector of his common law rights. It was impossible to escape from
this dilemma until sweeping reforms and changes had been made in
the English constitutional and legal systems. It was perfectly clear
that if the Commons were to be the sole judges of their privileges,
free from the restraints of the common law and the courts, they
might make whatever extensions they might desire, and the abuse
would become intolerable, for "when supremacy and impunity go
together, there is no remedy." Here was the "sophistical riddle that
perplexed many," and it defied all solution until changes were made
in the composition of the English supreme court. Had it not been
for this peculiar state of affairs, the problems of privilege would
undoubtedly have found a much earlier solution. As it was, the
judicial claims of the House of Lords blocked the way.

Among all their rights and privileges, there were none which
the Commons thought of more importance, or more necessary to
defend, than those which gave them the sole authority to decide
disputed election cases, and to determine who was entitled to a seat
in the House. In the Fortescue-Goodwyn affair, the king tried to
establish his right to pass judgment upon election returns, and the
House vigorously and successfully remonstrated.[32] To admit the
right of the courts to examine the returns, would be equally dangerous. In the great Aylesbury cases, the House gave unmistakable
evidence of its fear of the appellate jurisdiction of the Lords, and
resolved that "The Commons cannot but see, how your Lordships
are contriving by all Methods, to bring the Determination of Liberty
and Property into the bottomless and insatiable Gulf of your
Lordships Judicature; which would swallow up both the Preroga-

---

[32] See *ante*, 58.

tives of the Crown, and the Rights and Liberties of the People."[33]
In the Skinner-East India Company case, the two houses fought
long and hard over the question of the Lords' original jurisdiction.[34]
Though aided by the king, the upper house was forced to yield. In
the great Shirley-Fagg case of 1675, the issue in the conflict between
the two houses was the appellate jurisdiction of the Lords in matters of privilege.[35] It was on that occasion that Shaftesbury, in
prophetic words, warned the Lords that "This matter is no less
than your whole judicature, and your judicature is the life and soul
of the dignity of the peerage of England; you will quickly grow burdensome if you grow useless."[36] Both houses were fully awake to
the vital issues at stake. What bitter conflicts resulted has been
related in the preceding chapters. As late as 1880, when the real
danger had disappeared since the corps of legally-trained Law Lords
now constituted the supreme tribunal of England, a member of the
Commons, in a speech on the Bradlaugh case, called attention to
the old conflicts between courts and Parliament, and warned
against a course of procedure which might result in an appeal to the
House of Lords.[37]

Thus far, I have spoken largely of the danger to Parliament and
the lower house in particular, that might result from an infringement upon the field of privilege by either king or courts. There
is still another far more serious aspect of the matter. At times,
parliamentary privilege became a serious menace to the liberty of
the subject. Like most of the medieval "liberties," parliamentary
privilege was also an "oppression" for the people. If parliamentary
privilege existed by virtue of the *lex parliamenti*, a law separate
from and often held to be above the *lex terrae*, what could prevent
an abusive extension of the claims of either house? Ordinary courts
of law were clearly prohibited from interfering, for they were
"inferior," and had cognizance only of cases under the *lex terrae*.
What other power was there to prevent encroachment by the *lex
parliamenti* upon the law of the subject? If the law of privilege
is known only to Parliament, if it exists only in "the mouth and
breast" of Parliament-men, and if no other court or agency of government has a right to interpret it or question its application or

---

[33] 14 *Com. J.,* 563.
[34] *Ante,* 77.
[35] *Ante,* 81.
[36] *Ante,* 87.
[37] *Ante,* 161 *et seq.*

prevent its abuse, what is there to prevent unwarranted encroachments upon even the most sacred guarantees of individual liberty?
Cases are on record, and have been cited earlier, wherein the law
of privilege was made the justification for abuses of the rights of
the subject, as flagrant as those committed under the law of prerogative ever were.[38]

What was the injured subject to do? He could hardly expect
to secure a redress of grievances by petitioning the Parliament
house which had inflicted the injury. He might go to the ordinary
courts of the kingdom and ask the judges to protect his common
law rights. Certainly no resolution of a single house could alter
the law of the land, for legislation, to be valid, must be by King,
Lords, and Commons. But unfortunately for the victims of parliamentary tyranny, the tribunals of the common law were "inferior" to the High Court of Parliament, and therefore could not
pass judgment on its acts. Moreover, almost any extension of
privilege could be justified under the *lex parliamenti*, for it made
each house the sole judge of its privileges. Changing the law of
the land, or taking exception to it under a resolution of privilege
passed by one house, was without question usurping the function of
the whole Parliament, which alone had the legislative power. Such
a practice often became a serious menace to personal liberty, but
the injured subject found himself without a remedy. The courts
for a long time rigidly refrained from passing upon the action of
either house when based upon the *lex parliamenti*, even though it
clearly affected the principles of the common law. They refrained
because they held to the view that there were a number of separate
laws in the kingdom, each enforced by its own set of courts, and because *lex parliamenti* could be interpreted and enforced only by
Parliament, the highest court in England. Little concern was manifested for the rights of the subject. Only occasionally a judge of an
ordinary court, without directly claiming the right to limit Parliament's privileges, insisted upon exercising jurisdiction in the
cases before him, and applying the law, whether his judgment
clashed with a claim of privilege or not. Naturally, he would apply

---

[38] See the discussion in Chapters V and VI on *Lex Parliamenti* versus *Lex Terrae*, and
especially the cases cited from the *Journals of Parliament* in Chapter II, *ante*. On June 23, 1647,
the officers of the Army, distrustful of Parliament, included in their Remonstrance the statement "that Parliament privileges as well as royal prerogatives may be perverted and abused, to
the destruction of those greater ends for whose protection they were admitted or intended, viz.
the rights and privileges of the people." Rushworth, *Hist. Coll.*, VI, 587, quoted in C. H. Firth,
The House of Lords During the Civil War, 240.

the *lex terrae*, which frequently was at variance with the law and custom of Parliament. Neither house could stop such a case in the ordinary courts by any legal process, so other means had to be devised. The result was inevitably a violent conflict between courts and Parliament, each claiming exclusive jurisdiction, and each insisting on its claim with all the power at its command. Between the two contenders the individual had to choose. The result was that he often lost his remedy altogether, and frequently suffered additional injuries from the party in the contest whose rights he had questioned.

Ordinary cases of trespass and petty thefts—entering a member's land, stealing a bit of timber, breaking a fence, catching fish in forbidden waters, and many other petty offences that might be mentioned—were punished, time and again, *not* by the ordinary courts, where these cases belonged, but by a Parliament house as a breach of privilege. They were thus removed to a special jurisdiction, where a special law applied, and to a tribunal from which there was no appeal. Parliament could take cognizance of almost any offence under the *lex parliamenti*, punish it as a breach of privilege, and thus invade the field of jurisdiction that rightly belonged to the judges of the *lex terrae*. Later, when Parliament actually allowed the issuing of "protections" to members' servants and some who had absolutely no connection with either house or its membership, thus practically giving them the right to sin at will against the common law, the abuse of privilege became intolerable. It became intolerable, but this was the natural result of the logical application of the *lex parliamenti*, and a carrying to extreme, but still logical conclusions, the theory that lay behind this peculiar law.

Under a strict application of the law of privilege, privileged publications of a house of Parliament, no matter how slanderous upon individuals, were considered to be free from all interference of the courts. The legislature thus became "a libel shop," and its reports "vehicles of slander" against individuals, and under the *lex parliamenti* the subject was left without his common law right of action. In the early days, privilege was extended to members' servants as well, and it was conceivable that hundreds of individuals might, by the logical application of this process, be freed from all amenability to the common law courts. In this respect, privilege of Parliament resembled the old privilege of clergy, and the system of a special administrative law which exists on the Continent of Europe. The term "servant" moreover might include almost any one, from a member's actual attendant, to his tailor, or the keeper or workman on his estate. At times, a regular traffic in "Protections," sold at fixed market prices, arose. Unscrupulous members issued and sold these "protections" indiscriminately and thus enabled individuals, in no way connected with Parliament, for a fixed sum to escape the penalties of the common law. It was like the sale of a form of Parliamentary "Indulgence," by which offenders took refuge behind the cloak of Parliamentary privilege.

Under a claim of privilege, Parliament thus removed individuals from the jurisdiction of the courts, and allowed them to escape the penalties they deserved. On the other hand, as already suggested, Parliament often punished individuals for breaches of privilege, who should really have been tried by the ordinary courts—if at all—and whose misdeeds were not of such a character as to warrant action by Parliament. In early centuries, the privilege of freedom from molestation was widely applied, and perhaps necessarily so. But in the eighteenth century, this was no longer necessary. By that time, however, a corrupt, time-serving Parliament had learned to use the law of privilege to punish personal enemies and petty offenders, for offences that should never have been noticed by either house. Cutting down trees, fishing without license, pulling down a scaffold, challenging members to duels, and many common law offences were in fact included under the law of Parliament, as breaches of privilege, and were prosecuted and punished in Parliament as such. Privilege became a real danger to individual liberty, for these cases brought under the *lex parliamenti* were tried by a different law and a different procedure than would have been used in the ordinary courts, and the accused was deprived of all opportunity to appeal to a higher court. The common law guarantees of the subject's rights and liberties proved of no effect when matched with a Parliament, determined to vindicate its claim of privilege.

In election cases, the right to determine who shall sit in the House, was extended, at times, to give the House the power to determine the right of an individual to vote, a matter properly cognizable only in the ordinary courts of law. Holt pointed out the dangers that lay in such an extension of privilege in his decisions in the

Aylesbury cases,[39] but his opposition had little practical effect. In the Wilkes cases, the royally-controlled majority in the Commons repeatedly excluded Wilkes from his seat in the House, thus depriving his constituents of their fundamental right to be fully represented in Parliament. Burke on that occasion pointed out how the liberties of the subject were being subverted, and how the legislative body had established itself into a "court of criminal equity," "going beyond the law," and reviving "all the evils of the Star Chamber."[40] Henry Cavendish fiercely denounced "as unconstitutional and illegal, the damnable doctrine that the House of Commons can make, alter, suspend, or abrogate the law of the land."[41] Junius wrote—"I hope I shall never see the time when not only a single person, but a whole county, and, in effect, the entire collective body of the people, may again be robbed of their birthright by a vote of the House of Commons. But if, for reasons which I am unable to comprehend, it be necessary to trust that House with a power so exorbitant and so unconstitutional, at least let it be given to them by an act of the legislature."[42] In the debates in the House, on the expulsion of Wilkes, Grenville argued that no resolution of the House could bind the people; it required a law to do that. "The legislature alone, which is the united power of the state, King, Lords, and Commons, can enact new restraints. Courts of judicature, and houses of Parliament, acting as courts of judicature, have only the power of declaring them; and in the use of that power are bound by the law as it stands at the time of making that declaration."[43]

Occasionally, the two houses were divided against each other, the Lords championing the *lex terrae*, in a struggle over privilege, the Commons supporting the *lex parliamenti*. Here again the nature of the English judicial system affords the key to this almost inevitable alignment. There was always this possibility that the two houses might make contrary declarations of privilege in the same case. If not a conflict between the two houses, there was almost certain to be one between one house and a common law court. A declaration of privilege, however unreasonable, contrary to the

[39] *Ante*, Chapter III, 65-67.
[40] Burke—*Works*, (Boston, 1865) I, 499-500.
[41] Quoted in Percy Fitzgerald's *Life of Wilkes*, II, 54. See also, pp. 63 and 64.
[42] *Letters of Junius* (Woodfall's Edition, London, 1915) I, 185. For a good exposition of the dangers from privilege and one-house legislation, see another letter, *Ibid.*, 328-339. Also, 255-270.
[43] *Parl. Debates*, XVI, 588-590.

law of the land, and without precedent, was nevertheless, under the orthodox interpretation of the *lex parliamenti,* unimpeachable. The result was one-house legislation, instead of legislation by King, Lords, and Commons in Parliament assembled. In many cases, privilege obstructed the common law right of the subject to obtain a writ of habeas corpus, with results dangerously like one-house legislation. Still another confusion arose from the uncertainty whether Parliament in legislating acted by the *lex parliamenti* or by the *lex terrae,* and these uncertainties in regard to privilege and the law of Parliament lasted for centuries. Occasionally some one caught a faint glimpse of the ultimate solution, but it took years to realize it in practice. Gradually it must have dawned upon men's minds to inquire why privilege alone should remain unlimited and undefined by law, long after the royal prerogative and the rights and liberties of the people had become fixed and circumscribed by acts of Parliament and decisions of the common law courts.[44]

The ultimate solution was to make the law of Parliament subordinate to, or a part of, the great all-embracing, fundamental common law of the land. But it was impossible to realize this solution, as I have tried to show, until the members of the House of Lords had been shorn of their judicial power as the supreme court of England; until the notion of such a common law had been evolved, and the law of Parliament had lost its "separateness;" and until men came to see more clearly the difference between Parliament's activities as a sovereign legislature, and the remnants of its judicial powers. With the creation of a small body of expert, legally-trained Law Lords, and the exclusion of all other members of the upper house from participating in a judicial decision, the greatest obstacle in the way of a sane interpretation of parliamentary privilege was removed. Further, by the great reforms of the nineteenth century, the House of Commons became more and more a truly representative body, the organ of the people, and the real power in the state. As such, its position became more and more secure, and sweeping claims of privilege were no longer so necessary to protect it in the exercise of its legislative activities, and to guard it against encroachments from Crown, Lords, and courts.

---

[44] Prynne was aware of this state of affairs. He asks why members of Parliament alone should be free from suit, when—"The King himselfe, the head and chiefest Member in the High Court of Parliament, who hath the highest, largest privileges of all others, from whose grace and indulgence all the other Members Parliamentary Privileges only flow"—is hot. Prynne, *Brief Register,* IV, 695.

Prynne seems to have had some vague idea of the proper relation between the law of Parliament and the law of the land, although his views are not always entirely clear. He believed "That every private subject in cases of pretended ancient Custom and Privilege of Parliament, though recited in Writs of Privilege under the Great Seal of England, to retard or delay him in his just sutes and proceedings in Law in publike Courts of Justice against the Great Charter and common Rules of Right, may lawfully traverse, deny, and join issue thereupon, whether there be any such ancient custom or privilege of Parliament or not, without any breach of Privilege or dishonour to the Parliament or its Members; and the King's sworn Judges, not rashly, precipitately, but upon solemn deliberation and advice with their fellow judges, may and ought judiciously to resolve, whether it be a real Custom, Privilege, or not."[45] In another place, Prynne observed—"Parliament, being the supremest Court of Law and Justice, ought to proceed legally according to the course of Law, and not to enlarge or extend the Privileges of Parliament beyond their ancient, just, legal bounds, nor alter the Law therein by their absolute power."[46]

Clarendon believed that the Commons should be the judges of their privileges, but added "there can be no privilege of which the law doth not take notice, and which is not pleadable by, and at law."[47]

The brilliant opinions of Lord Holt in the Aylesbury cases and the Knollys case have already been sufficiently discussed. His decisions had little practical effect at the time they were announced, but the modern solution follows substantially the same reasoning. It required almost two centuries more to bring Parliament and the courts to adopt the solution Holt offered in 1701. "Both Houses of Parliament," he said in *Regina v. Paty*, "are bound by the law of the land, and in their actions are obliged to pursue it." In short, no

---

[45] Prynne, *Brief Register*, IV, 765.

[46] *Ibid.*, 685. On page 694 of the same volume, Prynne writes—"I cannot possibly apprehend nor believe that the true, genuine Privilege of Parliament did ever extend to deny or obstruct common right, justice and legal processe against any Members, Assistants, Officers or their Menial Servants, whatsoever, either in real, personal, or mixed actions, demands or sutes against them whether in, or out of Parliament in other Courts of publicke Justice, where their persons were not arrested nor their right or titles prejudiced by surprise or circumvention: and that upon these General Considerations . . . because the Parliament is the most Honourable, Supream, and highest Court of Justice in the Realm, the fountain from whence all Lawes and Statutes for the speedy execution and distribution of common right, justice to all, etc. . . . originally flow."

[47] See *ante*, 106, footnote.

claim under the *lex parliamenti* could give any interruption to the law of the land. The Stockdale-Hansard cases (1837-1842) were decided on substantially the same principle, and at last gave a definition to matters of privilege that seemed to have the appearance of finality. Between 1701 and 1837, Holt's theory was disregarded completely, save in the arguments of a few able lawyers, and was never advanced by Parliament or the courts during this period as the real solution for the problems of privilege and its relation to the common law. These years include the reign of the Whig Oligarchy, still resting serenely on the prestige which the Glorious Revolution had brought them. Parliament was their stronghold, and they clung tenaciously to their power. It was unreasonable to expect them to support a principle that would rob them of their arbitrary powers in Parliament, and bring them under the restraints of the law. Privilege of Parliament proved one of the convenient aids in maintaining and prolonging an autocratic rule.

In the nineteenth century, it became evident that the only possible solution for these troublesome problems arising from privilege of Parliament, lay in bringing that privilege within the cognizance of the ordinary courts, and in making *lex parliamenti*—like the *lex prerogativae*—a part of the law of the land and no longer superior to it. Courts to-day admit no superior except those which revise their judgments for error. This conclusion, and this settlement of the relation between privilege and the law, could be brought about only after the idea of separate codes of law had disappeared, and the notion that *lex parliamenti*, like the rest, was part of the common law, had been evolved; after the nature of the English Supreme Court had been radically altered; and after the democratization of the lower house had made substantial progress.

At present, the application of privilege has been greatly limited. Members' servants have long been denied the protection of Parliament. To-day practically any process that does not affect the *person* of a member or prevent his actual attendance in Parliament, may be issued. Courts may be compelled out of necessity to pass upon the validity of a claim of privilege. Neither house can hope any longer to create a new privilege by a mere resolution. The dangers of one-house legislation are past. Officers of the House, in carrying out the orders of their body, may become exposed to the "censure of the law," should it develop that their orders were based on an unjustifiable claim or on a wrong interpretation of privilege. There is an interesting similarity between this double liability of officials of Parliament and the liability of the English soldiery, who, like Parliamentary officials, act under a special set of rules (martial law), and yet may become liable, under certain circumstances, to the penalties of the common law.[48] At present, there can be no privilege of Parliament that is not pleadable at law, and examinable by the common law courts, should it come before them in a judicial way. *Lex parliamenti* has at last become a part of the *lex terrae*.

It required almost five centuries to complete this process. From the history of parliamentary privilege, one gets many interesting suggestions as to the history of Parliament, its origin and early functions, the gradual rise of the Commons, and the decline of the Lords. A study of privilege furthermore throws much light upon many of the struggles between king and Parliament, and on the nature and defects of the English judicial and constitutional system. Sometimes out of a claim of privilege there grew a bitter struggle between the royal prerogative and the law of Parliament, each claiming to be "above the ordinarie course of the law;" sometimes a prolonged conflict between a jealous and powerful House of Lords and a struggling, but slowly rising House of Commons. Privilege has been both the bulwark of English liberty and the most ruthless oppressor of the rights of the subject. It has proved a means for the advancement of democracy and representative government and institutions in the hands of some, and again, it has been a tool of oppression in the hands of a corrupt, mercenary, time-serving oligarchy of politicians desirous of perpetuating their power. The proper adjustment of privilege to the other existing laws and institutions was worked out very slowly. With the rise of a sovereign Parliament in a democratic state, where all persons and all institutions seek protection under the aegis of one great common law, privilege of Parliament has lost its vital importance.

England now has an all-embracing law of the land, which protects the subject and the just privileges of Parliament as well. Fear for the appellate jurisdiction of the House of Lords has been dispelled, and with it, the enmity between courts and the Commons, in matters of privilege, has practically disappeared. Parliament has become the unquestioned sovereign legislature of the state, the judicial functions which colored its activities for so many hundreds

---

[48] For excellent summaries of the modern status of privilege, see Broom's *Constitutional Law* (2d Ed.) pp. 107-109, 161; May—*Parliamentary Practice* (11th Ed.) 145, 146.

of years have largely disappeared or have been absorbed by other bodies and agencies of government, and the confusion between Parliament's legislative and judicial powers is no longer apparent or significant. Parliamentary privilege exists to-day only under the rules and limitations of the law. As a comment upon the remarkable evolution of English institutions, institutions which have their origin in the very dawn of history, and whose development seems never to be quite completed, the history of parliamentary privilege is almost without a parallel.

BIBLIOGRAPHY

1. Sources

Rolls of Parliament.
Journals of the House of Commons.
Journals of the House of Lords.
Cobbett's *Parliamentary History.*
Cobbett's *Parliamentary Debates.*
Hansard *Parliamentary Debates.*
Statutes of the Realm.

Law Reports

Adolphus and Ellis, *English King's Bench Reports.*
Barnardiston, *English King's Bench Reports.*
Barnewell and Alderson, *English King's Bench Reports.*
Brownlow and Goldesborough, *English Common Pleas Reports.*
Canadian Supreme Court Reports.
Carrington and Marshman, *English Nisi Prius Cases.*
Chancery Division, English Law Reports.
Chitty's, *English Bail Court Reports.*
Dow, *Reports.*
Douglas, *Election Cases.*
Dowling, *English Practice Cases.*
Dowling and Lowndes, *English Practice Cases.*
Durnford and East, *English King's Bench Reports* (Term Reports).
Dyer, *Reports.*
East, *English King's Bench Reports.*
Espinasse, *English Nisi Prius Reports.*
Fortescue's, *English King's Bench Reports.*
Fraser, *Election Cases.*
Glanville, *Reports of Certain Cases Determined and Adjudged by the Commons in Parliament.*
    (London, 1775).
Holt's, *English King's Bench Reports.*
Howell, *State Trials.*
Keble, *English King's Bench Reports.*
King's Bench Reports (English).
Knapp and Ombler, *Election Cases.*
Latch's, *English King's Bench Reports.*
Law Journal (Queen's Bench).
Law Reports (Ireland).
Law Reports, Appeal Cases (New South Wales).
Levinz, *English King's Bench Reports.*
Lower Canada Jurist.
Lower Canada Reports.
Luders, *Election Cases.*
Manning and Granger, *English Common Pleas Reports.*
Maule and Selwyn, *English King's Bench Reports.*
Modern Reports (English King's Bench).
Moody and Robinson, *English Nisi Prius Reports.*
Moore, *English Privy Council Cases.*
Moore, *English Privy Council Cases* (New Series).
Mylne and Craig, *English Chancery Reports.*
New South Wales Law Reports.
Noy, *English King's Bench Reports.*

Peckwell, *Election Cases.*
Perry and Knapp, *Election Cases.*
Philipps, *Election Cases.*
Queen's Bench Reports (English).
Raymond, Lord, *English King's Bench Reports.*
Russell and Mylne, *English Chancery Reports.*
Saunders, *English King's Bench Reports.*
Siderfin's, *English King's Bench Reports.*
State Trials (New Series).
Strange, *English King's Bench Reports.*
Stuart's Reports (Lower Canada).
Taunton, *English Common Pleas Reports.*
Vesey (Senior), *Reports* (English Chancery).
Weekly Reporter (London).
Wilson, *English Common Pleas Reports.*

2. PRIVATE JOURNALS, MEMOIRS, AND MISCELLANEOUS SOURCES

Burke, Edmund, *Works of* (Boston, 1865)..
Canada Sessional Papers.
Cowell, Law Dictionary, *The Interpreter.*
D'Ewes, Simonds, *Journals of Parliament.*
Greville *Memoirs.*
Hatsell, *Precedents of the Proceedings of the House of Commons.*
Junius, *Letters of* (Woodfall's Ed.) London, 1915.
Pemberton, M. P., *Letter to Lord Langdale* (1837).
Pepys, S., *Diary* (Wheatley's Ed.) 1912.
Prothero, G., *Statutes and Constitutional Documents* (1559-1625).
Prynne, *Brief Register of Parliamentary Writs.*
Rogers, T., *The Lords' Protests.*
Rushworth, *Historical Collections.*
Toynbee, *Letters of Horace Walpole.*
Townshend, *Proceedings of the Last Four Parliaments of Elizabeth.*

3. SECONDARY MATERIAL

(a) *General*

Adams, G. B., *Origins of the English Constitution.*
Amos, Sheldon, *Fifty Years of the English Constitution.*
Anson, Sir William R., *Law and Custom of the Constitution.*
Bagehot, W., *The English Consitution.*
Broom, H., *Constitutional Law.*
Cox, Homersham, *Ancient Parliamentary Elections.*
Dasent, A. I., *The Speakers of the House of Commons.*
Davis, H. C. W., *England Under the Normans and Angevins.*
Dicey, A. V., *Introduction to the Study of the Law of the Constitution.*
Dicey, A. V., *The Privy Council.*
Dickinson, G. L., *The Development of Parliament in the Nineteenth Century.*
Firth, C. H., *The House of Lords During the Civil War.*
Fisher, H. A. L., *The Political History of England* (1485-1547).
Gneist, R., *Student's History of the English Parliament.*
Gooch, G. P., *Political Thought from Bacon to Halifax.*
Holdsworth, W. S., *History of English Law.*
Ilbert, Sir Courtenay, *Parliament.*
Jennings, G., *Anecdotal History of the British Parliament.*
Keith, A. B., *Responsible Government in the Dominions.*
Low, Sidney, *The Governance of England.*
Maitland, F. W., *Constitutional History of England.*
May, Sir Thomas E., *Constitutional History of England.*

May, Sir Thomas E., *Parliamentary Practice* (11th Ed.)
McCarthy, Justin, *History of Our Own Times.*
McIlwain, C. H.,*The High Court of Parliament and Its Supremacy.*
Medley, D. J., *English Constitutional History.*
Palgrave, Reg. F. D.,*The House of Commons.*
Pike, L. O., *The Constitutional History of the House of Lords.*
Pollard, A. F., *The Evolution of Parliament.*
Pollard, A. F., *The Political History of England* (1547-1603).
Porritt, E., *The Unreformed House of Commons.*
Redlich, Joseph, *The Procedure of the House of Commons* (A. E. Steinthal's Translation).
Robertson, C. Grant, *England Under the Hanoverians.*
Shortt, A. and Dougherty, A. G. (General Editors), *Canada and Its Provinces.*
Skottowe, B., *A Short History of Parliament.*
Smith, G. Barnett, *History of the English Parliament.*
Stubbs, W., *Constitutional History of England.*
Trevelyan, G., *England Under the Stuarts.*
Turberville, A. S., *The House of Lords in the Reign of William III.*
Vickers, K. H., *England in the Later Middle Ages.*
Walpole, Spencer, *History of England.*
Wright, A., and Smith, P., *Parliament, Past and Present.*
Wright, Thomas, *Caricature History of the Georges.*

(b) Miscellaneous

Alexander, De Alva S., *History and Procedure of the House of Representatives* (United States).
Atkyns, Robert, *Parliamentary and Political Tracts.*
Churchill, W. S., *Lord Randolph Churchill.*
Clarendon, Lord, *History of the Rebellion* (Oxford Press, 1839).
Coke, Sir Edward, *Institutes of the Laws of England.*
Cushing, L. S., *Law and Practice of Legislative Assemblies.*
Dictionary of National Biography.
Dwarris, *On the Statutes.*
Elsynge, *The Manner of Holding Parliaments in England.*
Forsyth, *Cases and Opinions on Constitutional Law* (1869).
Fitzgerald, P., *Life of Wilkes.*
Hakewell, *Modus tenendi Parliamentum.*
Hale, Sir Mathew, *Judicature of the Lords' House.*
Hale, Sir M., *History of the Common Law.*
Hale, Sir M., *The Original Jurisdiction, Power, and Judicature of Parliament.*
Harford, R., *The Privileges and Practices of Parliaments in England* (1680).
Hargrave, Francis, *Collection of Tracts Relative to the Law of England.* (London, 1787).
Holles, Lord, *The Case Stated Concerning the Judicature of the House of Peers in Point of Appeal* (1675).
Lucas, R., *Lord North.*
Mitchell, W., *An Essay on the Early History of the Law Merchant* (Cambridge, 1904).
Paine, H. E., *A Treatise on the Law of Elections to Public Offices* (Washington, D. C., 1888).
(Petyt) G. P., *Lex Parliamentaria* (1698).
Rae, W. F., *Wilkes, Sheridan, and Fox.*
Ruville, A. von, *William Pitt, Earl of Chatham.*
Selden, J., *On the Laws of England* (London, 1760).
Smith, H. H., *Digest of Decisions and Precedents of the Senate and House of Representatives of the United States Relating to Powers and Privileges* (Senate Misc. Doc. No. 278, 53d Cong. 2nd Sess.)
Taylor, Fennings, *Are Legislatures Parliaments?*
Traill, H. D., *Life of Shaftesbury.*
Williams, Basil, *The Life of William Pitt.*
Winstanley, D. A., *Lord Chatham and the Whig Opposition.*
Wynne, Charles Watkins W., *Argument upon the Jurisdiction of the House of Commons to Commit in Cases of Privilege* (1810).

INDEX

211